Narrative, Identity, and Academic Community in Higher Education

Grounded in narrative theory, this book offers a case study of a liberal arts college's use of narrative to help build identity, community, and collaboration within the college faculty across a range of disciplines, including history, psychology, sociology, theater and dance, literature, anthropology, and communication. Exploring issues of methodology and their practical application, this narrative project speaks to the construction of identity for the liberal arts in today's higher education climate. *Narrative, Identity, and Academic Community* focuses on the ways a cross-disciplinary emphasis on narrative can impact institutions in North America and contribute to the discussion of strategies to foster bottom-up, faculty-driven collaboration and innovation.

Brian Attebery is Professor of English at Idaho State University, USA.

John Gribas is Professor of Communication, Media, and Persuasion at Idaho State University, USA.

Mark K. McBeth is Professor of Political Science at Idaho State University, USA.

Paul Sivitz is Lecturer of History at Idaho State University, USA.

Kandi Turley-Ames is Founding Dean of the College of Arts & Letters and Professor of Psychology at Idaho State University, USA.

Routledge Research in Higher Education

For a full list of titles in this series, please visit www.routledge.com

Working with Underachieving Students in Higher Education
Fostering inclusion through narration and reflexivity
Edited by Maria Francesca Freda, José González Monteagudo and Giovanna Esposito

Graduate Education at Historically Black Colleges and Universities (HBCUs)
A Student Perspective
Edited by Robert T. Palmer, Larry J. Walker, Ramon B. Goings, Charmaine Troy, Chaz T. Gipson, and Felecia Commodore

Transnational Education Crossing 'Asia' and 'the West'
Adjusted desire, transformative mediocrity, neo-colonial disguise
Phan Le-Ha

Experiencing Master's Supervision
Perspectives of international students and their supervisors
Nigel Harwood and Bojana Petrić

The Design of the University
German, American, and "World Class"
Heinz-Dieter Meyer

The Politics of Widening Participation and University Access for Young People
Making educational futures
Valerie Harwood, Anna Hickey-Moody, Samantha McMahon and Sarah O'Shea

Narrative, Identity, and Academic Community in Higher Education
Edited by Brian Attebery, John Gribas, Mark K. McBeth, Paul Sivitz, and Kandi Turley-Ames

Narrative, Identity, and Academic Community in Higher Education

Edited by Brian Attebery,
John Gribas, Mark K. McBeth,
Paul Sivitz, and Kandi Turley-Ames

LONDON AND NEW YORK

First published 2017 by Routledge

2 Park Square, Milton Park, Abingdon, Oxfordshire OX14 4RN
52 Vanderbilt Avenue, New York, NY 10017

Routledge is an imprint of the Taylor & Francis Group, an informa business

First issued in paperback 2018

Copyright © 2017 Taylor & Francis

The right of Brian Attebery, John Gribas, Mark K. McBeth, Paul Sivitz, and Kandi Turley-Ames to be identified as editors of this work has been asserted by them in accordance with sections 77 and 78 of the Copyright, Designs and Patents Act 1988.

All rights reserved. No part of this book may be reprinted or reproduced or utilised in any form or by any electronic, mechanical, or other means, now known or hereafter invented, including photocopying and recording, or in any information storage or retrieval system, without permission in writing from the publishers.

Notice:
Product or corporate names may be trademarks or registered trademarks, and are used only for identification and explanation without intent to infringe.

Library of Congress Cataloguing-in-Publication Data
A catalog record for this book has been requested

ISBN: 978-1-138-64736-7 (hbk)
ISBN: 978-0-367-19518-2 (pbk)

Typeset in Sabon
by Apex CoVantage, LLC

Contents

Acknowledgments	ix
Introduction BRIAN ATTEBERY, MARK K. MCBETH, AND KANDI TURLEY-AMES	1

SECTION I
Interrogating and Framing Reality: Identity and Cultural Perceptions — 15

1. Old and New Technologies of Asynchronous Communication: Virtual Narratives and "Presence" — 17
   THOMAS KLEIN

2. Onitsha Market Literature: Narrating Identity and Survival in a Colonial African City — 31
   RAPHAEL CHIJIOKE NJOKU AND KING YIK

3. Narrative Identities in India's Global Age — 47
   ALAN JOHNSON

4. Narrative Text and Photographs: A Case for Ethnographic Research Poetry — 68
   TERRY OWNBY

SECTION I SUMMARY
An Author Conversation — 83
RAPHAEL CHIJIOKE NJOKU, THOMAS KLEIN, TERRY OWNBY, AND ALAN JOHNSON

SECTION II
Narratives at the Intersection of the Public and Private — 89

5 Finding Story in Unexpected Places: Branding and the Role of Narrative in the Study of Communication — 91
JOHN GRIBAS, ZAC GERSHBERG, JAMES R. DISANZA, AND NANCY J. LEGGE

6 The "Not Yet Pregnant": The Impact of Narratives on Infertility Identity and Reproductive Policy — 111
KELLEE J. KIRKPATRICK

7 Letter-Writing and the Eighteenth-Century Scientific Community: Constructing Narratives and Identity — 129
PAUL SIVITZ

SECTION II SUMMARY
An Author Conversation — 143
ZAC GERSHBERG, PAUL SIVITZ, AND KELLEE J. KIRKPATRICK

SECTION III
Performing Bodies, Creating Stories — 149

8 Narratives of Pain — 151
GESINE HEARN

9 Narrative and the Performing Arts: A Symposium — 164
BRIAN ATTEBERY, VANESSA BALLAM, GRANT HARVILLE, AND LAURALEE ZIMMERLY

10 Stories and Objects: Narrative and the Construction of Connective Links in an American Quilting Guild — 176
SONJA LAUNSPACH

11 The Currency of Stories: Anthropologists, *Nawaals*, and the Strange World of Academe — 196
ELIZABETH CARTWRIGHT

SECTION III SUMMARY
An Author Conversation   207
GESINE HEARN, SONJA LAUNSPACH, GRANT HARVILLE,
AND ELIZABETH CARTWRIGHT

Conclusion: Narrative Diffusion   211
PAUL SIVITZ

   List of Contributors   213
   Index   214

Acknowledgments

The editorial team would like to acknowledge the considerable assistance of Emily Treasure in reviewing these chapters and providing valuable feedback. We would also like to thank all faculty, staff, students, and supporters—past and present—who are part of our ongoing story as an academic community. We appreciate all of you who have enthusiastically embraced narrative as part of the Idaho State University College of Arts & Letters through your scholarship, teaching, and academic exploration.

Introduction

Brian Attebery, Mark K. McBeth, and Kandi Turley-Ames

The best way to introduce a book about narrative is to tell a story. In this case, it is three stories, or, more precisely, a story in three parts, as told by a trio of the editors.

Narratives, Literature, and Everything Else: Brian Attebery

Just about the time I was finishing my graduate studies, a new kind of literary study caught the attention of many people in the academy. It was called narratology: the study of the underlying structures of stories and storytelling. Coming out of an education that was still based in the New Criticism—a form of interpretation developed in the early twentieth century to explain and to cheerlead for the Modernist poems of T. S. Eliot, Ezra Pound, and the like—I was more than ready for a new model of literary studies. Narratology offered a striking alternative.

It wasn't just suited to reading short lyric poems. It didn't privilege elite literary art over all other kinds of storytelling—examples were as likely to be fairy tales or bawdy jokes as novels by Proust. Narratologists drew upon linguistics and folklore more than aesthetics, and they didn't talk about verities that seemed more culture-bound than eternal. In contrast to the other critical fashion of the day, deconstruction, narratology was typically written in clear, down-to-earth prose like that of Robert Scholes or Seymour Chatman.

I was lucky enough not only to read those two scholars but also to study with them: Scholes at Brown University and Chatman in a National Endowment for the Humanities Summer Seminar at U.C. Berkeley. Both are sensible and humane, as well as brilliantly insightful: it is no wonder that I imprinted on them like a newly hatched duckling. I followed them back to their sources, such as the Russian sociolinguist Mikhael Bakhtin and the French structuralist Gérard Genette. Furnished with a whole new set of analytical tools, I was able to make a case for literary modes ignored or disparaged by the New Criticism. By posing narratalogical questions, I could write about popular fantasy and metafictional experimentation (categories that overlap more than one might expect). Narratology allowed me to demonstrate kinds of complexity and depth that more traditional readings were blind to.

But after a brief fling with narratology, most literary scholars moved on to other issues and other critical fashions. There was a general sense of having been there, done that. Narratology: that's so 1980s. Now we're all pursuing transgender identities or trauma studies, leaving behind a few specialists to tidy up the field.

Yet at the same time, narrative approaches were shaking up many other disciplines, from psychology to international relations. I began to hear about new ways to look at narrative from people outside of literature. Metahistorian Hayden White challenged historians to look at the narrative basis of their craft as something more than a mere container in which to pour historical information. Anthropologists were rethinking their foundational texts, looking at the way an ethnologist such as Claude Lévi-Strauss created plots and characters out of cultural confrontations. When my wife spent a term as a Fulbright distinguished chair at Uppsala University, we heard a talk by Rita Charon, founder of the Narrative Medicine Program at Columbia University. Back home, my colleague Mark McBeth gave a sabbatical report describing a collaborative project he had undertaken on political narratives and their power to change ideas and spur action. Narrative wasn't over; it was everywhere.

Wanting to find out whether my impression was accurate, in the fall of 2013, I invited a number of faculty members to come together to talk about the role of narrative in their work. I sent around a list of questions and invited people to give a five-minute précis addressing the following questions:

- How is narrative defined within your discipline?
- Do you analyze narrative as we do in literary studies: as both a series of events that comprise a plot and illuminate a group of characters and as a form of discourse that selects and arranges to give the events a pleasing shape and thematic significance?
- Does it make sense to talk about narrative as a way of knowing—perhaps equal to but different from logical argument or empirical observation?
- Is your work affected by new studies of cognition that look at the mental processes involved in creating, telling, and hearing stories?

We held a panel discussion in front of a packed room, and the panelists found both common ground and challenging differences in their approaches. At that first event, anthropologist Elizabeth Cartwright talked about inviting Peruvian Indians to tell stories of their illnesses as a way to bridge the gap between patient and practitioner as well as offering a source of insight into traditional cultural patterns. Psychologist Shannon Lynch spoke of the split in her discipline between those who value narrative evidence and those who stick to statistical methods. Political scientist Mark McBeth discussed the way competing narratives drive contemporary political and policy debates. Photographer Terry Ownby talked about telling stories visually and invoked Roland Barthes's ideas on cultural myth. Linguist and anthropologist Chris Loether told of his collaboration with members of the nearby Shoshone-Bannock tribe to preserve their stories and the languages within which those stories have form and meaning. Communication scholar John Gribas spoke of the role of storytelling in business and other organizations. Historian Stephanie Christelow talked about the narratives she finds in medieval texts and the narratives through which the historian in turn presents such materials. The audience was rapt, and after the presentations, everyone wanted to chip in from the perspectives of folklore or language studies or social work. Clearly, there was widespread interest and a need to keep this project going.

At that point, though, I was happy to step aside and have others take over. We in the newly formed College of Arts & Letters had found a common interest in language, metaphor, and storytelling; now it was time for people from all departments of the College to explore the place of these concepts within their respective disciplines. A single panel discussion was only the beginning of a long process of working through implications for research, classroom practice, curriculum, and departmental structures. The single panel discussion generated a three-year series of interdisciplinary colloquia, guided by historian Paul Sivitz, with participation from every department in the College and a few guests from other parts of the University as well.

As a result, I had a lot to think through with regard to my own understanding of the nature of narrative. What was it if it was not primarily a literary device? Was there more for my own discipline to contribute to this new endeavor? What did it mean for literary studies to acknowledge the role of narrative in everything from medical treatments to military campaigns?

The shift in my thinking was not dramatic. I have always been more interested in the cultural work of literature than in the elevation of specific texts to the rank of great works. My graduate program in American civilization encouraged awareness of interactions between literature and other arts, as well as the interlaced nature of elite, popular, and folk cultures. However, now when I invite students to investigate cultural contexts, as a result of our narrative project, I can draw on more concrete examples drawn from my colleagues' work in history, anthropology, or psychology. The result for me, and I hope for my students, is a broadening of the concept of literature. As Robert Scholes pointed out a couple of decades ago, we should think of literary art as a small part of the discipline of English: what we really study is the production and reception of meaningful texts, and those texts can as easily be Internet jokes or graphic novels as sonnets.

The same hunger for new perspectives that instigated the narrative panel has led me to stretch the boundaries of my narrative competence in order to advise thesis writers working with comics and computer games. Their chosen subject matter poses fundamental questions about narrative art, prompting me to return to narratology to see what has been going on since I was reading such theory intensively. We turn to theory when something isn't quite working in our practice. Inspired by our panel and looking for ways to guide my current crop of graduate students, I found, for instance, Rick Altman's revisionist idea of the "following unit" as a basic component of storytelling. Drawing on his study of film narrative, Altman notes that, like a movie camera, a narrator directs our attention toward selected individuals or groups and follows their actions until the scene shifts. He found that what works for cinema also works for visual narratives and conventional print fiction. Armed with Altman's ideas, my students have identified patterns in the work of Frank Miller's noirish superhero comics and Bill Watterson's *Calvin and Hobbes*. Similarly, seeking a way to examine the process of playing a character within a computer game, another student drew on psychological studies of identification, including recent critical applications of the psychological concept of theory of mind. Each of these concepts sends ripples through my entire model of reading by redefining notions of character and plot, and renewing my interest in the nature of narrative.

Listening to the various presentations in our colloquium series has similarly enriched my understanding of storytelling and made me aware of how much my field can benefit from work done in other disciplines. At the same time, it reinforces my sense that the field of English—broadly defined—has much to offer those in other areas of the arts and social sciences. I say broadly defined because "English" has always been a meeting point of various language-based studies. Our department at Idaho State University includes specialists in composition, linguistics, creative writing, folklore, and, by fortuitous historical accident, philosophy. Even among literature faculty, we harbor such extraliterary interests as ethnicity, ecocriticism, postcolonialism, and gender.

I would like other departments and other disciplines to think of the humanities in general and English in particular as resources, not in the sense of being a service department, a place to send illiterate students for remediation, but rather as a repository of knowledge about language and meaning. We have been working on this stuff for a long time. We have tools and terms for talking about stories and storytelling. We are happy to learn from our non-English colleagues who are engaged in such fascinating fieldwork on narratives of health and sickness, cultural clash and cooperation, political maneuvering and propaganda. We hope they are as willing to learn from us about unreliability and irony, and the manipulation of time.

Narrative runs through everything human beings say and do. This project focuses on the arts, humanities, and social sciences because those are the areas within the College of Arts & Letters at ISU. However, we hope to extend the project to other fields and other colleges within the University. We already overlap with and cooperate with the many health-related fields that are a traditional emphasis at our institution. Other interdisciplinary projects require interactions with geosciences, biology, and computer science. All use narratives in some way or another. Even the most abstract, mathematical forms of knowledge must be communicated, and communication invariably involves narrative. My own research on gender and science fiction includes a study of the ways the gendered body serves as a platform for knowing the universe, as pointed out by Donna Haraway and other historians of science. The so-called STEM disciplines—science, technology, engineering, and mathematics—can only function through linguistic and other codes. They must operate within human communities, and they are thus given meaning and purpose through narratives. If they are the STEM disciplines, we are the ROOT disciplines: no acronym, just a metaphor.

I hope that this project, which crosses departmental and disciplinary boundaries, will continue to remind our readers and us of the variety and inevitability of stories. Everything is rooted in narrative, but the branches are innumerable.

Political Science, Public Policy, and Narrative: Mark K. McBeth

By the late 1990s, as Brian stated earlier, the study of narratives had moved from being the exclusive province of literature programs to a wide variety of academic disciplines. Public administration and public policy were no exception to this movement, and much of the work on narratives in public administration and public policy came out of the postpositivist or postmodern school of thought. The publication of Fischer and Forester's *The Argumentative Turn in Policy Analysis and Planning* (1993), Deborah Stone's *Policy Paradox* (1988), and Fox and Miller's *Postmodern Public Administration* (1996) made narrative a buzzword at academic conferences and in departmental break rooms and college classrooms.

Of course, those of us in public administration and policy had no formal training in narrative, and the term "narrative" itself was used loosely and was often confused in the policy literature with discourse, framing, and rhetoric. Moreover, the field became increasingly divided on the use of narrative in the late 1990s when leading policy theorist Paul Sabatier published the first edition of his now seminal edited book, *Theories of the Policy Process* (1999). Sabatier, never one to avoid a good fight or to refrain from speaking his mind, excluded from his book any work on narrative (and the larger social construction school in which narrative was widely used) because in his view the postpositivists and postmoderns had used narrative in a manner that was unconnected to institutions, policy settings, or theories of the policy process. Most specifically, Sabatier did not believe that the study of narrative in public policy was scientific. The reaction to Sabatier's omission was intense and the formal reaction occurred mainly in the *Journal of European Public Policy* (see Radaelli 2000).

Since then, a more scientific study of policy narratives has emerged within the Narrative Policy Framework (NPF), which is a public policy theory framework that originated at Idaho State University. The NPF seeks to study the use of policy narratives by interest groups, media outlets, and others in public policy making, as well as how these narratives impact individual and public opinion. Surprisingly, however, as somebody who had studied policy narratives for nearly fifteen years, I had not asked for advice, cooperation, or input about narrative from my colleagues in communication, English, history, theater, or psychology (though I should have). It was not until 2012, when I gave a sabbatical presentation on the framework, that my colleague in the Department of English and Philosophy, Brian Attebery, approached me about his idea of putting together a panel on narrative in the fall 2013. Brian asked me if I wanted to participate and I did.

What I have learned since 2012 is that the use of narrative in the College is diverse and the interest among faculty seemingly has no limits. A series of monthly colloquia hosted by historian Paul Sivitz has allowed a diverse group of faculty to discuss narrative with colleagues in the social sciences, humanities, and fine arts. The collaboration has been tremendous and the feedback honest—and sometimes difficult to deal with. For example, after fifteen years of work, I was convinced that my NPF colleagues had truly defined a policy narrative and had successfully differentiated our work from rhetoric or discourse. Yet a well-respected colleague in English reported, after one of my presentations, that the NPF does not always study narrative (because the NPF does not spend enough time with plot), but instead the NPF seems to study rhetoric. Scholars in my academic field have accepted that the NPF studies narrative. But hearing criticism from my colleague in English has greatly impacted how the NPF approaches narrative. In particular, there are efforts to work on policy plot development. Criticism comes best from colleagues you know and respect, work with, and can walk across campus to talk to, and that is the idea of the College narrative project and specifically the narrative book project.

What can a public policy theorist learn from an actor, a photographer, a composer, a historian, or an English literature expert? What can we all learn from each other? The College narrative book project is an attempt to answer just that question, as well as the broader question of what everyone in academia can learn from faculty well outside their disciplines. As a bureaucracy, the academy has become increasingly compartmentalized over the past thirty years. Even within departments, room for collaboration has shrunk as subfields have become more specialized. In my home department of political science, we have faculty who specialize in political philosophy, network analysis, behavior, quantitative modeling, and postmodernism. This increasing academic specialization can inhibit collaboration. Academic conferences in political science are increasingly specialized affairs. Only those interested in a very narrow subfield attend panels, and unless you are in the same narrow subfield, you tend not to know or talk to other political scientists. If political scientists are no longer able to talk easily across their own subfields, we must ask whether collaboration across a college is even possible. What we have found, however, is that narrative is one concept (though, we disagree what it means) that connects the diverse departments in the College of Arts & Letters. This connection leads to increased collaboration, communication, and collegiality within the College. Since my own two appearances on narrative panels within the College, my own work has been consumed by rethinking how social scientists may indeed co-author the very narratives that they analyze, how plots may work within policy narratives, and how the audiences of policy narratives might play their own role in the interpretation of plots. My guess is that my colleagues within the College have much good advice to give me.

Of course, what I have learned over the past few years is not confined to my research. Narrative also consumes much of my thoughts about teaching: What are the best ways to encourage students to understand politics and democracy effectively? As a political science faculty member, I am particularly interested in self and political identity, as well as the relationship of identity to narrative. In the liberal arts tradition, we pride ourselves in giving students the ability to understand the values and beliefs of others and to develop empathy for others; the liberal arts serve an important role, as empathy is an important element of mature and responsible adults. But in addition to teaching about how to understand others, we also provide students the ability to understand their own values and beliefs. Self-reflection is as important as empathy in developing responsible and mature citizens.

As somebody who has taught politics for more than twenty years, I have found it very helpful to use narrative to help students understand the origins of politics and political conflict. While many years ago students questioned how a lecture and discussion about narrative applied to a class on US politics, today they seem to understand that contemporary politics is constructed as battles between (often self-proclaimed) heroic figures and villains. Here victims are supposedly harmed by the villain and waiting for help from the hero. Of course, such a situation does not lead to healthy outcomes in a democratic form of government. The ability to forge political compromise requires give-and-take and acceptance that the "other side" might have some value in their ideas and beliefs. Narratives in politics too often create dichotomous worlds of right and wrong, with the result being the bitter political polarization that we see today in US politics. It would be impossible (since humans make meaning through narratives) and undesirable to eliminate narratives in politics. However, democratic governance requires narratives that allow for some bridging between groups.

One of the best lessons that I have learned in my recent work with my political science colleague Donna Lybecker is that a narrative with a villain automatically is more contentious than a narrative without a villain. Villains divide, whereas heroes in a narrative provide a better chance of providing some unity between conflicting groups. Currently, some faculty members in the College are working on studying the restoration of a local river. What we have found is that when individuals talk about the river and assert blame about who polluted and degraded the river (in essence naming a villain), conflict and disagreement are exacerbated. However, when groups focus on solutions to the problem and instead of naming a villain provide a wide variety of different individuals who can fix the problem (heroes), a sense of cooperation rules the day. Just as some narratives polarize, other narratives can build cooperation.

Students are often resistant to accept that their own political beliefs and values are embedded in a narrative. Instead, students often try to hold on to the idea that their own political views are grounded more in empirical fact and evidence. It is the other side, they argue, that uses narrative. Thus I would argue that the most valuable teaching use of narrative is helping students understand the origin and construction of their own. Increasingly, in today's highly polarized political environment, individuals are literally trapped by their own political narrative, which is reflective of their self and political identity. While students are frustrated with the political party, media outlet, or interest group that they dislike, they tend to view themselves as more rational and logical than those that they oppose.

The chapters in this book all deal with identity and narrative. Narratives are very important in how individuals construct their own identities and how they construct the identities of others In addition, in the College, we are interested in how the narrative project itself has helped form the College's own unique identity as well as the identity of individual faculty in the College. One of the unique features of this book is that the authors of each section were given the opportunity to discuss each other's chapters in a facilitated dialogue at the end of each section. Just as the authors have learned from each other, I have learned much about my own teaching in both reading and listening to my colleagues' ideas about narrative. As I have participated in the narrative colloquia and in the development of this book, I have felt assured that my colleagues in other departments remain steadfastly committed to teaching core values that lead all of us to not only understand others but also to self-discovery. Understanding narratives aids in critical thinking and critical thinking is much more than a soft skill, it is again an essential element of democratic governance. As such, the liberal arts continue to play an essential role in society with narrative at the very center of this role.

One College's Response: Kandi Turley-Ames

These are interesting times in education. State budgets for higher education continue to shrink, creating less opportunity for those who most need that opportunity. In many states, especially rural states such as Idaho, the only way "up and out" is postsecondary education. Yet educational boards encourage students to go to school only to develop skills that lead to immediate employment. Rather than focusing on foundational skills and lifelong learning, governing bodies are investing in narrow, trade school training. Traditionally, higher education strives to provide students with the skills necessary to pursue a career rather than to "get a job." With a broad set of skills that include critical thinking and an aptitude for continued learning, students are better prepared for whatever the future might hold: more agile and better able to adjust to an ever-changing marketplace. Investing now in seemingly impractical studies will pay dividends in the end, as their narrowly trained peers require retraining for "new" entry-level jobs when their existing jobs become obsolete.

In this context, the story I will share with you is one that has been relived over and over again in the last decade. Over that time, many institutions have been forced to make significant changes to meet the expectations of state governing bodies. It is through such a process that the College of Arts & Letters at Idaho State University discovered its collective strength in narrative. The story begins in 2006 with a change in leadership and a difficult reorganization, mandated from above, that separated the humanities, arts, and social sciences from mathematics and the natural sciences. In response to those personally and professionally challenging conditions, the faculty rallied, taking ownership of their destiny and recreating their own reality . . . and this is our story.

Part of the current intellectual climate is a questioning of the value of a liberal arts degree and a corresponding favoring of technological degrees and certificates and STEM (science, technology, engineering, and mathematics) training. Many institutions, including ISU, have had to determine just how to embrace these changes in educational priorities. After our College of Arts & Sciences was dissolved, with many assuming that the new College of Science and Engineering would be the primary home for research and professional training, the objective for the College of Arts & Letters was much less clear. This newly formed College with a very old school name—what the heck are Letters?—had no defined mission or apparent relevance to the goals and objectives set by university leadership. We were not "hard" sciences; we were not engineering, and we were not health sciences.

The College of Arts & Letters was, at the time of the reorganization, primarily responsible for general education on the campus, and we remain so postreorganization and postgeneral education reform. However, our ability to interact regularly with our colleagues in the hard sciences became much more difficult. Many in the College lamented over the loss of biology, mathematics, and so forth, because their scholarly identities and interdisciplinary work aligned with those disciplines, which now reported elsewhere. Silos were created where opportunity for interaction had been plentiful.

With these challenges in mind, the new College of Arts & Letters determined to rediscover itself and its strengths. We had to come together to define our presence and relevance. It would have been very easy to allow ourselves to be marginalized, to be viewed as simply a service college, one responsible simply for teaching the fundamentals of general education. But the faculty in the College and its leadership knew we had skills and expertise equaling any and all areas of the academy. We also knew how important liberal arts education is for advancing new ideas and creating a world that we want to live in.

Even in today's digital world, professionals need to know how to think *critically*, to *communicate* effectively with others in speech and writing, to work effectively and *collaboratively* in groups, to engage in *creative* problem solving, and to understand and appreciate *cultural* differences (we sometimes refer to these as the 5 Cs). From our perspective, a scientist who cannot communicate ideas is not going to effect change. A physician unable to think critically will have difficulty treating his patients effectively, and an engineer who cannot work in groups or connect with others from different cultures will fall short of his or her professional goals. A liberal arts education is as valuable today as it has been for centuries.

Beyond meeting the foundational needs of our students and our institution, we knew we had exceptional faculty with skills that could be leveraged to create a new identity for the College and to bring distinction to our institution. However, we could not rely on university leaders to locate those strengths or to identify a path forward. The faculty would need to find its place, its voice, and its passion. We are still in the midst of this process, but we are much closer to redefining our mission and areas of excellence.

In one administrative meeting early on—in my mind a defining moment—the College was described as that junk drawer in your kitchen or laundry area where everything and anything ends up. That drawer holds lots of useful items, even treasures, but finding those items when you really need them can be difficult and time consuming. Our College needed to turn the junk drawer into a tool cabinet, identifying strengths that had been hidden in the previous structure. Unfortunately, there are no "how-to" books for this kind of situation and certainly no guidelines for how to reinvigorate a college that felt it had lost its identity.

The one thing we knew for certain was that it had to be a faculty-driven, bottom-up process. College leadership could create opportunities, facilitate discussion, and applaud outcomes, but we could not make it happen. After the reorganization, faculty had to have ownership and investment. They had to find a path forward.

We used the time of transition to allow faculty to create a collective vision for the College: to think through who we were now, not who we were before. One push was to identify areas of excellence in the newly formed College of Arts & Letters and to encourage innovation and collaboration along those lines via assemblies, college-wide meetings, chairs' meetings, collective policy development, and so forth. At the same time, the College invested a great deal of time and energy in educating the community, our local and state leadership, and our students about the critical importance of a liberal arts education. These discussions echo the debates that appear regularly in the *Chronicle for Higher Education* and other outlets devoted to issues facing higher education. In addition to partnering with community leaders, we encouraged faculty and students to play with new technologies as ways of enhancing existing curricula and instructional methods, instituting, for instance, a grant-funded technology initiative that created virtual resource centers to supplement regular classrooms.

Finally, and most directly tied to the theme of this book, one of our identified strengths led to the College's narrative project. The notion of narrative as an area of excellence—an idea first proposed by English professor Dr. Jessica Winston—was both intriguing and uncertain. The study of narrative throughout the College was diffuse and disorganized—not unlike the junk drawer in the kitchen. Once we began to look more objectively at what and how faculty studied in their scholarship, we became more confident that the College could indeed have a genuine concentration in the study of narrative. As a result of online discussions and informal conversations that ensued, a faculty member in the Department of English and Philosophy and a member of the editorial board of this book, Dr. Brian Attebery, organized a panel discussion on the study of narrative. A call was put out to enlist faculty presenters and to begin a dialogue about how faculty members throughout the College study narrative. The response to the first colloquium by both faculty and students was robust. The event was standing room only.

After that initial colloquium, there were questions about how to maintain interest and momentum. Fortunately, a colleague in the Department of History who is also a member of this editorial board, Dr. Paul Sivitz, volunteered to take on planning of a regular colloquium series as a means of continuing the dialogue and building mutual understanding. At each colloquium meeting, two to four faculty members discuss the role of narrative in their scholarly work, and the audience, led by discussant Dr. Sivitz, offers commentary and questions.

I have learned as dean of the College that it is one thing to have an interesting idea, but it is another to identify how best to bring that idea to fruition. With this lesson in mind, I was struggling, at one of the colloquia in 2014, to figure out a way to help our College share this unique effort with our local and academic communities. As I listened to the presentations, looking for underlying themes and considering opportunities to promote colleagues' work, I began to see an interesting parallel. Each faculty member in turn seemed to come back to the use of narratives to create a sense of identity. I realized that this is exactly what the study of narratives had done for our College. The study of narrative had brought very different disciplines together to create common ground. It started us down a path of sharing and collaboration. Now we, as a college, had a real opportunity to showcase this achievement. Could we turn the project into an interdisciplinary book focused on the study of narrative and the formation of identity?

I would argue also that the College of Arts & Letters has created a strong identity, and it has done so in a relatively short period of time. Just as our students are working to create their professional identities, we as a college have created an identity. We are—for better or for worse—the center of the

University, the foundation of a solid college education, and leaders in our local and campus community. Now, that has become our story.

I recognize that many other institutions have undergone significant changes, including reorganization. I also recognize that the disciplines in a college such as ours are often targets for critiques of higher education. But I believe that the process we have gone through and the common objective we have identified make us stronger and better able to serve our students. I believe our College has made significant strides in reframing and reaffirming the liberal arts, and that we have a story to tell—one from which others facing similar changes might learn.

The Book

The book that has resulted from our combined efforts highlights the diversity of the use of narrative in the College, and at the same time, reveals hidden continuities among our various projects. The first section of the book (Interrogating and Framing Reality: Identity and Cultural Perceptions) opens with one of three contributions from English and Philosophy. Thomas Klein studies how old and new technologies impact the consumption of narratives and how new technologies might shift attention away from the narrative itself and toward the device used in the reading. A historian, Raphael Chijioke Njoku, works with economist, King Yik to study narrative and the construction of ethnic identities in modern Africa, showing that during the nineteenth century, the newly educated African elite jumped on the opportunity to construct, reconstruct, and sometimes fabricate ethnic histories that were intended to privilege some while alienating others. The second contribution from English and Philosophy finds Alan Johnson exploring how characters in Hindi film and Indian fiction have conveyed various forms of identity since the country's independence in 1947 and how these narratives are both contradictory and reflect the complexity of today's narrative constructions of identity. The section concludes with a facilitated dialogue among the section's authors, where they discuss interconnections in the chapters.

Section two of the book (Narratives at the Intersection of the Public and Private) begin with a photographer from Communication, Media, and Persuasion, Terry Ownby, who studies ethnographic photography and examines one methodology for explicating underlying ideologies from photographs reliant on textual narrative. A second contribution from Communication, Media, and Persuasion finds John Gribas, James R. DiSanza, Zac Gershberg, and Nancy J. Legge focusing on the role that narrative plays in corporate identity and how this narrative is ultimately used to build a brand loyalty. Political scientist Kellee J. Kirkpatrick explores how and to what extent narratives are defining the identities of those facing infertility as well as the ways in which narratives influence how these individuals define themselves and make sense of their experiences with infertility.

Finally, the second historian in the book, Paul Sivitz, examines the narratives, or "conversations," that members of the eighteenth-century scientific community created within their letters. The study uncovers how scientific information moved through the community with great precision and demonstrated each practitioner's commitment to the community. The section then concludes with a facilitated dialogue among authors discussing the inner-connections between the chapters.

Section three (Performing Bodies, Creating Stories) opens with a chapter from sociologist Gesine Hearn, who studies how sufferers of chronic pain use narratives to search for meaning and ultimately construct not only a self-identity but a connection to community. Brian Attebery, from the Department of English and Philosophy, next presents his interviews with faculty in the performing arts, in which teachers of performance discuss the nature of storytelling within their particular fields. Another contribution from English and Philosophy finds Sonja Launspach discussing how narrative serves as an interactional function in a quilting guild and how a group uses narrative to construct group norms and group identity. An anthropologist, Elizabeth Cartwright, examines the role of narrative in fieldwork. The chapter deals with the author's encounter with a young Amuzgo Indian girl who was possessed by an animal spirit: a nawaal. From a medical anthropology perspective, the chapter explores the power and ethics of narrative in reconceptualizing and negotiating the world. The section closes with the final facilitated dialogue among authors recounting the inner-connections between the chapters.

Finally, editorial team member Paul Sivitz closes the book by tying together the different chapters and exploring themes that will advance the study of narrative in the liberal arts.

References

Fischer, Frank, and John Forrester. 1993. *The Argumentative Turn in Policy Analysis*. Durham, NC: Duke University Press.

Fox, Charles J., and Hugh T. Miller. 1996. *Postmodern Public Administration: Toward Discourse*. Thousand Oaks, CA: Sage.

Radaelli, Claudio M. 2000. "Public Policy Comes of Age: New Theories and Policy Process Symposium: Theories of the Policy Process." *Journal of European Public Policy* 7: 30–35.

Sabatier, Paul A. ed. 1999. *Theories of the Policy Process*. Boulder, CO: Westview Press.

Stone, Deborah A. 1988. *Policy Paradox and Political Reasoning*. Glenview, IL: Scott Foresman.

Section I
Interrogating and Framing Reality
Identity and Cultural Perceptions

1 Old and New Technologies of Asynchronous Communication
Virtual Narratives and "Presence"[1]

Thomas Klein

As will become clear over the course of this book, narrative can be defined very precisely or very loosely depending on who's discussing it and for what reasons. To *narrate* is to recount a story or series of events or facts. Stories have plots and characters, and beginnings, middles, and endings; they attempt to call upon or establish a common ground between tellers and audiences, which may include a shared understanding of settings and the rules by which narration may operate.

In the European Middle Ages alone (my general disciplinary area), writers and tellers created dozens of story types and forms, including chivalric and Christian romances, Arthurian tales, comic fabliaux, saints' lives, confessions, *exempla*, Breton lays, sermons, miracles, and beast fables, just to mention those found in Geoffrey Chaucer's *Canterbury Tales* (ca. 1390 CE). Those who simply study the Middle Ages call upon narrative in many ways as well. For instance, narratology, the systematic analysis of narrative structure, which has long focused on the post-seventeenth-century period, has become increasingly common in studies of medieval literature.[2] More profoundly, perhaps, thinking about broad cultural narratives has been one of the ways that medievalists have resisted the simplistic tendency to view the Middle Ages as a stultifying and oppressive time—a period hidebound by fear, ignorance, and church dogma. In short, medievalists recognize and resist, as Lee Patterson (1990) writes, "The gigantic master narrative by which modernity identifies itself with the Renaissance and rejects the Middle Ages" (92). In so doing, they attempt to create new narratives about the period, by which the Middle Ages (note the plural) cease to be the "other" against which modernity identifies itself.[3]

As a medievalist, I am particularly interested in studying textual and material artifacts, and in recovering meaning and intention from them. Studying these textual artifacts and immersing oneself in the technical details of earlier forms of writing inevitably draws one's attention the materiality of writing: how writing may be inscribed on metal, stone, or wax; how ink may be spread on vellum or paper; and how letter forms, such as runes, may be adapted to the surfaces on which they are written. From this comes the inspiration for the present chapter, which began by asking, what are some of the ways that technologies of writing, both ancient and modern, shape the experience of what is read? To what degree are writers and readers conscious of this shaping, and how has it affected the narratives they tell about themselves and each other?

Because space is limited here, I will concentrate on just one type of technology: forms of brief asynchronous communication. While short written messages (now in the form of texts, tweets, and e-mails) seem to govern our lives, they have in fact been part of human interaction since the beginning of writing. I wish in particular to consider the digital text message and contrast it with an arguably equivalent ancient technology, the Roman letter-tablet, and consider how these particular technologies promote distinct experiences of "presence": our sense that our correspondents are near and present to us. With the help of Wolfgang Iser, who explored the interaction between a text and its reader, I find that paradoxically, ready availability does not always seem to result in genuine intimacy, and may in fact diminish presence. I will be using a generous definition of what constitutes narrative, which I understand as an implied larger conversation—the *whole* story—that the writing only alludes to, leaving gaps for the reader to fill.

Reading Technologies and Virtual Narratives

One of the curiosities in the development of highly sophisticated technologies of writing and reading is that they frequently seem to contain and recapitulate the old technologies within them. This seems to be particularly true in the language that we use to refer to these objects. Thus the electronic *tablet* (literally, "little table") recalls wax, slate, and paper tablets (devices intended for temporary writing and drawing) on the one hand, and clay and stone tablets (intended for very permanent inscriptions) on the other. E-books mimic physical books (that is, the codex, the stacked side-bound collection of pages); especially interestingly, reading on computer screens has meant returning to *scrolling*, a type of reading technology that the codex had previously made obsolete. Digital styluses, bookmarks, keyboards, and desktops recall or reappropriate physical tools and environments of intellectual activity. The *icon*, a mystical object central to Eastern Orthodox worship, is repurposed (but now gives way to the *widget*—perhaps reflecting a tendency to favor terminology of industrial production). Perhaps one of the most interesting developments is the ubiquitous *screen*: originally designed to block drafts around fireplaces or to shield the altars of gothic churches from general view, the screen became a place on which to depict and then to project images; thus the screen no longer hides or stands in for the view, but is the view itself. This suggests a deeper shift in how we imagine where the textual or visual story is based. Earlier narratives existed either in the memory or on the page. It is hard to say where precisely digital texts and narratives have their foundations—where they "stand."

Having said this, we should acknowledge that, at least according to some perspectives on narrative, our experience of stories that we read has always been in some way virtual. In this regard, I have found Wolfgang Iser's (1972) analysis of the reading process to be especially provocative. According to Iser, a text may reside on the page (or screen), but this arrangement of symbols and spaces is really in essence a schematic framework for how the text may be "realized" (*konkretisiert*, to cite the useful German term) by the reader (279).[4] However, the literary text or narrative is not to be taken as equivalent to the individual and possibly idiosyncratic responses of a given reader; rather, it exists somewhere *between* the "words on the page" and the "reader's response," and this is what gives it its virtual character. Iser's idea allows us to focus on the way that reading is actually an ongoing process of anticipation and retrospection: as we read, "We look forward, we look back, we decide, we change our decisions, we form expectations, we are shocked by their non-fulfillment, we question, we muse, we accept, we reject," and in doing so we "recreate" the text; this is even true upon successive re-readings, where we continue to form new anticipations "by referring to our awareness of what is to come" (293, 286).

At the heart of this activity, spurring the reader into action, are the gaps in the text: the places where the text does not and perhaps could not ever entirely specify everything that would allow a complete and direct transference between the text and the reader's experience. As Iser (1980) notes,

> What is concealed spurs the reader into action, but this action is also controlled by what is revealed; the explicit in its turn is transformed when the implicit has been brought to light. Whenever the reader bridges the gaps, communication begins.
>
> (110–111)

Central to this process is the lack of "a common situation and a common frame of reference" between the text and the reader and the inability of the text to adapt itself to each individual reader. Iser suggests that this very quality makes the interaction between text and reader similar to other forms of interaction, which are brought on by a need to fill a gap in our direct knowledge and experience (109).

Brief Asynchronous Communication and "Backstory"

Although Iser was describing our experience of literary narrative (especially the novel), his theory may also describe our experience of the sort of writing that is intended to mimic or stand in for in-person communication. With brief written communication, the correspondents have still to contend with an ever-present asynchrony, even in those instances where the lag time is much reduced. The very brevity of the message and the absence of other signals (punctuation and emoticons aside) tend to augment our awareness of the asynchrony; the experience is not unlike communicating through a wall: we tap out our message and then wait anxiously for the reply.

Because of the constrictions of its format, asynchronous communication requires the communicants to create and then draw upon a certain "backstory" to supply what they know of "the rest of the story." While such communication does not necessarily involve storytelling per se, it does require us to proceed on the basis of interpretation of each other's motives given what we know makes a reasonable story: a sequence of events, experiences, and intentions that we mutually construct. For this reason, I suggest that we view the correspondents in an interchange of asynchronous communication as participating in an only partially visible narrative, which they allude to but which may never be fully developed in the course of communication.[5]

It is perhaps not surprising that the speed of communication and the technology-determined length of the message play into the correspondents' mutual sense of physical and psychological distance, as we will see. What is surprising, however, is that it appears to do so in inverse relation: greater speed seems to mean a greater fragmentation of the underlying narrative, with a corresponding loss of intimate expression.

Text Messages: Always Here, Never Away

The world of personal digital communication offers a dizzying, ever-expanding array of interfaces, at the heart of which is always the promise of newness and choice, as well as the sense that each service offers an entirely distinct experience (often an unsatisfactory one, if the online reviews are any indication). Text messaging, or texting, refers specifically to messages sent via Short Message Service (SMS). Although the "text" was first introduced in the 1990s, the form has greatly taken off since 2000, especially since the arrival of the smartphone. Text messages, of course, are characterized by their 160-character limit and the general speed of their delivery. Despite their speed, however, text messages are not truly "instant": a slight delay attends each sending, and composition and response speeds vary widely according to the availability, skill, and commitment of the correspondents.

The narrative aspect of text messages can be seen in a variety of ways. In the early 2000s, Rich Ling and Birgitte Yttri (2002) perceptively noted that the mobile phone was enabling a curious phenomenon of social interaction that they called micro-coordination. Here the phone eliminates the need to establish previously agreed upon meeting times and places, replacing it with the ability to give minute-to-minute updates on one's movements (139).[6] Instances of micro-coordination suggest the participants see themselves as involved in an unfolding, wide-ranging, coordinated narrative, their movements resembling pieces on a massive game board, each movement an episode with its own dramas and triumphs. These qualities may be seen in the following text interchange cited by Caroline Tagg (2012, 13–14):

Laura: Hello we are back waiting for luggage, not sure if will make the bus! Will let you know
Laura: We made it! Eta at taunton is 12.30 as planned, hope thats still okay?! Good to see you! :—xx
Charlotte: Yes i will be there. Glad you made it

Tagg suggests,

> Previously, you would arrange your trip from home and then set out on it. The mobile phone, however, allows people to set out with a vague idea as to where they are going, whom they are meeting and when, and to reach a "progressively exact arrangement . . ." as they go.
>
> (14)

Thus cell phones and texting allow us to range widely within a shared space and come together at crucial moments (if we were further apart we wouldn't need to synchronize; if we were closer together we wouldn't need to coordinate). There is a strong narrative component to these exchanges: the recipient is intended to follow them with interest, and the interest is generated by the gaps between the messages. These gaps, of course, oblige the recipient to fill the context, the movement between one point and the next, and the likely direction: the message "We made it!" requires the reader to fill in the gap that the sender has successfully moved from the airport carousel to the bus stand, the sender is now on the bus, and the bus is moving forward. In effect, each message offers the recipient a sort of narrative cliffhanger ("will let you know").

One effect of this is that text message exchanges encourage each correspondent to construct the situation and activity of the other, *as they are right now*. As with other kinds of correspondence, each becomes imaginatively present to the other. However, the brevity of the message format (as well as the fairly minimal range of emotional tones and signals that it allows) means that writers frequently make wrong guesses about each other's positions and intentions, as can be seen in another exchange cited by Tagg (2012, 103):

Chloe: Guess ur back now. Do u want to come here for around four?
Jo: Oh ok. I had visions of your coming here! But ok, see you then.
Chloe: Oh sorry, hadn't thought of that.

While each correspondent is making guesses and "having visions" of the other, they are actually doing so incorrectly, and it is only the speed of the message that saves them from total misapprehension.

New technologies of communication such as texting create the impression of constant presence: many commentators have described the impression of perpetual contact generated by text messages, and Carmen Frehner (2008) suggests that the absence of salutations in the medium in particular "indicates a certain *always-here-never-away* attitude towards one's friends or colleagues" (91). Consider the general absence of greetings (other than an opening "Hi") or sign-offs in the following exchange cited by Frehner (165):

> 20:03 Hi, didn't get the one I wanted but they liked me so they have sent my details onto Nhs professionals who will find me one.
> 20:05 that's good. Don't lose heart . . . easier said than done but keep pushin-one they know you're serious you'll impress them :-)
> 20:35 well I think it's better this way cause there doin the searchin for me! Saves me doin it! An ill have a job! How you doin? X
> 20:49 not so gd. Few problems at home and I've gotta stick around which is unavoidable but was sposed to b going to [name] in 3wks.

It is interesting that despite time delays ranging from two to thirty minutes, the conversation proceeds more or less as if it were a continuous spoken dialogue. However, despite text messaging's *always-here-never-away* appearance, it is in many instances illusory. In the example given earlier, we may observe that while the writers seem to know each other well and to be on familiar, even intimate terms, our impression of their sympathetic closeness ("Don't lose heart," "How you doin?") may be tempered by what we see of their ignorance of each other's current circumstances, and a deeper reticence ("not so gd. Few problems at home") that discourages further elaboration.

Perhaps it is simply the human condition to be absent even when present, but when one is absorbed in a digital activity, as Kenneth Gergen (2002) writes, "One is physically present but is absorbed by a technologically mediated world of elsewhere" (227). While some, such as sociologist Christopher Licoppe, see digital technologies such as the text message as a vehicle for something called "connected presence" in a space beyond the physical, "a permanent connection, an impression that the link can be activated at any time and that one can thus experience the other's engagement in the relationship at any time," such an impression is always one of projection, of filling the gap of the other's absence (quoted in Ling 2008, 171). Ultimately, if our friends are "always here," are we really "closer" to them?

The Vindolanda Tablets: *Greet from Me Our Friend*

The Roman letter-tablets discovered in the north of Britain, dating from the end of the first century and beginning of the second, offer an attractive point of comparison to the digital technology discussed earlier, especially when we approach their fragmentary evidence in a sympathetic and imaginative way. The first tablets were discovered in the 1970s in and around the Roman fort of Vindolanda, located roughly equidistant from modern Carlisle and Newcastle upon Tyne and near the site of the subsequently built Hadrian's Wall. The tablets are made of thin, rectangular sheets of wood (used apparently because imported papyrus was expensive), which happened be preserved by the anaerobic northern British soil (Bowman 1994, 15–16; Bowman, Thomas, and Adams 1994, 18–20).

The letter-tablet seems to have been widely used in the north of Britain by the Roman occupiers, and it takes a standard format: the message is written on one side, the tablet is folded in half, and the address is then written on the outside surface. While there are receipts, lists, and records of various sorts included among the tablets, the letter-tablets are generally comparable to, or slightly longer than, the modern text message: most tend to be in the range of about 80 words (or 350 characters), with elaborate salutations constituting a fair proportion of their message. When it comes to their delivery speed, however, they were (not surprisingly) considerably slower than digital forms of communication. It is true that the state administration did maintain a mounted courier system, the *cursus publicus*, designed for fast movement of messages; the ancient writer Procopius claims that this system might allow a courier to travel between forty and sixty-four Roman miles in a day, and Lincoln Blumell (2014) finds evidence "that some letters were transported a distance of almost 200 km on the same day" (55–56). It is thus conceivable that a letter might travel, for instance, from Lundinium (London) to Vindolanda in about a week, as Greg Jenner suggests (2015, 161), which is fairly prompt, all things considered. Many of the more personal messages, however, were probably included with other commerce and took a good deal longer.

Interestingly, even this slower technology allowed for a sort of microcoordination similar to that enabled by the text message. A command coming probably from Flavius Cerialis, the prefect of the Ninth Cohort of Batavians stationed at Vindolanda around 100 CE (Bowman 1994, 25),[7] to a centurion of his division, reads: "Come to Vindolanda tomorrow, early in the morning in order to [receive] the payment of the company . . . Farewell, my dearest Felicio . . . " (Tab. 242).[8] This message requires a fast turnaround time, and obviously, "Felicio" must have been fairly nearby to make this possible. Nevertheless, as we review the tablets, it becomes apparent that while senders and recipients view themselves as sharing a friendship, they are necessarily living separate stories. In general, writers and readers do not remark upon the fact of being distant from each other: physical distance (and the "travail" required to traverse it) is the essential unstated background to these letters.

As a result, the writers of many letters are vague about their own activities and do not seem inclined to ask about those of their correspondents, as though the time and distance between them precludes anything other than a general expression of goodwill. One letter to Cerialis from Aelius Brocchus, about whom we will hear more shortly, simply expresses the wish that "whatever you are about to do will be successful" (Tab. 248). Other letters are intended to prompt the recipient simply to keep the sender in mind and help him (or her) out in general: in one, the sender asks the recipient to "please either send or keep on one side anything which you believe useful for me" (Tab. 218); in another letter, Cerialis writes to a Crispinus, evidently a high-ranking officer with access to the provincial governor, requesting that "in whatever way you wish, fulfil what I expect of you and . . . so furnish me with friends that thanks to you I may be able to enjoy a pleasant period of military service" (Tab. 225). Here, specific directives would seem out of place and would perhaps be rude; instead, the recipient is expected to use his knowledge of Cerialis, and to act in his interest.

For our purposes, the most interesting tablets involve Cerialis and his wife Sulpicia Lepidina.[9] Although Vindolanda and nearby forts were chiefly military outposts, at least the high-ranking officers did keep their families there: this is attested by the finding of an elegant woman's sandal, some well-preserved children's shoes, and what appear to be juvenile writing-exercises with lines from Virgil (Bowman 1994, 57). While Cerialis received the bulk of correspondence, Lepidina appears to have been a person of some importance and influence.[10] Interestingly, Cerialis and Lepidina's personal names suggest that both of them (or their immediate ancestors) might have recently been enfranchised as Roman citizens (Bowman 1994, 27). As the head of the Batavian cohort, originating from the Dutch Rhine delta, Cerialis likely came from Germanic nobility; as such, the presence of the Batavians (and Tungrians, from further to the south) in Vindolanda reflects a larger, effective strategy, whereby "areas of the periphery of the empire were controlled and organized through the medium of troops from an area which was itself peripheral until relatively recently" (27).

We can assume that as foreigners in a strange land, the officers and their families stationed in the north of Britain formed close relationships among other such families there, and this emerges particularly in the correspondence of Cerialis and Lepidina and their particular friends, the Aelius Brocchus mentioned earlier and his wife Claudia Severa.[11] Brocchus and Severa appear to have lived fairly nearby, either at a place called Briga or perhaps at Coria (modern Corbridge), just fifteen miles away (Bowman, Thomas, and Adams 1994, 262; 2003, 82). The couples appear to have visited each other regularly: Brocchus for instance appears in one of the records as having been present at Vindolanda several times over the course of several months, presumably as a guest, and having consumed a number of geese and chickens (Tab. 581).

More importantly, when they were not together, the couples corresponded regularly. The subjects of these letters are charmingly mundane: in a draft of a letter to Brocchus, Cerialis pleads, "If you love me, brother, I ask that you send me some hunting-nets" (Tab. 233); other letters, as we will see, contain the details of future visits and of an upcoming celebration. For our purposes, it is particularly interesting to consider the various rhetorical gestures the individuals in the correspondence make in order to maintain their relationships over the intervening distance and space. For instance, it is important for all involved not only to formally greet the addressee of the letter but also to extend good wishes to the recipient's spouse and child, and to pass on greetings from his or her own family. Thus in one letter, Brocchus writes to Cerialis, "My Severa greets you both," and in another, "My little son greets you" (Tab. 622). Likewise, Severa opens a letter that reads, "Claudia Severa to her Lepidina greetings" and writes further on, "Give my greetings to your Cerialis. My Aelius and my little son send him their greetings" (Tab. 291). Often, given the fragmentary nature of the tablets, only these salutations survive: piecing together one series of fragmentary texts from Brocchus to Cerialis, we read, "Aelius Brocchus to his Cerialis, greetings brother"; "my Severa greets you"; "Greet your Lepidina from me. May you be well, my lord and dearest brother" (Tab. 243, 244, 247). In another series (given this particular order by the editors of the tablets), only the names and possessive adjectives survive: "Aelius Brocchus to his Cerialis"; "my Claudia"; "your Lepidina" (Tab. 624, 626). It is clear that aside from any informational message-giving, these letters are centrally concerned with affirming familial and friendship bonds—the mutual "backstory" that I mentioned earlier.

Stanley Stowers (1986) proposes a classification of ancient letters that distinguishes letters of friendship from family or household letters (58–76). Perhaps because they are so brief, these letters do not allow for any such clear distinction: they are being passed between friends, but their references to and involvement with their respective families make them a combination of the friendship and family letter types. The various salutations I just mentioned, however, do show them to be participating in recognizable formulaic practices in ancient letter-writing. Stowers describes the typical shape of ancient letters in this way,

> Most extant Greek and Latin letters begin with a prescript or salutation that contains the name of the sender, the name of the addressee and a greeting . . . This may be embellished or either abbreviated or expanded in various ways. Often the greeting was followed by a prayer for the recipient . . . The letters usually end with the word "farewell." Sometimes the farewell is preceded by a wish for the health of the recipient or a request for the recipient to greet family members, friends, or others named by the sender.
>
> (20)

It makes sense that the Vindolanda letters should match the generic expectations of ancient (and even modern) letters. In describing the letters home of Swedish immigrants to the American West, Jennifer Eastman Attebery (2007) notes that "Writers of letters do not just sit down and allow words to flow onto the paper . . . They write to produce a text that satisfies their and their recipient's idea of a letter" (21).[12] They do so, however, even as they play with, strain, and occasionally violate the expectations of the genre's form. What makes the Vindolanda letters unique is their particular way of breaking the familiar address patterns, and it is here that they get especially interesting. Perhaps the most famous of the Vindolanda letters is Tablet 291, where Severa extends a birthday invitation to Lepidina:

> On 11 September, sister, for the day of the celebration of my birthday, I give you a warm invitation to make sure that you come to us, to make the day more enjoyable for me by your arrival, if [you are present].[13]

Most of Severa's invitation to Lepidina appears to have been written by a scribe, but the message concludes another hand, which is certainly that of Severa and is perhaps the earliest piece of Latin writing by a woman. She says, "I shall expect you, sister. Farewell, sister, my dearest soul, as I hope to prosper, and hail." Alan Bowman (1994) explains that "although most of our letters were not written by their authors but by clerks or amanuenses, the authors normally add the closing greetings (which show some variety of expression) in their own hands" (88–89). This is the case in the Severa letter, and virtually everything about her concluding farewell is unique. Her use of *sperabo* for "I shall expect," her expression *ita ualeam* for "as I hope to prosper," and her ending *haue* or "hail" when she has already said *uale* or "farewell"—all of these are otherwise unattested; even calling Lepidina *anima mea*, "my soul," is fairly rare (Bowman, Thomas, and Adams 1994, 258). As Bowman (1994) notes, the variety of such closing greetings speaks to a more than basic literacy among the men *and* women in the far north of the Roman Empire (and by implication elsewhere in the empire): it suggests that "the authors and writers were masters of their material, not the other way round" (89). In this case it allows us to perceive, at a distance, the apparently genuine and abiding affection between the two women.

It does not appear to be the case, however, that the correspondence was a full and satisfactory substitute for the physical presence of the other. In her book on modern technologies of presence, Esther Milne (2010) suggests,

> In the course of communication by letter, postcard and email readers construct an imaginary, incorporeal body for their correspondents. . . . At times, subjects believe the body imagined in these exchanges is more real, more expressive of the writer's emotions and soul . . . [than] the actual body encountered in face-to-face communication.
>
> (2)

This statement, however, does not seem applicable to our Vindolanda correspondents. Everything they say suggests that they are eager to be in each other's company. Brocchus writes to Cerialis that he should "Come with your Lepidina in this way so that you may stay with us [beyond] the New Year" (Tab. 622). In Tablet 292, Severa reports to Lepidina,

> Just as I had . . . promised that I would ask Brocchus and would come to you, I asked him and he gave me the following reply that it was always readily (?) permitted to me . . . to come to you . . . in whatever way I can.

She then promises, "You will receive my letters by which you will know what I am going to do" (thereby giving evidence of their extended correspondence); however, she alludes intriguingly to "certain essential things" (*necessari quaedam*) that she apparently will only communicate in person (thus creating her own narrative cliffhanger). Her conclusion, written in her own hand, is again striking and unprecedented. She writes, "Farewell, my sister, my dearest and most longed-for soul." For Severa, Lepidina's soul is not present: it is "longed-for" (*desideratissima*).

For Severa and Lepidina, "physical absence is no impediment" to their relationship; "despite their physical separation . . . they construct an intimate relation" (Milne 2010, 1). However, the letters exchanged between them seem to be a stand-in, and a poor one at that, for the actual intimacy that they can only fulfill in person, thereby reactivating their shared story. In this respect, the Vindolanda tablets make an interesting contrast to later communication technologies. It might be said then that the Vindolanda tablets seem to give us an example of a technology that is somehow *more* intimate than many modern forms, but that is curiously not sufficient for its users. By contrast, a technology such as the text message promotes a casual relationship between correspondents and is therefore less intimate, yet somehow its users find it sufficient. Perhaps this is something akin to what Martin Heidegger (1971) had in mind when he observed that in the modern world "all distances in time and space are decreasing . . . but the hasty elimination of all distances does not bring about nearness, for nearness does not consist in shortness of distance" (164). The Vindolanda tablets remind us that the gains we have made in speed, convenience, and coordination in communicating with each other has not necessarily meant a corresponding increase in intimacy.

Conclusion

I hope this chapter offered a broad illustration of one project of the liberal arts in general and the humanities in particular: in part recovering but more especially "un-othering" the past. Just as modernity has used the Middle Ages (and even earlier eras, as examined here) as a period to define itself against in telling its own narrative, so the present moment continually tells us that that which is most recent is better: the latest gadget, the newest method, the most cutting-edge research. This is true within the University, where innovation seems to be always celebrated, regardless of its outcomes, as well as the culture at large. As we remind our students, however, when we carefully study the past, we come to recognize both its familiarity and its strangeness; we also acquire a healthy skepticism with regard to what is said to be genuinely new and the virtues of what the present day produces.

Thoughtful comparison is nearly always a productive activity. For instance, given space, we might also think about how the e-reader, book, and ancient scroll promote different kinds of reading experiences of what would otherwise be the same narrative, or how various technologies of writing, such as Microsoft Word or the wax tablet, suggest distinct metaphors of narrative composition.

Doing so causes us to see that one technology is not necessarily "better": it is simply *different*, subtly shifting our physical and mental activities.

Thinking carefully about the past can also alert to us to the dangers of what we might call "present" bias. When one encounters an antique artifact in its concrete reality, usually in the context of a museum, it seems not only venerable and fragile but also smaller than expected. Whether the object is the Mona Lisa, the Book of Kells, or a Clovis point, museum objects often seem less vibrant than digital images or reproductions seen previously. While some ancient objects, such as the pyramids at Giza or Machu Picchu, do not fail to impress, artifacts from the past often seem to undergo a kind of shrinkage. The story the humanities tells is that these objects are nonetheless comparable with present-day technologies, in the senses that they are available for comparison and that they performed equivalent or parallel functions.

This is, of course, not to say that ancient and modern technologies and the activities they engender are essentially the same. Placing the Roman letter-tablet next to the text message allows us to see how different technologies of written communication promote distinct experiences and actions. In this case, perhaps the most interesting difference is a shift in narrative, from one involving desire for presence, to another that self-consciously foregrounds the technology ("Just got your text") and the activity ("Text you later!").

As a postscript, I might add that we should of course resist the opposite impulse: the desire to create an idealized past, conveniently forgetting those aspects that were at their best messy and at their worst vicious. In the case of Vindolanda, we remember that life on the frontier was hard and that the people involved were part of an invading and occupying force. Tellingly, there is little evidence for the presence of native Britons in and around the fort, and Tablet 164 contains a slight reference to the *Brittunculi*, the "wretched little Britons," who were so unsophisticated as to lack armor and to not "mount in order to throw javelins."[14]

If I may extend this thought to the context of the present book, the narratives that we create about our institutional history and our current moment need to recognize that our past (when we had money to travel, fewer pressures for service, more time for research, always-eager and well-prepared students, etc.) was probably never as good as we may be inclined to imagine at our most pressured moments, and that the un-othered past was as messy—for good and for ill—as the present.

Notes

1 I would like to thank my colleague Matthew VanWinkle for his invaluable help, encouragement, and insight in reviewing many drafts of this chapter, as well as John Gribas, my contact with the College of Arts & Letter's editorial board for this project.

2 See Eva von Contzen (2014).

3 For a recent installment of that master narrative, see Greenblatt (2011); for an example of the critical response, see Hinch (2012).

4 Iser was drawing upon the work of the Polish philosopher Roman Ingarden.
5 Along these same lines, we may also cite Walter Fisher's (1995) theory of the narrative paradigm, whereby "all forms of discourse can be considered stories, that is, interpretations of some aspect of the world occurring in time and shaped by history, culture, and character" (170); see also Fisher (1984, esp. 7–8).
6 Caron and Caronia (2007, 172–175) illustrate micro-coordination especially well.
7 As Bowman (1994) says, "The Batavians, from the region around the mouth of the Rhine / Scheldt, . . . were renowned for their horsemanship and had been heavily used in Britain in the conquest period" (26).
8 Tablets are cited by the numbers given them by Bowman and Thomas. Translations are by Bowman and Thomas, modified for clarity: the texts of tablets 118–573 are from Bowman, Thomas, and Adams (1994); tablets 574–853 are from Bowman and Thomas (2003); tablets 854–869 are from Bowman, Thomas, and Tomlin (2010); and tablets 870–889 are from Bowman, Thomas, and Tomlin (2011).
9 People in the tablets are named by their *gentilicium* (family name) and *cognomen* (distinguishing personal name); after giving the two names, writers tend to refer to each other by their personal names, although one couple alternates between *genticilium* and *cognomen*.
10 For instance, in Tab. 257, a woman named Valatta appeals to Cerialis for clemency by calling upon Lepidina's name: "I ask my lord that you relax your [severity] and through Lepidina that you grant me what I ask . . . "
11 For extensive discussion of the people figured in these particular letters, see Birley (2002).
12 See also Bowman (1994, 85–87).
13 Birthday celebrations seem to have been significant events at Vindolanda: in Tab. 628, an officer apologizes to Cerialis for having missed his wife's birthday, and in the draft of Tab. 227, Lepidina herself apparently begins a message explaining that Cerialis's birthday prevented her from doing something; she subsequently cancels "birthday," and substitutes "health," as a better excuse (Bowman, Thomas, and Adams 1994, 204).
14 Adams (2003) does note the occurrence of some Celtic-derived terms among the tablets, but he suggests that these words might "have been transferred from Gaul to Britain by soldiers of Celtic origin" (572).

References

Adams, J. N. 2003. "The New Vindolanda Writing-Tablets." *The Classical Quarterly* 53 (2) (November): 530–575.
Attebery, Jennifer Eastman. 2007. *Up in the Rocky Mountains: Writing the Swedish Immigrant Experience*. Minneapolis: University of Minnesota Press.
Birley, Anthony. 2002. *Garrison Life at Vindolanda: A Band of Brothers*. Stroud, Gloucestershire: The History Press Ltd.
Blumell, Lincoln. 2014. "The Message and the Medium: Some Observations on Epistolary Communication in Late Antiquity." *Journal of Greco-Roman Christianity and Judaism* 10: 24–67.
Bowman, Alan K. 1994. *Life and Letters on the Roman Frontier: Vindolanda and Its People*. New York: Routledge.
Bowman, Alan K., J. David Thomas, and J. N. Adams. 1994. *The Vindolanda Writing-Tablets (Tabulae Vindolandenses II)*. London: British Museum Press.
———. 2003. *The Vindolanda Writing-Tablets (Tabulae Vindolandenses III)*. London: British Museum Press.

Bowman, Alan K., J. David Thomas, and R. S. O. Tomlin. 2010. "The Vindolanda Writing-Tablets (Tabulae Vindolandenses IV, Part 1)." *Britannia* 41: 187–224.
———. 2011. "The Vindolanda Writing-Tablets (Tabulae Vindolandenses IV, Part 2)." *Britannia* 42: 113–144.
Caron, André H., and Letizia Caronia. 2007. *Moving Cultures: Mobile Communication in Everyday Life.* Montreal and Kingston: McGill-Queen's University Press.
Fisher, Walter. 1984. "Narration as Human Communication Paradigm: The Case of Public Moral Argument." *Communication Monographs* 51 (March): 1–22.
———. 1995. "Narration, Knowledge, and the Possibility of Wisdom." In *Rethinking Knowledge: Reflections across the Disciplines*, edited by Walter Fisher and Robert F. Goodman, 169–192. New York: State University of New York Press.
Frehner, Carmen. 2008. *Email, SMS, MMS: The Linguistic Creativity of Asynchronous Discourse in the New Media Age.* Bern: Peter Lang.
Gergen, Kenneth J. 2002. "The Challenge of Absent Presence." In *Perpetual Contact: Mobile Communication, Private Talk, Public Performance*, edited by James E. Katz and Mark Aakhus, 227–241. Cambridge: Cambridge University Press.
Greenblatt, Stephen. 2011. *The Swerve: How The World Became Modern.* New York: Norton.
Heidegger, Martin. 1971. "The Thing." In *Poetry, Language, Thought*, translated by Albert Hofstadter, 164–184. New York: HarperCollins.
Hinch, Jim. 2012. "Why Stephen Greenblatt Is Wrong—and Why It Matters." *Los Angeles Review of Books*, January 12. Accessed June 2, 2015. https://lareviewofbooks.org/review/why-stephen-greenblatt-is-wrong-and-why-it-matters.
Iser, Wolfgang. 1972. "The Reading Process: A Phenomenological Approach." *New Literary History* 3 (2) (Winter): 279–299.
———. 1980. "Interaction between Text and Reader." In *The Reader in the Text: Essays on Audience & Interpretation*, edited by Susan R. Suleiman and Inge Crosman, 106–119. Princeton: Princeton University Press.
Jenner, Greg. 2015. *A Million Years in a Day: A Curious History of Everyday Life.* London: Wiedenfeld & Nicholson.
Ling, Richard. 2008. *New Tech, New Ties: How Mobile Communication Is Reshaping Social Cohesion.* Cambridge, MA: MIT Press.
Ling, Richard, and Birgitte Yttri. 2002. "Hyper-Coordination via Mobile Phones in Norway." In *Perpetual Contact: Mobile Communication, Private Talk, Public Performance*, edited by James E. Katz and Mark Aakhus, 139–169. Cambridge: Cambridge University Press.
Milne, Esther. 2010. *Letters, Postcards, Email: Technologies of Presence.* New York: Routledge.
Patterson, Lee. 1990. "On the Margin: Postmodernism, Ironic History, and Medieval Studies." *Speculum* 65 (1): 87–108.
Stowers, Stanley. 1986. *Letter Writing in Greco-Writing Antiquity.* Philadelphia: Westminster.
Tagg, Caroline. 2012. *Discourse of Text Messaging: Analysis of SMS Communication.* London: Continuum Books.
von Contzen, Eva. 2014. "Why We Need a Medieval Narratology: A Manifesto." *Diegesis: Interdisciplinary E-Journal for Narrative Research* 3 (2). Accessed June 2, 2015. http://www.diegesis.uni-wuppertal.de/.

2 Onitsha Market Literature
Narrating Identity and Survival in a Colonial African City

Raphael Chijioke Njoku and King Yik

This chapter examines the role of a genre of African literary collections commonly known as the "Onitsha market literature" in the construction of gender and identity discourses in the late colonial and early postcolonial eras. These writings had a significant effect in shaping postcolonial notions of women, gender, identity, and cultural practices among the Igbo of southeastern Nigeria in particular and Africans in general. Here we argue that the ideas expressed in the writings that mostly tried to cast African women in demeaning terms are embedded in the wider resonance of colonial culture of promoting masculinity or male dominance. The views held by the Onitsha literature authors mirror a gendered struggle for access to power and economic opportunities created by the colonial encounter. For us, narrative, as a procedural method to research, is at the soul of all socioeconomic endeavors and historical events. It represents a storied approach to the unfolding of events, including the issues projected in the Onitsha market literature. In this study, we see the works of economists and historians as intricately complementary rather than separate spheres of inquiry. Economics provides lenses to deciphering motives or profit and losses driving everyday human activities across time and space. Historians survey motives to either corroborate or dismiss a story line.

Personal Story: Use of Narrative in History and Economics

As economists and historians, we are mindful of the potency of stories in propagating ideas into the world. Whether through bedtime stories our parents told us or the moonlight stories that characterized the African village squares or the rumors people peddle in offices and private spaces or even the tones of novels and academic essays and books we digested in college and graduate school, we have learned that stories can empower, dehumanize, challenge, and inspire. On the function of storytelling, Chinua Achebe (1987) once noted that only the story can survive after "the war and the warrior" are gone.

> It is the story that outlives the sound of war-drums and the exploits of brave fighters. It is the story . . . that saves our progeny from blundering

like blind beggars into the spikes of the cactus fence. The story is our escort; without it, we are blind. Does the blind man own his escort? No, neither do we the story; rather it is the story that owns us and directs us.
(13)

Passing through graduate schools and as students with more focus on colonial and postcolonial studies, we have learned how narrative could mold economic and historical perceptions and reactions. It has the clout to impose notions of authenticity or lack of it, and to set boundaries in the production of economic and cultural knowledge, especially with regards to a preliterate society in transition from colonial rule to independence. Frederick Cooper (2000) and others have cautioned that the sources of information on Africa's pasts is multifaceted, and the colonial archives are not only incomplete but fraught with invented traditions, which comes with the baggage of obfuscation and modifications shaped by elite voices as opposed to subaltern/silenced voices.[1] In light of this, T. B. Bottomore in *Elites and Society* (1993) advanced the view that the elite of every society holds the power to shape society after their whims and caprices.

Starting from the late nineteenth century when the missionaries brought Western education and writing skills to the continent, we have realized, as also documented by other studies, that the newly educated African elite jumped on the opportunity offered by colonial education to construct, reconstruct, and sometimes fabricate ethnic histories and gendered practices that were intended to privilege certain groups, while alienating others.[2] This reminds us of Benedict Anderson's (1983) characterization of identity as "an imagined community." As we illustrate with the Onitsha market books and chapbooks, the lettered Africans leveraged the power accorded them by Western education to construct a peculiar form of narrative that tried to shape or even impose ideas and behaviors, including how women should and should not behave. Our study reveals that ideologies and perceptions propagated by these writings—whether real or fictional—were powerful instruments of sociopolitical and cultural ordering and alterity; they conjured emotive and potent imageries that structured how certain individuals and groups have come to understand who they are today.

Sir Francis Bacon (1561–1626), the esteemed English author, courtier, and philosopher, once cautioned readers to

> read not to contradict and confute; nor to believe and take for granted; nor to find talk and discourse; but to weigh and consider. Some books are to be tasted, others to be swallowed, and some few to be chewed and digested.
>
> (Vickers 1996, 439)

Thus as scholars on a quest for a balanced narrative, we are trained to be prudent and to question sources and their motives. How we use genres of narratives—personal stories or official releases preserved in written, oral or other forms—make a lot of difference in the kind of knowledge we produce. In our journey as scholars, we have learned that because narratives have the power to befuddle our understanding of reality, it is important for us to observe cues and prejudices, and acknowledge those trends shared across cultures, while underscoring the nuances of local differences and cross-cultural connections.

History and economics are contingent upon patterns and connections. It is only by tracing these linkages that the story becomes a sequence rather than an interlude and passing echoes. Narrative or historiography (i.e., how historians study events and interpretations they assign to them) is encountered in two models: the "traditional" and the "modern." Traditional narrative is compelled by events and focuses on the sequential unfolding of history in the Hegelian tradition. The adaptors of traditional narrative place more attention on individuals as history makers and the incentives that drive their actions. Just to illustrate, a historian who uses the traditional narrative approach may perceive European imperialism as a single episode in the progression of African history or even in the specific context of Euro-African relations, which in most instances is driven by market forces.[3] Such a historian may choose to see less of African agency in the making of the colonial encounter and more of the British role in modeling the evolution of modern Africa—that is, if we rely more on the accounts of prominent colonial officials such as Sir Frederick Lugard (1858–1945) and/or business profiteers such as Cecil Rhodes (1853–1902), the former prime minister of the Cape Colony. In other words, the narrator either consciously or unconsciously chooses certain sources of information that tend to support this received notion of history.

On the other hand, modern narrative follows a meta-narrative. In the idiom of post-structuralism, modern narrative interrogates structures or dispersed centers of power and politics, as well as evolving cultural emblems, economic and social classes, and general trends (Derrida 1988, 133; Foucault 2002). The aim is to transcend the rigid and Manichean compartmentalization of historical events and economic activities into such notions as elite versus masses, men versus women, "we" and "them," or colonizer verses colonized dichotomies.[4]

In connection with this study of the Onitsha literary collections, we adopted an eclectic approach in distilling how African women were narrated in the colonial and early postcolonial eras. This allows us to employ interdisciplinary tools to reveal why the authors would privilege one gender over the other and either support or oppose colonialism and the sociocultural and economic transformations it enthroned. Contrary to the traditional narrative, proponents of the modern narrative have argued that their adversaries put too much emphasis on what happened rather than on causality. In this study, our method is to provide the historical and economic basis for the women's subaltern position in colonial society and then highlight the reasons behind the authors' ideas in light of the struggle for power and control. We took pains to bring to the fore both privileged and silenced voices within the broader context of colonial and postcolonial discourses.

Contextualizing the Onitsha Market Chapbooks

In line with Karl Marx's dialectical materialism, we posit that political and historical events result from the clash of social forces—specifically accumulation of material needs—and are interpretable as a series of incongruities and their solutions. The Onitsha literary works emerged in the late colonial era as an attempt by the emergent educated elite (some of them semiliterate in the real sense) and urban dwellers in this densely populated West African commercial city to claim a commanding voice in the ongoing sociocultural reordering that defined the colonial encounter between Europe and Africa.

Located on the Niger River and open to the development of markets along the waterfront, Onitsha itself is a city of about half a million people but hosts one of the largest markets in West Africa. With the power to generate ideologies and material cultures that could travel far and wide in a globalizing world, Onitsha of the 1950s and 1960s was a space that embodied cultural propagation as well as rumormongering. A studied observation by Misty Bastian (1998) in the 1980s revealed that Onitsha "embraced profound contradictions and used those contradictions to generate power" (111). The writings of this self-appointed "modernizing community" of thinkers constituted a force in image making, educational fantasy, and social reordering. The locally owned printing presses in Onitsha published the collections comprising stories, poems, plays, comedies, pamphlets, letters, and opinion papers, as well as pieces of commentaries on morals.[5]

A 1990 study, *Market Literature from Nigeria: A Checklist*, observed that publishing output in Onitsha, which is located about three hundred mile from Lagos, was naught as at 1949 compared to nineteen for Lagos, the former capital city of Nigeria. Both cities are among the largest commercial centers in the country. Between 1950 and 1954, Lagos, the capital city of colonial Nigeria and the most cosmopolitical seat of Western education, accounted for thirty books while Onitsha had merely seven titles. But from 1955 to 1959, Onitsha gained predominance with fifty-six books as opposed to thirty-one from Lagos. Among other things, the expansions in Western education, rural-urban migrations, quests for new opportunities for employment in the modern sectors of the economy, and interests in emergent sociocultural dynamics accounted for this development in Onitsha. In the boom years of 1960 to 1966, Onitsha issued 411 titles while Lagos printed 65 books (Hogg and Stenber 1990). Sales of the Onitsha market pamphlets averaged three thousand copies per title. Best sellers such as Ogali A. Ogali's hilarious play *Veronica My Daughter*, featuring the verbose Bomber Billy, recorded about one hundred thousand copies in sales (Uzoatu 2012).[6]

The style of the Onitsha literary works is firmly grounded in "African oral traditions with plays, riddles and jokes as common features" (McCarthy 1984, 22). John Middleton (1997) has rightly noted that this genre of writing is special because they are located "among the masses, and it is their voices that we hear" (v, III). The audience was the product of the colonial schools that formed a reading public. They included people of all walks of life: pharmacists, taxi drivers, politicians, roadside auto mechanics, white-collar clerks, schoolteachers, small-scale entrepreneurs, students, and traders and their customers (Middleton 1997, 452). Focused on everyday matters such as social etiquette, traditional customs, sex and marriage, money, and lifestyles, politics, fiction, poetics, plays, and verses, as well as current affairs, language primers, religion and morals, history, biography, illness, medicine and healing, proverbs, letter-writing, money-making, and lots more, the authors captivated a lively cross-section of Nigerians while proudly exhibiting their newly acquired writing skills (Thometz 2001, xviii). Scholars hail this popular literature, in part "conditioned and compromised by the marketplace," as a major impetus for an eager literate public to experiment with more serious and dynamic works of creative writing (Middleton 1997, 444–445). In fact, the Onitsha market literary corpus inspired a new generation of postcolonial African writers who have dominated the field of African novels since independence.

We argue here that beneath the narration of women in the Onitsha writings is a muted economic discourse centered on power, survival, and control. A great majority (about 75 percent) of the writings were preoccupied with an idealistic construction of an African woman as opposed to her specie, which evolved from the colonial order. The Onitsha market authors often narrated African women as "dangerous," "parasitic," "lazy," "treacherous," and "expensive."[7] The problem, however, is that such images of women held by the writers were not peculiar to Igbo/African women. They were the products of colonial rule, which privileged men as superior to women.

Across the continent, colonial rule granted men access to education, employment, and political and religious leaderships. African women were compelled to remain at home and nurse children while their husbands took up employment opportunities in the urban centers. Scholars such as Schmidt (1991) have asserted that the colonial state allied with African men to control women's mobility. A study by Theresa Barnes (1992) on Zimbabwe reveals that in 1936, only 6 percent of African women were formal wage workers in Salisbury (now Harare). While most African women complied with this sit-at-home rule, some younger women defied the restrictive order to seek opportunities in the cities. In the urban centers, a few of them sold sex, but the majority were there to explore new economic opportunities, ask for those employment openings they were qualified for, and sell food and vegetables. The more business-minded among them opened mobile food services and beer parlors. But the male authorities, some of whom were regular patrons to the brothels, characterized all the urban women as prostitutes.[8]

The discourses found in the Onitsha market writings touch on numerous crosscutting levels of gender and identity. Some of the authors focused on what they perceived as authentic Igbo/African culture as opposed to alien ones. For example, Okenwa Olisah's *The Igbo Native Law and Customs* (1963), which is today a handy resource material on Igbo history and culture, covered such topics as title-taking, marriage, funeral ceremony, wrestling, religion and worship, riddles and jokes, popular legends, war songs, and birth ceremony. It also depicts some ideas about popular Igbo names and towns, practices considered abominable, capital thefts, social relations, salutations, and manners of greetings. It further devoted space to Igbo market days, salutations, the kola nuts rituals, feasts, and property inheritance. Also covered are ideas about what an Igbo wife is expected to be, as well as gender relations. In a foreword to the book by an Onitsha-based lawyer, Barrister Metuh noted that there have been some works on Igbo customs including *Omenuko* published in 1933 by Peta Nwana, but argued that only this book deals exclusively with the Igbo native law and custom (Olisah 1963).

Indeed, ethnographic and anthropological studies by European scholars were a crucial part of colonial rule as the Europeans grappled with understanding the indigenous people they colonized. While the works of scholars such as Richard Henderson and M.D. Jeffreys set the agenda for modern Igbo/African studies, the Onitsha collections were notable for attempting to shape and reshape what we might consider here as remnants of precolonial customs.[9] Over the decades of colonialism, the indigenous customs and habits had engaged the newer trends in a process of dialogue, and adaptation.[10] Often the boundaries between the "old" and "new" were confused and misplaced to the result that new cultural orders and traditions were invented.

One of the species of the Onitsha literary works that falls within the scope/purview of alterity is that concerned with courtship and marriage.[11] J. Abiakam's *How to Write and Reply Letters for Marriage, Engagement Letters, Love Letters and How to know a Girl to Marry* (1965), bears all the evidence of cultural reordering. In the book consisting of thirty-three letters covering diverse stages of courtship and marriage, the author claimed that for many years he has been receiving pleas from the public including men and women of all ages "asking me to teach them how to write and reply letters for marriage, Engagement letters, Love letters and how to know a girl to marry" [sic] (Abiakam 1965, 4). While our focus here is not to challenge the validity of Abiakam's claim, the overriding fact is that in the traditional society, it was not customary for the bride and the bridegroom to negotiate a marriage. Rather, it was the primary duty of parents, aunts, uncles, kin, friends, and acquaintances to act as go-betweens, while the bride and bridegroom were more or less passive participants (Olisah 1963, 15–19). What Abiakam is implying in his book then is that in the early 1960s, those newly educated young people had begun to turn the indigenous culture upside down, using letter-writing to try to seize the initiative in the process of courtship and marriage. In his book, Abiakam claims,

A man can be disappointed by educated girls if he does not know how to write good letters for marriage. From your letter a girl will be able to tell the type of man you are and whether to say yes or no.

Before you write such letter to a girl, she must be somebody you know or met sometime in a train, on the way, in the market, in the school, in the taxi etc. And she must know you as well. You cannot write to unknown girl asking for marriage [sic].

(Abiakam 1965, 5)

An observer may note that in the 1960s, letter-writing in general was very popular as a means of communication among the more educated urban dwellers and their kin in the countryside. Also students at the primary and secondary school levels have embraced this form of communication for various purposes, including friendships, dating, and marriage. However, the traditional culture of contracting marriage relations through middlemen remained resilient. A good case to cite is the marriage of former Nigerian federal minister Dr. Kingsley Ozurumba Mbadiwe in 1950. Despite his Columbia University education and political status as one of the most prominent Nigerian politicians of the first republic, K.O., as he was popularly known, was not involved in his own choice of a spouse. Rather, his elder siblings and kinsmen were responsible for choosing a bride he never met prior to the wedding (Mbadiwe 1991, 41).

Stephanie Newell (1996) has argued persuasively that the Onitsha market publications were arenas "where contradictory notions of masculine power jostled for dominance, adapting to the altered social relations and new female identities accompanying decolonization and urbanization in Nigeria" (50). This summation is apt in light of such works as *A Woman's Pride Is Her Husband* by Chinwe Akaosa (1960). The author claimed his book was the collective idea of Nigerian women aspiring to make marriage a more successful endeavor. "It will in the main, assist men and women when married, to live together, happily" (Akaosa 1960, 3). With that caveat, Akaosa provided "a list of suitable charms" for a successful marriage. These include dos and don'ts that the woman must observe in order to enable a happy married life as perceived by the author: (1) She must be clean both in appearance and behavior. (2) Women are supposed to cook and not allow servants to go and manage that. At the same time, women are to teach their children the best domestic work; for the kitchen is the most reasonable office for any married woman. (3) She should see that her husband takes his meal on time. (4) She should keep her children clean by bathing them and also make them have their meal on time. (5) She is expected to be on good terms with her neighbors. This will promote a social life. (6) On no account should she make it a policy to keep on purchasing things on credit. For such behavior might degrade her and at the same time affect the prestige of her husband [sic] (3–4).

The so-called set of charms remind us more about the gender ideals of the Victorian Age (1850–1914), which was about expectations of certain manners held of the genders and family ideology. Among other things, the Victorian ideals placed emphasis on marriage, love, and romance, as well as masculine ideals of strength and courage contrasted with feminine virtues of beauty and kindness. These were not the exact gender and family ideals held in the Igbo/African precolonial society. Thus Akaosa, as his peers, comes across as an Anglophile apologist using alien ideologies to promote a masculine agenda in Africa. This point is evident at the end of his book, with words that were aimed to buttress its primary goal of enthroning male dominance:

> Whatever might be the rank of any woman, she ought not [to] forget that her pride is her husband. He may be rich or poor. But he should not be neglected. For, it is on him, that the respect of the woman lies.
> (Akaosa 1960, 29)

Akaosa's push for absolute respect for men irrespective of their economic status underlies an observed social phenomenon in contemporary Nigeria in which parents aspiring for their daughters to marry up, sought for wealthy suitors. Often pursued with desperation, the prospective in-law is expected to carry all the financial burdens of his wife along with those of his in-laws, including the cost of education or vocational training for the younger members of his wife's family. Separate studies by Michael Echeruo (1977) and Kristin Mann (1985) on colonial Lagos illustrate the fact that social class of the suitor played a substantial role in marriage. Echeruo's book details the pattern of what was perceived as "civilized life" in colonial Lagos. The book conveys the cultural and intellectual pretensions of urban lifestyles in general and the "strongly felt and keenly cherished passion of the native Lagosians of the period to have a local version of what they considered to be established civilized habits" (Echeruo 1977, 17).

Similarly, in her examination of marriage among the educated elite in colonial Lagos, Kristin Mann highlights the sweeping socioeconomic and political changes that produced the elite and shaped its subsequent development. Mann concludes that the sexes responded quite differently to marriage, because Christianity, Western education, and colonial legal and economic changes impacted heavily on the roles and opportunities of women and men differently. According to Mann (1985), Lagos witnessed a "new kind of union among educated men and women characterized by distant conjugal roles and carefully circumscribed and clearly defined areas of domestic interaction" (18). Much the same can be said of many marriages among the Igbo elite in the early postcolonial era as the urban settings offered many attractions including opportunities for employment.

In *Why Boys Don't Trust Their Girl Friends* (n.d.c), Nathan Njoku, an Onitsha market literary star, argues that his work was "the first of its kind specially to deliver boys from the hands of our girls, who are in the habit of duping, bluffing and asking for much gifts from the boys [sic]" (Njoku n.d.c, 2). The author further claims that "girls' love towards boys is only, to eat them and get their needs from them, mostly to get clothes and money because without clothes girls cannot be regarded [sic]" (Njoku n.d.c, 2). What the author did not take the pains to explain, however, is that because colonial rule denied women equal access to education and opportunities for employment, women became economically marginalized and as a result tended to be overreliant on men. Gloria Chuku's (2005) study, *Igbo Women and Economic Transformation in Southeastern Nigeria, 1900–1960*, informs us that there were "major changes in gender relations and ideological transformations within local and regional economic networks and structures occurred" (3) as a result of this form of colonial gender practices. "The period witnessed an influx of men into economic activities hitherto dominated by women," and, consequently, "women never regained the control of the oil palm industry that was hitherto their main domain" (3). The Igbo women's frustrations boiled over in 1929 when a rumor emerged that they were going to be subjected to taxation despite the fact that only a few of them were engaged in government-owned waged labor. Across the region, Igbo women embarked on demonstrations targeting warrant chiefs or local colonial officials who represented the status quo. Several of the protesters were shot dead by security personnel, who in the official reports described them as "lawless women armed with all sorts of dangerous weapons" (NNAE 1938). This is a good example of measured misrepresentation in narrative aimed to legitimize use of deadly force against women who were demonstrating with no weapons except palm fronds, sticks and leaves.

Women's disempowerment under colonial rule was in contradiction to the precolonial order when women were in fact economically better off than the men. With their financial power, they took care of their children's welfare in the often polygamous African family settings (Chuku 2005, 3–9). By deliberately or erroneously ignoring the dynamics that produced women's attitudes and actions under colonial rule, the Onitsha market writings on women and gender relations were substantially skewed. Nonetheless, Nathan Njoku (n.d.c) also had some advice for men who are flirts. "It is really a fact that some women are just the same thing, but remember that if you follow street and public women you cannot marry your own wife who can help you when you are in trouble" (36).

In *My Seven Daughters Are After Young Boys*, a satire by N. Njoku (n.d.b), the author continued to portray women as good for nothing and at best looking for men who will bear the costs of their burdens or material needs. Despite the seriousness with which the subject should be reviewed, Njoku introduces his book as

> a funny and interesting drama intended to make your leisure time very enjoyable. It is also designed to ban your anger. Whenever you are annoyed, take up this booklet and go through it. You will come across very funny items that will make you forget all about your anger [sic].
> (preface)

The play dramatizes how the daughters and wives of a king tried to lure one of the male palace servants to bed. A scene that highlights the entire play depicts the women hitting hard on the male servant who, apparently in awe of his master, decided to report the incident to the king.

> They [the women] are interested in me and have been asking me for friendship. When I said No! Some of your wives started to hate and trouble me. Anything I do, they find faults in it merely because I refused to be their secret lovers.
>
> (Njoku n.d.b, 13)

Such a skewed statement represents women as dangerous, unreliable, shameless, and amorous. This is more so when the king replied with the statement that he believed the servant's story rather than the explanation offered by his children and wives.

In a similar tone, *Beware of Women* further tried to present women as a source of trouble for young men, especially the male Casanovas. The author claimed,

> When you travel to other continents of the world you see that women of [those] parts, behave better and more lovely than our mongerish African Women (sic). Our women know nothing than to pretend, to talk lies. To trick and say, "give me money" if you don't give them the money your word will be ignored. They don't know how to serve, to obey, to love, to pet and talk the truth. They are rather licensed liars. Only very few are fair. In order to discipline them, this little but effective booklet, has been produced.
>
> (Njoku n.d.a, 2)

From an economist's perspective, one may underline the implicit struggle for access to opportunities and survival in a society in transition. In this social milieu, the male counterparts held all the aces in terms of access to education and employment opportunities. While the African men sought to guard the immense privileges and new opportunities bequeathed to them by colonialism, the women fought back within the limited space at their disposal in an attempt to recover some grounds. The discourse and struggle mirror on the implicit anxieties inherent in the new postcolonial society as class, identity, gender norms, and etiquettes transformed.

Under colonial rule, social etiquettes gained new values as Judo-Christian/Western values wrestled with traditional norms and values. In a novel, *They Died in the Game of Love*, Cyril Umunnah (n.d.) depicted a tragic story of a teenage love affair that resulted in unwanted and multiple pregnancies, deaths, and suicides. Apparently, the author's motive was of good intention—namely, to advise teenagers to eschew decadent lifestyles, especially early sex. As Umunnah stated in the preface, "This Novel, is designed to serve as a lesson to some of our boys and girls who feel that there is another heaven in the game of love" (1). The novel depicts a boy called Thony, who was the only child of his parents. Thony had fallen in love with a schoolmate called Cathe. Not long afterwards, Cathe got impregnated by Thony, and in an attempt to abort the pregnancy, Cathe lost her life in the hospital. As a result, a big fight broke out between the two families. Thony's mother died, and others inflicted serious injuries on themselves. Soon after, the entire episode repeated itself as Thony got another girl called Agnes pregnant. After Agnes died trying to deliver the baby, Thony drank poison and died in his bedroom. In conclusion, the author advised young people to be very careful with reckless lifestyle, especially lovemaking. Poetically, the author wrote,

> When love and peace join together.
> To stamp nature's desire.
> A sympathetic lover.
> Is the man's best pride.
> (Umunnah n.d., 8)

In another play by Motulumanya J. Okafo (n.d.) entitled *The Struggle for Money*, the author highlights his gratification in challenging dominant social norms. Okafo was wary of the moralizing themes that have dominated other writings in Onitsha, including issues related to women, marriage, and hard work as a road to success. Okafo's contrary idea about industriousness and riches is glaring as he rather favors "opportunity and chance and not high sensibility" (Okafo n.d., 1). In the play, which portrayed Bueze as a young man who lost his life in a desperate attempt to make money through violent crimes, the author decried the pervading notion that pursuit of wealth is supreme above everything in our new society. During his funeral, the relatives of the deceased announced to the public that it should not be viewed as a surprise that they have decided not to accord the deceased with the traditional rites of passage as was customary.

> Let it not surprise you that we announced [his death] without ceremonies. This is simply because Bueze was killed while he was robbing people in Lagos. You all know that our society here hate thieves. Such a death is regarded or should be regarded by us as death by suicide. Bueze is responsible for his own death. We need not mourn him. Thank you ladies and gentlemen.
> (Okafo n.d., 23–24)

Other writers such as Marius Nkwoh (1965) tackled corruption as a problem of development. Citing the work of Dr. Nnamdi Azikiwe, *Renascent Africa* (1937), he noted that similar problems have been noted with other African countries including the Gambia, Sierra Leone, Nigeria, and Ghana, where some leaders have perished "on alters defied with the stench of corruption, chicanery, egocentrism, tribal prejudice, cowardice, get-rich-quick philosophy" (Nkwoh 1965, vii). Nkwoh explains that his primary concern was to highlight and possibly reform the numerous social ills plaguing his society.

> I see into and through the conceits, hypocrisies, weakness, selfishness, and wickedness of mankind and laugh or weep. What can I do? I can't change the course of life were I even a Hercules. But I can comment and tell the truth as I see it; without hypocrisy, without sentimentality, without any ulterior motive, without malice or bitterness.
>
> (vii)

Robert Tignore (1993) who has made a study of corruption under colonial rule in Nigeria observes that political corruption was widespread and perhaps "the most single obstacle to economic development and political integration" (175–202). Along this line, Nkwoh maintained, "every Nigerian today agrees that bribery, corruption, injustice, jobbery, nepotism, favoritism, partiality, selfishness and other kindred social evils are wrong." In a rhetorical question, Nkwoh (1965) wondered how Nigerians tend to "condemn these evils in the daylight when so many of us are arch-givers or receivers of bribes in the secret of darkness? Are we really sincere and do we really mean what we say" (vii)?

Narrative as an Identity in the College of Arts & Letters

In this chapter, we have surveyed the role of Onitsha market literature in shaping our notions of identity and gender discourses in Africa as it emerged from the late colonial and early postcolonial eras in a society that was in rapid flux. Biased as they may have been, these stories influenced postcolonial notions of gender and identity, including cultural practices among the Igbo of southeastern Nigeria in particular and Africans in general. We have made the argument that the ideas conveyed in the writings tended to cast African women in certain negative and often derogatory terms. This ideology was taken from the wider resonance of male dominance over women under colonial rule. This discourse and the resultant struggle was engendered by a quest for access to economic opportunities and power as colonial institutions such as education and cash economy impacted on precolonial institutions, including gender relations.

While there are different layers of identity, including culture and gender, narrative has been a powerful tool for (re)construction of exclusion and belongingness. Scholars whose areas of expertise crisscross the social sciences and humanities have successfully connected intellectual kinships across the disciplines as they explore these and other themes in the academe. As our exploration of the Onitsha literature shows, history and economics are intricately inseparable, as together they provide insights into human behaviors and actions, and how these impact on social institutions. If we choose to ignore the historical and economic context in which African women operated under colonial rule, the views espoused by the Onitsha market literature may appear vindicated. But with proper consideration of the socioeconomic milieu in which the women found themselves, one can see that the Onitsha authors were guilty of "The Dangers of a Single Story" (Chimamanda 2009).

Overall, the works of historians and economists have helped provide insights into the fields of social sciences, humanities, and natural sciences. Within the College of Arts & Letters, narrative as a model of research and interpretation bestows upon us multiple identities as social scientists, literary critics, humanists, and interdisciplinary/multidisciplinary enquirers. Our audience cuts across diverse interest groups and subject fields including political science, sociology, literature, psychology, development studies, and anthropology. In other words, being trained as either an economist, political scientist, or historian does not preclude scholarly forays into anthropology, sociology, literature, or political science. Given that each of these disciplines provides unique lenses to understanding the broader picture that a single disciplinary expertise often stifles, it is important to promote collaboration across the disciplines vigorously in an increasingly complex and globalized world.

Notes

1 For an engaging work on the invention of tradition and falsification of history in colonial Africa, see Ranger (1983).
2 In Nigeria, one of these dynamics saw to the publication of an ethic history of the Yorubas by Rev. Johnson, a rescued slave who lived in Sierra Leone and became an Anglican priest. See Johnson (1921). In Uganda, individuals such as Sir Apolo Kigwa cashed in on this opportunity to set a new agenda for political power and influence in which the Buganda people were extolled above other groups as the bearers of civilization. See Kagwa (1918).
3 See Conant (1898).
4 See for example Marchand and Papart (1995), Papart (1986), Stoler and Cooper (1997).
5 Chinua Achebe once described the writers and the social milieu in which they wrote as a "modernizing community." See Obiechina (1973).
6 Growing up in the 1970s and 1980s, my peers were fascinated by Bomber Billy's jawbreaking words in ordinary conversations.
7 See Kahmann (1985).
8 See Aderinto (2015) and White (1990).
9 See Henderson and Henderson (1966) and Jeffreys (1956).
10 See C. Njoku (2006).
11 The Onitsha collections also have pure academic writing such as Wilfred Onwuka's *How to Study and Write Academic Letters* (Onitsha: Gebo Brothers, n.d.), which the author offered as "good for all ages," although intended for students in primary and secondary schools and teacher training colleges.

References

Abiakam, J. 1965. *How to Write and Reply Letters for Marriage, Engagement Letters, Love Letters and How to Know a Girl to Marry*. Onitsha, Nigeria: J. C. Brothers Bookshop.
Achebe, Chinua. 1987. *Anthills of the Savannah*. London: Heinemann.
Aderinto, Saheed. 2015. *When Sex Threatened the State: Illicit Sexuality, Nationalism, and Politics in Colonial Nigeria, 1900–1958*. Urbana, IL: University of Illinois Press.
Akaosa, Chinwe. 1960. *A Woman's Place Is in the Kitchen; Revised and Enlarged by Felix N. Stephen*. Onitsha, Nigeria: P. E. Onaigwe.
Anderson, Benedict. 1983. *Imagined Communities: Reflections on the Origin and Spread of Nationalism*. London: Verso Books.
Azikiwe, Nnamdi. [1937] 1968. *Renascent Africa*. London: Routledge.
Barnes, Teresa A. 1992. "The Fight for Control of African Women's Mobility in Colonial Zimbabwe, 1900–1939." *Signs* 17 (3): 586–608.
Bastian, Misty L. 1998. "Fires, Tricksters and Poised Medicines: Popular Culture of Rumor in Onitsha, Nigeria and Its Markets." *Etnofoor* 11 (2): 111–132.
Bottomore, T. B. 1993. *Elite and Society*, 2nd ed. London: Routledge.
Chimamanda, Ngozi Adichie. 2009. *Chimamanda Ngozi Adichie: The Danger of a Single Story* [Video file]. https://www.ted.com/talks/chimamanda_adichie_the_danger_of_a_single_story?language=en.
Chuku, Gloria. 2005. *Igbo Women and Economic Transformation in Southern Nigeria, 1900–1960*. New York: Routledge.
Conant, Charles A. 1898. "The Economic Basis of Imperialism." *The North American Review* (September): 326–340.
Cooper, Frederick. 2000. "Africa's Pasts and Africa's Historians." *Canadian Journal of African Studies* 34 (2): 298–336.
Derrida, Jacques. 1988. "Afterwards." In *Limited, Inc.*, 111–154. Evanston, IL: Northwestern University Press.
Echeruo, Michael J. C. 1977. *Victorian Lagos: Aspects of Nineteenth Century Lagos Life*. London: Macmillan.
Foucault, Michel. 2002. *The Archaeology of Knowledge*. London: Routledge.
Henderson, Richard N., and H. K. Henderson. 1966. *An Outline of Traditional Onitsha Ibo Socialization*. Ibadan, Nigeria: Ibadan University Press.
Hogg, Peter C., and Lise Stenberg. 1990. *Market Literature from Nigeria: A Checklist*. London: British Library.
Jeffreys, M. D. W. 1956. "The Umundri Traditions of Origin." *African Studies* 15 (3): 119–138.
Johnson, Samuel. 1921. *The History of the Yorubas from the Earliest Times to the Beginning of the British Protectorate*. London: C.M.S Bookshop.
Kagwa, Apolo. 1918. *Ekitabo kye mpisa za Baganda [The Customs of Buganda in the Luganda Language]*. Kampala: Uganda Printing and Publishing Co. Ltd.
Kahmann, Annette. 1985. "Beware of Women!: Presentation of Women in Onitsha Market Literature." *Nommo* 2 (1): 40–48.
Mann, Kristin. 1985. *Marrying Well: Marriage, Status and Social Change among the Educated Elite in Colonial Lagos*. Cambridge: Cambridge University Press.
Marchand, Marianne H., and Jane L. Papart, eds. 1995. *Feminism, Postmodernism, Development*. London: Routledge.

Mbadiwe, Kingsley Ozurumbe. 1991. *Rebirth of a Nation*. Enugu, Nigeria: Fourth Dimension.
McCarthy, Cavan M. 1984. "Printing in Onitsha: Some Personal Observations on the Production of Nigerian Market Literature." *African Research and Documentation* 35 (August 1984): 22.
Middleton, John. 1997. "Popular Culture: Popular Literature." In *Encyclopedia of Africa South of the Sahara*, Volume III, 452. New York: Scribner's Sons.
Newell, Stephanie. 1996. "From the Brink of Oblivion: The Anxious Masculinism of Nigerian Market Literature." *Research in African Literatures* 27 (3): 50–67.
Njoku, Nathan O. n.d.a. *Beware of Women: Why Women Are Not Trusted*. Onitsha, Nigeria: Njoku and Sons.
———. n.d.b. *My Seven Daughters Are After Young Boys*. Onitsha, Nigeria: Njoku and Sons.
———. n.d.c. *Why Boys Don't Trust Their Girl Friends*. Onitsha, Nigeria: Chinyelu Printing Press.
Njoku, Raphael Chijioke. 2006. *African Cultural Values: Igbo Leadership in Colonial Nigeria, 1900–1966*. New York: Routledge.
Nkwoh, Marius. 1965. *Bribery and Corruption: Bane of Our Society*. Enugu, Nigeria: International Press.
NNAE (Nigerian National Archives, Enugu), OKIDIST 11/1/373. 1938. File N. 789. Report on Origins and Causes of the Tax Demonstrations in the Isuochi, Nneato, Umuchieze clans of the Okigwe Division by the Officer in Charge of No.2 Escort. R. C. Wilkenson, A.D.O. and Captain Ballantine, Ag. Commissioner of Police.
Obiechina, Emmanuel. 1973. *An African Popular Literature: A Study of Onitsha Market Pamphlets*. Cambridge: Cambridge University Press.
Okafo, Motulumanya J. n.d. *Struggle for Money*. Onitsha, Nigeria: City Printing Press.
Olisah, Okenwa. 1963. *The Igbo Native Law and Customs*. Onitsha, Nigeria: Okenwa Publications. University of Kansas, Rare Book Collections. C3561.
Onwuka, Wilfred. n.d. *How to Study and Write Academic Letters*. Onitsha, Nigeria: Gebo Brothers.
Papart, Jane L. 1986. *Women and the State in Africa*. East Lansing, MI: Michigan State University Press.
Ranger, Terence. 1983. "The Invention of Tradition in Colonial Africa." In *The Invention of Tradition*, edited by Terrence Ranger and Eric Hobsbawm, 211–216. Cambridge: Cambridge University Press.
Schmidt, Elizabeth. 1991. "Patriarchy, Capitalism, and the Colonial State in Zimbabwe." *Signs: Journal of Women in Culture and Society* (Special Issue on African Women) 16 (4): 732–756.
Stoler, Ann Laura, and Frederick Cooper. 1997. "Between Metropole and Colony: Rethinking a Research Agenda." In *Tensions of Empire: Colonial Cultures in a Bourgeois World*, edited by Frederick Cooper and Ann Laura Stoler, 1–58. Berkeley: University of California Press.
Thometz, Kurt. 2001. *Life Turns Man Up and Down: High Life, Useful Advice, and Mad English: African Market Literature*. New York: Pantheon.
Tignore, Robert L. 1993. "Political Corruption in Nigeria before Independence." *Journal of Modern African Studies* 31 (2): 175–202.
Umunnah, Cyril. n.d. *They Died in the Game of Love*. Onitsha, Nigeria: Njoku and Sons Bookshop.

Uzoatu, Uzo Maxim. 2012. "The Transition of Onitsha Market Literature to Home Movies." *Premium Times* (Abuja, Nigeria) December 4, 2012.

Vickers, Brian. 1996. *Francis Bacon: The Major Works Edited with an Introduction and Notes*. Oxford: Oxford University Press.

White, Luise. 1990. *The Comforts of Home: Prostitution in Colonial Nairobi*. Chicago: University of Chicago Press.

3 Narrative Identities in India's Global Age[1]

Alan Johnson

Prologue: Shared Identities

This chapter discusses my particular relationships to India, to storytelling, and to a sense of self in a rapidly globalizing world in order to address the two interwoven concerns of this book: the cross-disciplinary, cross-cultural vitality of narrative in both academia and our rapidly changing world. I turn to India because that is where I was raised and the country whose literary cultures I study, to storytelling because of its formative role in shaping both my own life and the layered biography of a nation, and to the challenge of crafting meaningful self-identities in the global age—one that India's recent history powerfully helped to shape. A guiding premise of this chapter, then, is that our personal, institutional, and global identities are inescapably interwoven, and that narrative, as both object of study and practiced art, enables us to communicate our "shared" experiences—those of our pasts and our present, and of our disciplines and institution (see Klein, Gershberg, and Hearn in this volume).

India today, filled with cell phones and multinational companies, is in many ways starkly different from the India I grew up in. The writings and films that have accompanied this change have a lot to do with how I perceive my past and present, the texts I teach, and my ideas about national and global boundaries. For if social and historical contexts determine the form and content of a story (see Klein), it is not surprising that storytelling in India—in films, novels, plays, poems, television serials—has been shaped by the country's dramatic transformation and has, at the same time, shaped the narrative of this transformation. For my generational peers and me, this has required an adjustment of our memories to align with the present. For my teaching, this means an ongoing parsing of India's cultural expressions. It is these challenges and concerns that I examine here, not so much in order to arrive at a singular conclusion as to illustrate the dynamism and importance of narrative in our global lives.

The resulting visions of our past are often distortive, with memory grafting onto today's reality to create contradictory emotions and strange (though compelling) tales. A recent *India Today* magazine cover story on

Mumbai (Bombay) is a case in point. "There was a Bombay once," the writer, Kunal Pradhan, laments. "A city of fables. A landscape where myth met realism... To live in Bombay was to... love it." He goes on to say that the city is now "going through a troubling transformation," "bursting at the seams" and "let down by its residents." But the author's memories of "a tinsel-tinged Neverland" shaped by a "melting pot" of migrants who "had devised [their] own language" is, he concludes, being superseded by other cities, with their "multiplexes, malls, pubs, tall glass-fronted buildings . . . variety of jobs." On one hand, he longs for the city of storytelling ("fables") and mythic realization (as the country's movie-making capital). On the other hand, he codes this presumptive cultural decline in terms of infrastructure, since other cities "across India" are fattening themselves on building projects. Bombay, for the author, was simultaneously a product of individual dreams and impersonal uniformity. Such contradictory views are familiar to anyone of a certain age, no doubt, but they are especially glaring in the wake of India's commercial wave. While India has always had an especially big challenge of balancing its industrial aspirations and geopolitical unity with its myriad traditions and languages, the speed of its changes today makes this challenge seem nearly unsustainable. For this very reason, the country's storytellers possess a "cornucopia," less of entrepreneurial dreams, as Pradhan says of Mumbai, than of possible tales.

I cite these examples to illustrate the peculiar blend of personal memory and present reality, artistic vision, and economic convulsion that shapes my identification with India and my approach to its literatures. In what follows, I begin by describing my own first encounters with stories and then summarize some of the broad literary perspectives about narrative. I then take up readings of some well-known Indian novels and films from different eras to illustrate the different values they espouse and different meanings they've acquired over the years. Specifically, I discuss how these stories, despite clear differences, express and negotiate the aforementioned changes through multilingual and multi-spatial registers that continue to evolve. I conclude by reflecting on some lessons we can take from such a discussion, particularly concerning the goals of a liberal arts education that a College of Arts & Letters appears best suited to meet.

Narrative Entrances

I entered the ocean of stories through folktales such as "The Monkey and the Crocodile," first set down in the great Indian collection *Panchatantra* and children's books passed down by my older sisters (English nursery rhyme collections, for instance). But it was India's festivals that lit up my eyes, since you could see stories acted out on streets and neighborhood stages—stories about Rama battling Ravana, or Hanuman finding Sita. Flatbed carts pulled by tractors or bullocks were moving stages for actors portraying some of these scenes. In the cortege behind the carts, swordsmen fought scary animals and, sometimes, one another. On Diwali, the festival of lights, my friends and I (under our parents' watchful eyes) burst firecrackers and stuffed ourselves with *laddoos* and other sweets; during Holi, we squirted bottlefuls of colored dyes on friends and anyone in our way. Bakr-Eid, the festive Muslim day marking the end of Ramadan, meant my fill of a favorite sweet, the hot and milky *kheer*. Christmas was triangles of colored tissue strung across narrow streets, paper stars shining light through tiny holes, and fruit cake (with forbidden coffee). My child's eye ran the festivals together: Diwali-Eid-Christmas, *laddoos-kheer*-cake. But the best festival was kite day on January 14, when thousands of paper kites, red, yellow, blue, green, took over the sky. *Manja*, kite string sheathed in crushed glass, allowed you to battle other kites and, if you were good (or lucky), sever the umbilical connection to their flyer. Each kite had a persona reflecting its owner—a bond whose breaking meant painful loss and shame, or, if you were a multiple victor, the honor of sustaining a kind of lineage, with lesser flyers singing praises to you and your kite. I distinctly remember a thick-armed, voluble man (a designation of ancientness amidst a gaggle of boys), who had cut down more kites than we could count and so deserved the right to strut through his neighborhood like a rooster. We chased after kites among cars and rickshaws and bicycles; boys were sometimes killed, and low-hanging *manja* could cut a scooter driver deeply. The stories circulated, a genre in their own right (perhaps awaiting research!).

Hindi films were a vital complement to this fare. I watched my hero, the famous wrestler Dara Singh, fight bad guys and told my father he'd be no match for Dara, who with his bare hands could hold back an escaping Jeep at full throttle. I sang the songs of Rajesh Khanna (usually voiced by Kishore Kumar) and of Sharmila Tagore (sung by the ageless Lata Mangeshkar). And I reenacted my favorite "picture" fights at home, complete with the sound of punches—*dishum! dishum!* Like many in India, film for me was a part of life and visiting the cinema an excursion into fantasy. My mother would Brylcreem my short hair into a perfect puff and adjust my dress shirt, and, in the company of a parent or other adult, I was off. At the interval—a necessity for a three-hour film—we relished the ritual of "espresso" (which I would learn later was really latte) with a pastry or samosa. Certain films for this reason will always have a particular flavor.

The first books I remember reading on my own were set not in India, but mostly in the land of its one-time suzerain, Britain. I sank into Enid Blyton children's adventures (the "Famous Five," the "Secret Seven"), Alistair Maclean thrillers, and Agatha Christie mysteries; went through the wardrobe with Peters, Susan, and their siblings; and happily followed Dr. Watson and Sherlock. England was an exotic land, filled with crumpets, sleuths, and jolly (if weirdly proper) children, where adventure awaited. (America, in contrast, was strange-smelling boxes—pudding mix, Kool Aid—shipped by relatives, and India was, well, the ordinariness of home.) If I had been able to then, I would have seen in those British tales Victorian presumptions about India and its neighbors—that Watson's old Afghanistan wound, for example, sustained in the 1880 Battle of Maiwand, was a reminder of Britain's imperial ambitions, or that characters such as Calormen in Lewis's Narnia stories are based on a mishmash of Ottoman, Indian, and Persian stereotypes. And this is to say nothing of Blyton's embarrassing depictions of race and class. I would also have seen, however, that these authors were part of a much larger web of enculturation, such as the Golliwog children's doll (ubiquitous in Britain and Australia until the 1970s) and tales from the Arabian Nights (which Disney until recently continued to adapt in troubling ways). All of which is to say that I, too, was at this time enculturated to some degree by vestiges of colonial England.

It wasn't until I was in high school that I found stories by British-Indians such as Kipling and by Indian writers such as Nayantara Sahgal interesting (though I never tired of Christie). Like most readers, my shift in taste accompanied my slow fall into adulthood—into a world where the specter of death was not a mere prop but a real presence. It was not that I had been shielded from death: I had seen bodies before the age of six—two on the street, two in coffins—and, with my fellow fourth graders, I attended the funeral of a student who had died after a short illness. But the dead seemed only to be asleep. As we sat quietly in the back of that school chapel, I had a vague sense that the boy was gone for a short time and would show up in a few weeks. Naturally, this changed in high school. Like everyone else in my school, I read about the million murdered in the course of the subcontinent's Partition (as family friends separated from loved ones could tell us), Jews gassed en masse (at a time my own father was drafted to serve), and slaves and Native Americans cut down like grass (the last incident, Wounded Knee, occurring when my father's mother was six). These facts did not, however, do away with the craving for adventure stories. What they did do was widen my worldview so that England, for instance, seemed to shrink in reach while India (and many other realms) expanded. It's what we who teach want our students to experience as well. By "worldview" I mean an open-eyed embrace of stories that cross borders and checkpoints, and a recognition of how these tales change in the crossing, mixing with the cultures, times, and personalities in which they're told. I also understand this term to mean a critical appreciation for the multiple viewpoints such an embrace requires us to inhabit, even if only in the space of each story.

There is one sentiment, however, that many storytellers convey but which I once believed I did not possess and that is an intimate connection to a specific home ground. My sensibilities have been shaped by India as a whole, producing an attitudinal stance that is itinerant, as was my somewhat nomadic upbringing, ranging from midwestern Maharashtra to northwestern Gujarat to the southern end of Tamil Nadu and points in between. As a result, I've been able to see regional biases that were invisible to others, even as I've lamented my lack of an identifiably grounded culture. My childhood Hindi, for instance, included (as I came to see in later years) words from several different neighboring tongues. I don't regret this now; in fact, I like to think it has enriched my approach to the characteristic hybridity of postcolonial literatures. I do, however, appreciate the local inflections that make so many narratives particularly memorable, whether these are the Greek islands of Homer, the Mississippi county Faulkner called Yoknapatawpha, or the Calcutta (Kolkata) of writers such as Amitav Ghosh. These narratives, in fact, become my own (become ours), affording me the local inflections I once thought I did not possess. In giving us access to locally grounded sensibilities, to versions of home, these writers grant us, as Salman Rushdie (1992) puts it so well, "imaginary homelands" that, like Alice's rabbit hole, provide "new angles at which to enter reality" (17). Each narrative, and each reading of that narrative, therefore attests to the fact that our identities are inescapably both "plural and partial" (14). This point has always appeared as a threat to some, who fiercely, sometimes violently, defend the illusion of an exclusive identity or homeland, whether this be national, racial, linguistic, or religious. Because those of us in academia are no less susceptible to self-enclosure, it's the common engagement with narrative that enables us to be at once in place and out of place, "in" our discipline of English or psychology or sociology and also trans-disciplinary. The resulting bifocal vision is a vital antidote to blinkered sight.

Narrating the Nation

Just as each reading of a text opens up a new angle of vision, so is each narrative not simply a telling, but a retelling. This is more obvious in oral storytelling, but equally true of the printed page. We have Sherlock Holmes, for instance, recounting his skills of detection to Dr. Watson, who then tells us what has occurred. There is also our own active reading of Conan Doyle's story, onto which we project our particular wants and expectations. Narrative, in Peter Brooks's (1984) words, thus "presents itself as a repetition and rehearsal . . . of what has already happened" (25). The paradox, then, is that while a story seems to be given to us whole, in a fixed form, it is actually a process in time—the time we take to read it as well as the imagined time of the fictional world's events. We know, too, that an event, whether traumatic or joyful, "gains meaning by its repetition" (99). All of which indicates that narratives, and narration, are inextricable parts of our experiences and thus, in short, our identities. Strangely, another person's story, no matter how unfamiliar the setting is to us—Dr. Watson's Victorian London, Edith Wharton's 1890s New York—resonates in uncanny ways with our twenty-first-century lives. What we imagine and recount, in other words, is part of what we call "reality."

These points are familiar to attentive readers and to teachers of literature, and they are at the core of a liberal arts education, which compels us to see through others' eyes imaginatively. But is it enough to characterize all narratives, ancient and modern, short and long, in this way? Yes and no. Yes, because voices from other times and places, whether in poems or novels, speak through, and to, our shared humanity. No, because literary expression is tied to each text's specific cultural, historical, and circumstantial moments. This is no less true of reading: actors and audiences at different times have, for instance, viewed Shakespeare's Shylock in very different ways, depending on such shifting factors as the degree of anti-Semitism, contemporary views of justice, and influential commentary on the play. (Which explains the witticism that the twentieth-century poet T. S. Eliot "influenced" Shakespeare.) Each of these broad terms—narrative, identity, nation, and globalization—thus connotes different meanings at different times, just as Shylock does. I expand on this in the context of India, whose cultures I study, to show how the country's rapid globalization, refracted through fiction and film, has complicated the seemingly self-evident distinctions between local and global, Western and non-Western, as well as Western assumptions about visual representation.

In turning to India in order to illustrate the complexity of living in a global age, I will make a case for why our students must understand this complexity as part of their university education, which, to be true to its "universal" roots, requires the cross-disciplinary perspectives that a College of Arts & Letters so richly provides. As Dean Kandi Turley-Ames rightly observes in her preface to this volume, a College of Arts & Letters such as ours is ideally suited to producing "well-rounded students with a passion for learning" and the tools of critical thinking that "are in high demand in this country." We can all agree that well rounded here means not simply gaining proficiency in a particular skill or discipline, but being members of an interconnected community. Narrative—especially, I will argue, fiction—is perhaps the key ingredient here since, as the psychologist Barry Schwartz (2015) has recently said (echoing many others), in putting us in others' shoes, fiction not only stretches our empathetic understanding but also refines our ability to evaluate the challenges characters face (B6–7). The word "evaluate" means to establish, to the best of our abilities, the value of an object, person, or action. To evaluate is, in other words, an ethical act—one that demands the range of intellectual tools familiar to a student of the liberal arts. Schwartz calls these tools the "intellectual virtues" that make doctors more empathetic to patients and scientists more attuned to the ethical implications of their work (B8).

The Global in the National

In the classic 1955 Hindi film *Shree 420*, the lead character Raj, played by the great Raj Kapoor, walks from his country home to the modern metropolis of Bombay to find his fortune. India was just eight years into its post-British independence, and the themes of its cinema not surprisingly reflected a "progressive" notion of democratic rights alongside traditional values (themes that would be burnished most explicitly two years later, in the iconic film *Mother India*). Along the way to the shining city, filled with national pride and individual hope, the hero of *Shree 420* sings his famous Hindi song "Mera Joota Hai Japani," with the opening stanza "*Mera joota hai japani, yeh patloon englishtani. Sar pe laal topi roosi, phir bhi dil hai Hindustani.*" [My Shoes are Japanese, these trousers English. The red cap on my head is Russian, but my heart's still Indian.] The song quickly became, and to some extent remains, a patriotic favorite among many northern Indians. It is also referred to by writers and filmmakers, often in surprisingly different ways. Salman Rushdie's Indian character Gibreel Farishta, in his 1988 novel *The Satanic Verses*, recites it as he falls through the air onto London, as does the Indian astronaut in the 2013 film *Gravity* who, as the actor tells us, enjoys its "celebratory" mood ("Raj Kapoor's Song"). Even Bengali writer and tribal rights activist Mahasweta Devi (2006), a famously harsh critic of state-level governance in India, quoted from it at the 2006 Frankfurt Book Fair to emphasize India's distinctive cultural vitality despite the rise of unrestrained global consumerism: "This is truly the age when the *joota* is *Japani*, the *patloon Englishtani*, the *topi Roosi*. But the *dil*—the *dil* [heart] is and always will remain Hindustani."

The words of this song of postcolonial pride have thus enjoyed a curious career that highlights the interconnected themes on which this chapter focuses. The song is, in its original historical and filmic context, an understandably well-intentioned but (as we can say in hindsight) predictably contradictory indictment of the modern city. Its criticism is predictable because, as in most national narratives, the city simultaneously represents corruptive temptations and cynical opportunism, but also—here is the contradiction— "learning" and "civilization," as Raymond Williams puts it (1). The countryside, by contrast, has in most nations been associated with "peace, innocence, and simple virtue," but also "backwardness, ignorance, limitation" (1). *Shree 420* explicitly echoes these attitudes. To be sure, there is a big difference between the ambivalence our hero Raj feels for the duplicitous city at this particular moment in India's journey as a postcolonial nation-state and the broad attitudes Williams summarizes. Yet Indian films and literary texts of the 1950s, despite overt celebrations of national consciousness and unity, often advance a more nuanced, many-sided understanding of what Homi Bhabha (1990) has called every nation's "Janus-faced" outlook (3).

For if, as Bhabha puts it, "Nations, like narratives, . . . only fully realize their horizons in the mind's eye" (1), and if we regard national belonging through the unavoidably bifocal lens of traditions rooted in the past alongside progressiveness and change, then it follows that national narratives are inescapably ambivalent. Literature has, broadly speaking, reflected this ambivalence, and together with film, including *Shree 420*, it projects this onto the city and the country. Williams has reminded us that the natural associations of the rural as pastoral, anti-industrial (and therefore pure), and, in the case of American settlers, wilderness, were given life in verse that erased the labor that went into those landscapes. The Elizabethan poet

Sidney, for example, wrote *Arcadia* 1590, which first expressed English neo-pastoralism, "in a park which had been made by enclosing a whole village and evicting the tenants" (quoted in Williams, 1973, 22). One might say that the countryside encapsulates a nation's ideals, but the city expresses and produces those ideals. Walter Scott's novels most famously illustrate this ambivalence in revising and reproducing for Scotland "an earlier period in the civil imaginary" that he believes must inform the nation's historical consciousness (During 1990, 147). It was Scott, in fact, who inaugurated the modern novel, specifically the romance, as a powerful means of invoking a shared "national life" through a "unified," "modern reading public" (Duncan 2001, 28, 31).

Ironically, the valorization of an Indian form of pastoralism arose with, as Vinay Dharwadkar (2003) observes, an "Indian print culture within the framework of colonial subjugation" (232). Perhaps not surprisingly given their colonial education, it was urban Indians writing in English who published some of the first expressions in the country of modern nationalism. Although oral tales and songs as well as indigenous writing technologies such as palm-leaf books had long voiced regional sentiments, the beginnings of Indian-English literature, coinciding as it did with the introduction of the printing press, was primed to take up a modern conception of India as a unified nation-state. Broadly speaking, Indian-English writers did so in the way their European models had. But because they faced the particular challenge of balancing the country's myriad regions, classes, castes, educational backgrounds, and linguistic inflections with their cosmopolitan outlook (including faith in the ideals of liberal humanism), these writers represented India not only in terms of the countryside-city dialectic described earlier but also in reference to the village and the empire (Dharwadkar 2003, 243). As Dharwadkar notes, Indian-English writers sought subject-positions that reflected what they variously saw, imagined, and idealized about their surroundings, with the unsurprising result that their visions often clashed with one another (242). There were great differences, for instance, between the sensibilities of Bengali and Tamil writers, which continue to this day. What they all shared, however, was a yearning for national and linguistic autonomy.

In fact, many of those writers did not write only in English. India's first modern novelist was Bankimcandra Chatterji, who had produced novels in English, but who turned to his native Bengali for his groundbreaking (and controversial) 1882 novel *Anandamath, or The Sacred Brotherhood*—illustrating both the rise of robust print cultures in Indian languages and the development of overtly nationalist narratives.[2] Published fiction enabled writers like him to reach a wide audience who could share their interests in, for example, nationalist aspiration, regional folk traditions, and Sanskrit classics. *Anandamath* contained the lyrics to India's iconic nationalist song "Vande Mataram" (Praise to Mother [India]), which animated anti-colonial demonstrations beginning in the late nineteenth century, when it was put to music, and which is still popular throughout the country. (The other great Bengali writer and thinker, Rabindranath Tagore, would pen the lyrics to India's national anthem, whose Bengali words every Indian still learns by heart.) Yet Chatterji's appeal to the ideal of an overtly Hindu nation, as the Hindu holy warriors in the novel exemplify, was after all expressed in the form of the novel—a genre he deliberately chose because of its resonance with Western scientism and modernity. As Sudipta Kaviraj (2003) has observed, the idea of modernity, being associated with British colonial rule, was itself contested by Indians (555–556). More to the point for this discussion is the characteristic ambivalence of Chatterji's nationalist novel, championing on one hand an indigenous (non-European), avowedly Hindu, and non-urban outlook while, on the other hand, wishing to appeal to the historical meliorism and cosmopolitanism of the author's nineteenth-century moment.[3]

This disjunctive outlook is still visible among the generations of Indian-English writers succeeding Bankim Chandra and his peers, though the advent of emboldened, well-organized, anti-colonial resistance—most famously, Gandhi's successful boycotts of British goods—meant that these successors possessed the percipient tools and confidence necessary for their expression of "vernacular cosmopolitanisms," as Ankhi Mukherjee (2014) puts it (154). R.K. Narayan, Raja Rao, Mulk Raj Anand, and other novelists "found that their interests and energies required the liveliness, immediacy, malleability, and capaciousness of prose," and chose realism (in Narayan's case, comic realism) as a dominant mode to articulate their progressive vision (Dharwadkar, 244). This does not mean, of course, that they wrote the same kinds of novels. In fact, Narayan's quietly self-assured voice, which in fifteen novels established his fictional South Indian regional town of Malgudi on the world stage, drew indirectly on Hindu myths to evoke a quotidian, pastoral world that did not depend on Western tropes (Mukherjee 2014, 245–246). Rao, in contrast, did not disguise his sense of "self-alienation" in his novels, using English as a "compromise formation between estrangement from the legacy of imperialism and a process of mutation, translation, and a new cross-cultural relation" (Mukherjee, 154). At the same time, socialist and Marxist writers, especially in Hindi, turned to social realism as a means of exposing societal inequities, such as caste discrimination and poverty, which Hindi films would take up in succeeding decades (until the 1970s). Hindi literature's greatest practitioner, Premchand, seems to refract several of the ambivalent outlooks mentioned earlier: he read English and translated European socially conscious novelists such as George Eliot and Tolstoy, advocated pan-Indian Gandhianism while being resolutely regional in his championing of Hindi and Urdu (he wrote in both), and seems to alternately uphold traditional and modern secular attitudes (Trivedi 2003, 1010–1011).

The settings and themes of this rich literary production show the importance of the village and the city as the spatial references for negotiating a specifically Indian modernity—a process that continues to this day. In the immediate wake of India's independence in 1947, writers variously espoused the secular socialist cosmopolitanism of the first prime minister, Jawaharlal Nehru; forms of democratic Marxism; and liberal humanism (see Dharwadkar, 249). Novelists grew ever more mindful of the role and perception of India in the world, responding variously by, for example, describing the failure of nation-state ideals (such as in Rohinton Mistry's *A Fine Balance*, published in 1995); bemoaning the hold of parochial traditionalism (as in Sri Lal Shukla's 1968 Hindi novel *Raag Darbari*); depicting the cynicism of elites and subjection of women (in Nayantara Sahgal's *Rich Like Us*, which appeared in 1985); or describing the horrors accompanying the subcontinent's 1947 Partition into India and Pakistan (in Bhisham Sahni's classic 1975 Hindi novel *Tamas*). The city and the village in these works are no longer presented in stark contrast to one another, as they tended to be in earlier novels. Later writers, more focused on colonial consequences and national ideals, present both spatial markers more complexly in relation to identity formation, a treatment effectively analogous to the complicating role played by creole Onitsha Market Literature in Nigeria in the 1950s and 1960s, immediately before and after independence, as Raphael Chijioke Njoku and King Yik describe in the previous chapter.

The history of the novel in India is, of course, only part of the narrative picture. Novels were soon joined by what would prove to be a far more powerful medium of national dissemination in India, film, whose influence on both the popular imagination and literature is, as I've indicated, exemplified by *Shree 420*. Within a few years of the 1896 arrival of film on the subcontinent, enterprising Indians in Bombay, notably Dadasaheb Phalke, were producing their own films, which under British rule could only express nationalist sentiments vicariously, such as by turning to Hindu epics. It is worth noting that India's film industry was "the only major [one] to emerge under colonialism" (Armes, qtd. in Desai and Durdah 2008, 6). India's national narratives were thus given a powerful visual form early on in the country's nationalist history, which had solidified just a decade earlier, in 1885, with the founding of the Indian National Congress. Significantly, the popularity of Indian films was greatly enabled by pre-existing visual cultures, which had a long and unique history in the subcontinent.[4] A vital, familiar feature of Indian spectatorship is *darshan*, which in "'seeing the divine in an image, in a person, or in a set of ideas' emphasizes 'the interdependence of the visual and intellectual'" (McDermott and Buck, qtd. in Freitag 2001, 45). The important point here is the relational and democratic aspect of this worshipful gaze, for viewers—of religious paintings, statues, persons, or films—is beheld by the image. Darshanic power only "works," moreover, if there is a shared, assumptive narrative that undergirds the image, such as the story of a goddess or the biography, however idealized, of a film star (which helps explain India's especially fervent fandom). Although this darshanic regard for film has weakened and even, among younger metropolitan viewers, perhaps disappeared, it was a powerful factor in the first half of the twentieth century, just as India's nationalism was in full swing. Thus, the first viewers to see our *Shree 420* film hero Raj singing joyfully would in addition to enjoying the lyrics, have also trained their darshanic vision on Raj's costume: a Chaplinesque, westernized concoction of (just as the song tells us) Russian hat, English pants, and Japanese shoes, along with a Western coat, and, thanks to Hollywood, hobo's bindle. Kapoor's celebration is as much about global imagery as his patriotic heart and hopes, and sums up the nation's ambivalence with regard to modernity. Yet the darshanic element helped make Raj Kapoor, the actor, an iconic persona synonymous with national pride as well as with "the pleasures of [modern] consumerism" (Prasad 1998, 83).

It is difficult to recapture exactly how the film's original viewers consumed this eclectic image, especially given the different class sensibilities of audiences then and now, and the rapidity with which film iconography evolved. What is clear is that Kapoor's character initiated a repertoire, extending over several decades of Hindi cinema, of similarly eclectic characters who affected a mix of Western and Indian accoutrements and habits. It is a repertoire that had a powerful effect on the country's evolving self-reflection, and which helps explain why the aforementioned song continues to serve as nostalgic shorthand for a distinctly Indian identity. I suspect this is so, in part, because Kapoor's eclectic character embodies so much of what we attribute to Indian narratives in general: a vitality marked by the absence of one oppressively dominant language, and, correlatively, by the presence of a multilingual openness and sense of play that animates the best of India's countless stories—a situation from which monolingual Americans can learn a great deal. The popularity of dialogues and song lyrics in Hindi film in fact forestalled the predicted (in the 1970s and '80s) obsolescence of Urdu, Hindi's sister language, both because of the Hindi's practical reach and the attempts of Hindi (and mostly Hindu) purists. Instead, Hindi cinema has unintentionally revived Urdu poetry, especially through the great *ghazal* form that had been a jewel of Mughal-era (and to some extent, pre-independence) India, emerging in the 1970s and '80s, as Harish Trivedi notes, as "a form of popular music that provided the first real alternative to Hindi film music" (Trivedi, 981). I can attest to this by citing the example of the linguistically and musically marvelous 1977 Hindi film *Amar Akbar Anthony*, which, along with a few other films of the period, remains a powerful ingredient of cultural sensibility in northern India.

How and why, then, should these backstories about Indian narratives matter to a liberal arts mission—and, indeed, to any university education? There are several interrelated reasons. Such a program of study matters first of all, as Cecilia Gaposchkin (2015) observes, because more than any other kind of education, it actually "makes you smarter" by "expos[ing] you to different types of thought" that "hone a student's skills of discernment" (1). Such exposure to "nimble" thinking better enables one "to distinguish between fact and opinion," exercising the brain "like any muscle" (Gaposchkin 2015, 4). Any real advancement of knowledge thus requires us to identify and critique our "pre-existing assumptions" (Gaposchkin 2015, 1)—a point I make in every class I teach. A key means of doing this is to compare one's own specific culture to other cultures, as all College of Arts & Letters courses do in one way or another. A recent (2015) introductory psychology textbook for this reason explains to students that it "weave[s] narrative threads through every chapter" (Coon and Mitterer, 2015, xviii), just as a typical political science class asks students to identify the logical fallacies in political narratives. Literature classes are all about reading a wide range of stories, of course, but also require students to discern how these stories fall into groups, or genres, and what this implies about our cultural assumptions; to understand exactly what stylistic and narrative devices they use to compel us to look through the eyes of characters very different from ourselves; and what, finally, this tells us about both our own cultural outlooks and those of the characters and narrator. A process like this necessarily entails some knowledge of the text's cultural and historical context, so that a student can make sense of, for example, the implications of Gibreel Farishta's song in Rushdie's *The Satanic Verses*—without which the character loses some of his empathetic energy and the story's impact is correspondingly reduced.

How does this description fit with such a scene, exactly? Why should Rushdie highlight this particular song in the context of his plot, and how are we to read it adequately? It matters, first of all, that Gibreel is an Indian actor, a "tuneless soloist," who, like all Indian film stars, mimes songs sung by playback (i.e., voice-over) singers. (In Raj Kapoor's case, the singer is the famous Mukesh.[5]) Gibreel translates the song into English "in semiconscious deference to the uprushing host nation," which is an image that conveys the "absurd" predicament of immigrants whose assimilation results in "severed mother-tongues" and "sloughed-off selves" (Rushdie 1988, 41). Rushdie's famously diasporic vision may at first glance seem to clash with Kapoor's homegrown variety. Yet the words of the song, like the plot of Kapoor's film, exemplify the cacophony of change in two countries (India and England) that have, as I've said, shaped one another's cultures. Indeed, Kapoor's sartorial hybridity foreshadows the global accoutrements and settings that later Hindi films would come to exaggerate even more. In a similar way, his linguistic playfulness echoes Rushdie's own exuberant style. (It's no coincidence that Rushdie's works are peppered with allusions to popular Hindi films and film songs, not to mention Western rock music.) Equally significant is Kapoor's aforementioned journey from village to city, which later films would likewise echo in a global register, one that no longer mourns the loss of a rural "heart" (indeed, the village in recent films often seems as corrupt as the city) but that is nevertheless acutely aware—arguably even more so—of the contradictions that avowedly national narratives can never forego. Rushdie's protagonists persistently embody and verbalize many of these contradictions, though from a privileged, transnational vantage point that has no patience with national visions.

These comparisons do not, however, mean that we should see Rushdie as a later avatar of Kapoor's character, or that the filmmaker Kapoor is, in turn, simply a different, prior version of younger Hindi filmmakers. As I've argued, India's profound changes in recent years are reflected in the variations of its modern narrative forms, which begin in the nineteenth century. Indian literature today thus recapitulates certain features of traditional narratives, including such ancient classics as the *Mahabharata*, but it does so with a sensibility and openness to rhetorical experiment that are distinctly modern. Several of Rushdie's works can, in fact, be described as innovative, postmodern palimpsests through which traces of the earlier career of modern Indian narratives are visible. For all their blind spots, particularly in terms of religion, earlier narratives by Bankimcandra Chatterji and others aimed, as we have seen, to transform their narratives in order to suit their quickly changing times (see Kaviraj, 539–540). The key distinctions to note here between Rushdie's and Kapoor's outlooks are, I believe, their attitudes to national identity (given Rushdie's avowedly diasporic self-identity) and their different generational perceptions (with Kapoor a generation older than the novelist). Rushdie is himself now a veritable elder statesman among writers of the subcontinent, his memories of Bombay and other cities are very different from today's lived realities, as Pradhan's words cited at the start of this chapter indicate.

Narrating Identities in Global India: *The White Tiger* and the Act of Reading

Aravind Adiga's 2008 novel set in modern India, *The White Tiger*, was published in the West to much acclaim, winning the Booker Prize and thus ensuring a widespread readership. Akash Kapur (2008) describes it as "a parable of the new India," where Adiga's novel was, as it continues to be, controversial because of its unabashed criticism of, in Kapur's words, "a resurgent economy and nation" that is nevertheless mired in "corruption, inequality and poverty" (n.p.). Kapur, writing in the *New York Times*, lauds its "penetrating ... social commentary, attuned to the inequalities that persist despite India's new prosperity" and its dig at "middle-class India's collective euphoria" (n.p.).

There is no doubt about India's resurgent self-confidence on the world stage, a perch that Prime Minister Nehru had always espoused, though by means different from the global marketization his own grandson helped inaugurate, and which took firm hold in 1991. Nor is there any question of deep-set problems in a vast, diverse country, which like America has been described as more an "idea" than a unified whole. Yet I also believe, as does Kapur, that the narrative's unrelenting glumness is a "blunt instrument" that eclipses the "complexity" of lives and moments of unaffected cheer. The novel's grim outlook matters in the context of my essay because, given its familiarity to American readers (perhaps partly because it appeared the same year as a film that presumed to tackle much of the same subject matter, *Slumdog Millionaire*), it presents precisely the kind of example a liberal arts instructor can offer to students as an object of critique—not as a reflection of "India," but, to use Kapur's words, as a one-sided, "incomplete portrait of a nation and a people grappling with the ambiguities of modernity" (n.p.). Its one-sidedness can only become clear if, as I've done, we read it alongside another, more wide-angle novel such as Amitav Ghosh's *The Circle of Reason* (1986). For as we have seen, India's storytellers in no way shy away from descriptions of the country's endemic difficulties, notably poverty, casteism, and corruption. Yet most of these same writers and filmmakers balance these depictions with others that exhibit the buoyant heterogeneity of everyday moments.

The introduction of two very different representations of an unfamiliar (to most American students) country such as India requires that they apply all their tools of evaluative scrutiny, practicing the kind of nimble critique so essential to the intellectual virtues I cited earlier. Even the debate over the merits of Adiga's novel—whether, for instance, he reproduces colonial-era stereotypes that Indian writers have long worked to undo, or whether he in fact makes valid points—serves as an instructive example of disagreements among Indians themselves about the specific themes and features that constitute a faithful rendering of modern Indian society. The challenge for the instructor in this case is to provide students with, in addition to customary interpretive tools, enough information about India's literary history and cultures to allow them to discern the issues at stake in such debates adequately. This is challenging due both to finite class time and to the sometimes daunting comparative-interpretive approach that obliges readers to be simultaneously sensitive to multilingual registers, national emergence, double consciousness, and the local-global overlap.[6]

Adiga presents his novel as a series of letters from the rags-to-riches protagonist, Balram, to China's prime minister, Wen Jiabao, who is about to make an official visit to India. Balram essentially chooses a confessional mode for his stated wish to describe to the premier his own "success" story in the global marketplace. We thus learn that he has come from a small village, where an impressed educator equates his intelligence to the rarity of a white tiger to become the driver for a wealthy, upper-caste, American-educated businessman. Balram's resentments accrue along with the temptations of the city, so although his boss is comparatively more benign than other members of the family, Balram, eyeing a bag of cash intended as a bribe to a politician, stabs him to death and makes off with the loot. Balram justifies the murder as the vengeful act of an oppressed worker and karmic payback.

All of which is, of course, recounted by Balram in letters that we are privy to, and that a statesman such as Prime Minister Jiabao would never read. Balram's retelling is therefore a working out on the page and, in time, of his self-conception. This working out is arguably a dramatized version of what all readers in today's changeable world experience, all the more so in

Balram's intensely transformative world. The reading of these letters thus compels us to ponder their narrative status. As Mukherjee asks, "Are we reading the letters as they are written, or in the form in which the intended addressee reads them? Does the fact of the letters' publication and dissemination in the public sphere imply that the missives were intercepted?" (1986, 167). Indian critics in particular have, as I point out to students, rightly complained of the "falsity" and "dissonance" of Adiga's conceit, as Sanjay Subrahmanyam (2008) observes, since a self-taught villager would hardly write in such a style (42). Subrahmanyam believes this is because the author has "no sense of the texture of Indian vernaculars" despite "claiming to have produced a realistic text" (Subrahmanyam 2008). The absurdity of Adiga's artifice is likely lost on most Western readers, but presents a point of discussion about the variable status of languages in a postcolonial nation, the aforementioned cultural amalgams, and, more broadly, an author's narrative choices and their consequences. One could, for instance, agree that while Adiga's approach is not entirely successful, the very unlikelihood of Balram's presentation in today's global language in fact highlights the absurdity of expectations and perceptions in contemporary India. Moreover, as Toral Gajarawala (2009) observes, Balram can be seen to "articulat[e] a political ideology that challenges . . . the liberal discourse of rights and privileges," some of which his boss Ashok, ironically, espouses (22).

Besides these textual and cultural considerations, the novel's plot demands a consideration of its ethical thrust. In what ways is it the "penetrating social commentary" Kapur sees it to be, and why should fictional narrative be an effective means of addressing this? Should it be the burden of any novel to do so? I suggest to my students, as I did earlier in this chapter, that literary evaluation is necessarily an ethical act, so that while a novel's content need not be explicitly concerned with moral justice, attentive reading cannot avoid it. On this score, Adiga makes it easier for us. For instance, the prospect of being labeled a murderer forever afterward haunts Balram, but perhaps no more than the label of "villager makes good." The very repetition of the murder and of his self-justifications at the time attest to the continuance, and even heightening, of Balram's guilty conscience despite his avowed identity as a hugely successful entrepreneur. Balram's very impetus for using English, a language, as he acknowledges to the Chinese leader, "Neither you nor I can speak" (3),[7] attests to his recognition of the language's global (in this case, written) utility. On the other hand, his self-taught affection for great Urdu poets such as Ghalib, whose works he is proud to "know by heart" (5), reflects his yearning for an Indian literary expression unfettered by worldly commerce. In a profound way, the novel shows us that Balram's relationship to "choice" is not entirely "free": he is born into village poverty, largely predetermining his societal rank. The decision to kill, though his own, is borne of a constellation of intense pressures that are far clearer than, for example, the factors driving Camus's Stranger or Dostoyevski's Raskolnikov, two fictional analogues that come immediately to mind. For all these reasons—a questionable depiction of modern Indian society, the theme of globalized change, Balram's self-taught linguistic abilities, and its narrative presentation—I have found the novel to be a worthwhile offering for my liberal arts students.

Balram's literal journey from village to city is, like Raj Kapoor's character, both a literal and imaginative version of the symbolic distance between these spaces in Indian popular imagination. Both characters move from naivety to knowing awareness—or, in Balram's case, cynical savviness. Balram styles the city-village distinction as a contrast between "Light" and "Darkness," echoing the similar eighteenth- and nineteenth-century Romantic characterization of Europe's industrializing pressures. However, as we saw in the glimpse at Raymond Williams's analysis of the city-countryside dialectic, Europe's countryside was in many ways already "in" the city, and the city "in" the country, since in reality capitalism began on the backs of rural laborers—a point Adiga's novel indirectly makes. The result is that figures such as Balram possess not so much a double consciousness, which presupposes a distinction between two worldviews, but a consciousness that harbors conflicting relationships to the world from an early age. Balram's focus on displacement, his embrace of urbanism as a way forward, and his implicit rejection of any sentimental attachment to rural life refute any notion of the countryside as innately innocent. Balram's animal nicknames for those in power, such as the Mongoose and the Stork, together with his own White Tiger moniker, conflates, in an ironic tone, these supposedly separate realms. This blurring of boundaries speaks to the chronic condition of displacement in modern India and, indeed, across the globe, and is in effect a recent rejoinder to the valorization of village life we find in Raja Rao and R. K. Narayan.

Thus by accentuating the textuality of his view of the world—through his letters to the Chinese premier, reciting of Urdu ghazals, and pungent descriptions—Balram Halwai's narrative, far from being "cartoonish," as one critic claims (Kumar, qtd. in Gajarawala, 21), highlights how such conventional dualistic tropes as country/city have very real consequences. In telling his story in this particular way, Balram exposes the distortive power of these tropes, which condition our perceptions of both physical and literary environments (Kumar, qtd. in Gajarawala, 22). As Balram writes to the Chinese premier, the "Indian village" is "paradise" only if you ignore its realities (Adiga 2008, 16). When his rich employers gush that "they"—Balram and his fellow villagers—"worship nature" and that this is "beautiful" (78), Balram's exasperation with ecological cliché is confirmed. For the real paradise is, in his view, the city, with its "nice car[s]" (58). True, it is a "jungle," but it is also "the Light" (268–269). At this point, we may smile at the young Balram's understanding of paradise even as we catch our own complicity in the rhetorical complements of this commodifying process. Even after Balram masters the hypocrisies of modern life and says at the end of his narrative, without apparent irony, that he is "in the Light now"

(269), the author is winking at us, making us doubt the sincerity of Balram's closing declaration that "it was all worthwhile to know, just for a day, just for an hour, just for a minute, what it means not to be a servant" (268).[8]

The novel in this way highlights the importance of figural language in our understandings of other cultures, and of our expectations about genre. This is why Balram's visit to a bookstall in Delhi is a catalyst for his enchantment with Urdu poetry, and, implicitly, for his motivation to write down his experiences. In the same way that he attempts to describe for his reader the inexplicable white tiger encounter, he finds that poets such as Iqbal and Ghalib "spill out secrets that allow the poorest man on earth to conclude" that he is no different from a rich man (217). Balram then asks the bookseller if "a man can make himself vanish with poetry"—by which he means erase the social boundaries that relegate him to the "animal" sphere (217). The bookseller says nothing, merely "narrow[s] his eyes." "He knew too much already," Balram declares (218). The bookseller clearly insinuates that Balram can never hope to erase those boundaries. But in spilling out his story—his secrets, as it were—Balram wants to approach the kind of "magic" he attributes to his beloved poets (217). One secret he learns is that life in the city amounts, as it did in his village, to a winner-take-all competition that he labels the "Rooster Coop." The city's "jungle law" means that only "those that [are] the most ferocious" take over (54). "I am now one of those who cannot be caught in India," Balram declares (275). But for the servant to "replace" the master (275), it is also necessary, clearly, to control language, as Balram attempts to do by writing his story—a story that is also necessarily that of his boss, Ashok. When Balram signs off as Ashok Sharma, using his dead boss's name, followed by The White Tiger, he signals his completion of a process of identification with Ashok that began the moment Balram chose to steal the bag of cash. As students can see once they have contextualized the novel in the ways discussed here, Balram's act is necessarily both a moral choice and a rhetorical move that is conditioned by, but does not in itself characterize, the role of narrative in figuring today's India.

Conclusion: The Liberal Arts, the Art of Thinking

In the 2013 hit Hindi film *Dhoom 3*, the cosmopolitan protagonist, Sahir, played by superstar Aamir Khan, robs the branches of a high-value bank in Chicago in order to avenge his father's humiliation years ago at the hands of the same bank in the city. Sahir works with his autistic twin, Samar (also played by Khan), in order to throw off the police. The brothers thus simultaneously honor their father's legacy, which is a long-standing Hindi cinema theme, and respond to a corrupt global financial system. We root for them because their action is presented as the justified redress of a past wrong. More significantly, for my discussion, the twins are cut off from the anchor of home culture—living (and dying) far away from India. As Rosie Thomas (1995) observes, Indian film characters who range abroad are often shown to be susceptible, wittingly or not, to the dangers of rootlessness (170). The twins are, in a sense, an updated version of Kapoor's eclectic village-to-city persona described earlier. Although they reside comfortably in look-alike global metropolises and are bilingual and seemingly well educated, it is clear that they have lost an essential orienting perspective. In place of a journey from innocence to experience, as for Kapoor's character, the twins' loss of a morally firm home culture leaves them vulnerable to the errancy of today's global existence. And whereas their acts of retribution echo Balram's in being similarly rooted in a past injustice, the justification for these acts is amplified by the universal post-2008 distrust of financial institutions.

What is striking about these oppositions of rootlessness and rootedness, urban amorality and familial bonds is the way they permeate one another, intentionally or not. The sleek "glass-fronted buildings" that Kunal Pradhan, in his eulogistic essay on Mumbai (noted earlier; Pradhan 2015), sees as lamentable displacements of a more provincial and friendly city, are in *Dhoom 3* and in most Hindi films the symbols of aspirational success. The "abroad" in which the thieving twins live is, visually anyway, exchangeable with the "at home" facades of Mumbai or Delhi, but is meant to be ineffably different. More interestingly, Pradhan's lament is for a city of stories, or "fables," rather than a particular property or edifice. Just as the film is ambivalent about global culture, so Pradhan mourns a Mumbai that is eclectic and real, yet distinguished by storytelling and multilingualism. The takeaway, I believe, following on the points in this essay, is that our descriptions of a place are just as important as its physicality and that these descriptions both reflect and are shaped by our self-identities.

The locations and dislocations of the protagonists discussed here illustrate these points. Kapoor's character sings his way into being, as it were, arriving in the city as already both provincial and global. His recognition of urban corruption would thus seem to depend on his ability to recognize the foreign pieces of his clothing while also, by their very foreignness, confirming his Indian "heart." Balram acquires the trappings of global commerce but can never let go of his village, including the nickname he gained there. And Sahir and Samar, embodying in their doubleness the ambivalence of modern belonging, consolidate their natal identities far from India. All these personas can be described as "provincial cosmopolitans," as Saikat Majumdar (2015) says of the Indian intellectual and autobiographer Nirad Chaudhuri (271). The difference between Chaudhuri, who was already fifty at the time of India's independence, and the figures I've described is that the latter could imagine, or actually inhabit, global spaces (such as Mumbai) that are no longer haunted by comparisons to imperial England. The narratives of both countries have changed, and continue to change. If the memories of some, such as Pradhan, sound mournful, their very recollection keeps alive the city that has ostensibly disappeared—just as today's Mumbai, in its physicality, will have vanished by tomorrow, but remain alive in its telling and retelling. Without critical discernment, it would be easy to miss the difference.

It's precisely this critical discernment that the humanities and humanistic sciences nurture, providing us with the evaluative tools—in short, the perspective—necessary to differentiate an idealized past, such as a fabled Bombay, from a more multidimensional and lifelike one. For although narrative composition is, arguably, what makes us human, it does not exist in a moral vacuum (see Gershberg's caveat in this volume, for example). If we're to examine narratives properly as objects of study and to construe meaning from them, we must resist the temptation to reside in cultural and disciplinary enclosures. My intellectual journey, described earlier, and my current interest in how Indian writers depict natural environments, have generated ever-widening circles of engagement with other disciplines, including history, anthropology, sociology, and geography. It's a necessarily humbling process. The work of my College of Arts & Letters colleagues, such as those represented in this volume, continually helps remind me of what I don't know and of the limitations of any single field of inquiry. This is why it's vital for us to communicate across disciplinary boundaries, and to feed off each other's ideas. This doesn't avoid every blind spot, of course. It does, however, ensure that we listen. For without listening, as I like to remind my students (even as I remind myself), there's little learning and therefore little perspective. When we listen closely, in the way that a liberal arts program encourages us to do, we gain the bifocal vision that allows us to discern our path (or course, to use the related term for a plan of study). Only by thus moving beyond "narrowly defined cultural frontiers," as Rushdie puts it in "Imaginary Homelands" (1992, 19) can we understand that while we may initially think, as Alice does in Lewis Carroll's (1866) classic, that we "know" who we were "this morning," we see how we've "changed several times since then" (60).

Notes

1 I thank the editorial team for this volume, especially John Gribas, for invaluable support and Emily Treasure for help with editing.
2 Bankimcandra Chatterji, *Anandamath, or the Sacred Brotherhood*, Trans. and ed. Julius J. Lipner (Oxford: Oxford University Press, 2005). Lipner notes that because his book is an English translation, he retains the English spelling of the author's name, since this is how it originally appeared (and how Chatterji himself used it), rather than the more Bengali-sounding Bankim Chandra Chattopadhyay that scholars sometimes use.
3 Stuart Blackburn (2003) summarizes the predicament facing early nationalist writers and their readers: "On the one hand, folklore represented what modernity would have to leave behind; on the other, it supplied the materials for constructing nationalist identity" (145).
4 For a detailed analysis of this, see Sandria B. Freitag (2001), 35–75 passim.
5 All actors in South Asian films lip-sync their songs, and playback singers are often famous in their own right. This is what Rushdie had in mind, and this knowledge enriches both the comedy and pathos of his character.
6 Ankhi Mukherjee (2014), in her discussion of *The White Tiger*, cites David Damrosch's use of the term "glocal" for such an overlapping interest, where a novel

may, in Damrosch's words, either "treat local matters for a global audience," as Adiga does, or offer "their locality as a microcosm of global exchange" (172).
7 All subsequent parenthetical page references are to the 2008 edition of *The White Tiger*, as cited under references.
8 Given the Hobbesian world Adiga describes, his turn to the motif of predation is apt. The image connects both to the long history of game hunting in the subcontinent and to global economic history as a characterization of capitalist voracity. In this vein, Balram resembles the protagonist of Indra Sinha's (2007) novel about the 1984 Bhopal gas disaster, *Animal's People*, which my students have found to be equally eye opening. Sinha's disfigured narrator, who calls himself Animal, presents us with a similarly rough-hewn, lower-class persona who looks unflinchingly into the "darkness." Although both protagonists find their way out of the morass of harsh circumstances, they express strikingly different visions of the journey. Animal embraces the collectivity of life, identifying with "his" people, as the book's title indicates. "We are the people of the Apokalis," he declares at the end, and "Tomorrow there will be more of us" (366). Balram, by contrast, is all about "me," the pronoun that, along with "I," sets the tone of his narrative—a tone that echoes the world of the rich (the "Light") that he usurps. Balram's voice sounds, in other words, very much like that of a modern urbanite.

References

Adiga, Aravind. 2008. *The White Tiger*. New York: Free Press.
Bhabha, Homi K. 1990. Introduction. In *Nation and Narration*, edited by Homi K. Bhabha, 1–7. New York: Routledge.
Blackburn, Stuart. 2003. *Print, Folklore, and Nationalism in Colonial South India*. Delhi: Permanent Black.
Brooks, Peter. 1984. *Reading for the Plot: Design and Intention in Narrative*. Cambridge, MA: Harvard University Press.
Carroll, Lewis. 1866. *Alice's Adventures in Wonderland*. London: Macmillan.
Chatterji, Bankim Chandra. [1882] 2005. *Anandamath, or the Sacred Brotherhood*. 1882. Translated and edited by Julius J. Lipner. Oxford: Oxford University Press.
Coon, Dennis, and John O. Mitterer. 2015. Preface to *Introduction to Psychology: Gateways to Mind and Behavior*, 14th ed., xvii–xxxi. Boston: Wadsworth.
Desai, Jigna, and Rajinder Dudrah. 2008. "The Essential Bollywood." In *The Bollywood Reader*, edited by Desai Jigna and Rajinder Dudrah, 1–20. New York: Open University Press and McGraw-Hill.
Devi, Mahasweta. 2006. "The Republic of My Dreams." Frankfurt Book Fair 2006. Reprint *Tehelka* Archives. July 12, 2015. http://archive.tehelka.com/story_main20.asp?filename=hub102106The_republic.asp.
Dharwadkar, Vinay. 2003. "The Historical Foundation of Indian-English Literature." In *Literary Cultures in History: Reconstructions from South Asia*, edited by Sheldon Pollock, 199–267. Berkeley: University of California Press.
Dhoom 3. 2013. Directed by Vijay Krishna Acharya. Mumbai: Yash Raj Films.
Duncan, Ian. 2001. *Scott's Shadow: The Novel in Romantic Edinburgh*. Princeton: Princeton University Press.
During, Simon. 1990. "Literature—Nationalism's Other? The Case for Revision." In *Nation and Narration*, edited by Homi K. Bhabha, 138–153 New York: Routledge.
Freitag, Sandria B. 2001. "Visions of the Nation: Theorizing the Nexus between Creation, Consumption, and Participation in the Public Sphere." In *Pleasure and*

the Nation: The History, Politics, and Consumption of Public Culture in India, edited by Rachel Dwyer and Christopher Pinney, 35–75. Delhi: Oxford University Press.

Gajarawala, Toral. 2009. "The Last and the First." *Economic and Political Weekly* 44 (50) (December 12–18): 21–23.

Gaposchkin, Cecilia. 2015. "Train the Brain." *Dartmouth Alumni Magazine* November–December 1–4. http://dartmouthalumnimagazine.com/articles/train-brain.

Ghosh, Amitav. 1986. The Circle of Reason. London: Hamish Hamilton Ltd.

Kapur, Akash. 2008. "The Secret of His Success." *New York Times* Sunday Book Review November 7. http://www.nytimes.com/2008/11/09/books/review/Kapur-t.html?_r=0.

Kaviraj, Sudipta. 2003. "The Two Histories of Literary Culture in Bengal." In *Literary Cultures in History: Reconstructions from South Asia*, edited by Sheldon Pollock, 503–566. Berkeley: University of California Press.

Majumdar, Saikat. 2015. "The Provincial Polymath: The Curious Cosmopolitanism of Nirad C. Chaudhuri." *PMLA* 130 (2) (March): 269–283.

Mukherjee, Ankhi. 2014. *What Is a Classic? Postcolonial Rewriting and Invention of the Canon.* Stanford: Stanford University Press.

Pradhan, Kunal. 2015. "The Megapolis that Lost Its Way." *India Today* October 28. http://indiatoday.intoday.in/story/the-megapolis-that-lost-its-way/1/509748.html.

Prasad, M. Madhava. 1998. *Ideology of the Hindi Film: A Historical Construction.* Delhi: Oxford University Press.

"Raj Kapoor's Song 'Mera Joota hai Japani' Was Perfect for 'Gravity': Phaldut Sharma." *DNA* November 1, 2013. Web. http://www.dnaindia.com/entertainment/report-raj-kapoor-s-song-mera-joota-hai-japani-was-perfect-for-gravity-phaldut-sharma-1912358.

Rushdie, Salman. 1992. Imaginary Homelands: Essays and Criticism 1981–1991. London: Penguin Books.

Rushdie, Salman. [1988] 2008. *The Satanic Verses.* New York: Random House.

Schwartz, Barry. 2015. "Intellectual Virtues." *The Chronicle Review* June 26: B6–B9.

Shree 420. 1955. Directed and performed by Raj Kapoor. Bombay: R. K. Studios.

Sinha, Indra. [2007] 2009. *Animal's People.* New York: Simon & Schuster.

Subrahmanyam, Sanjay. 2008. "Diary." *London Review of Books* (November 6): 42–43.

Thomas, Rosie. 1995. "Melodrama and the Negotiation of Modernity in Mainstream Hindi Film." In *Consuming Modernity: Public Culture in a South Asian World*, edited by Carol A. Breckenridge, 157–182. Minneapolis: University of Minnesota Press.

Trivedi, Harish. 2003. "The Progress of Hindi, Part 2: Hindi and Nation." In *Literary Cultures in History*, edited by Sheldon Pollock, 958–1022. Berkeley: University of California Press.

Williams, Raymond. 1973. *The Country and the City.* New York: Oxford University Press.

4 Narrative Text and Photographs
A Case for Ethnographic Research Poetry

Terry Ownby

> Within this Wunderkammer
> all of my teammates and opponents alike, were White
> I had no concept of race
> It was just the way things were then
>
> —T. Ownby

Photography and ideology have danced with one another since nineteenth-century European and American practitioners crafted their earliest images. Underlying British political ideologies can be gleaned from the propagandistic photos created by Roger Fenton during the Crimean War of the 1850s. Similarly, during the American Civil War of the early 1860s, capitalistic ideologies manifested themselves in photographs created by Mathew Brady and Alexander Gardener in their attempts to secure monetary reward by showing dead bodies at the expense of those soldiers. During the twentieth century, Roosevelt's political ideologies came through in the famous FSA (Farm Security Administration) photographs of the Great Depression and World War II. Thus ideologies underlie both still or moving photographs, and we find they directly impact one's sense of social or personal identity. We may not consciously consider how these identity-informing ideologies are presented during the course of our everyday lives, but institutions capable of delivering mass-mediated messages such as the educational system, the church, or the news and entertainment media lie at the heart of ideological dissemination. Given the historical moment and geographical location one finds oneself on during the course of one's life, ideologies and identities may shift.

The summer of 2013 marked the golden jubilee of the March on Washington for Jobs and Freedom rally, at which Martin Luther King Jr. delivered his famous "I Have a Dream" speech (1963) before an audience of nearly three hundred thousand participants. As such, film producers timed the release of the much-acclaimed 2013 motion picture Lee Daniels' *The Butler* to coincide with fiftieth anniversary remembrances of King's speech. Although the film was fictionalized, it was loosely based on real characters and true events, thus exposing younger generations of moviegoers to turbulent times from our collective American history and social identity. Many Americans are interested in their recent history, seeking to understand the progresses and failures of the American civil rights movement during the intervening decades.

However, recent events in Ferguson, Missouri; New York, New York; and Baltimore, Maryland, paint a different picture. Rioting over decisions not to indict white police officers who fatally shot and or killed black males have made global news headlines. Konstantin Dolgov (Russian Foreign Ministry's human rights envoy) claimed, "Racial discrimination, racial and ethnic tensions are major challenges to the American democracy, to stability and integrity of the American society" (Isachenkov 2014). Clearly, American society has not progressed in closing the racial divide as many had hoped during the past half century. There remains a need to critically examine texts and photographs addressing these issues and how one understands their own sense of personal identity within the American cultural milieu.

Thus the narrative of this nuanced dance between photography and ideology can be observed directly through denotative subject matter in some photographs, and at other times, it needs to be coaxed from the second order of significance through image connotations. The question then arises: How do we understand the visual narrative and extract its ideological meanings from photographs functioning at a higher order of significance? My previous research (Ownby 2011) has investigated the intersection of textual narrative and photographic representation through autoethnography, also known as the scholarly personal narrative (Nash 2004), as it relates to understanding this conjunction between ideology and personal identity. Specifically, my art exhibit in 2010, *Wunderkammer: Specimen Views of My Postmodern Life* visually and textually explored personal identity. The impetus for this work centered on childhood experiences of growing up Southern during those seminal years of racial tensions during the American civil rights movement and the author's concomitant acculturation journey of self-identity to the present moment. I have written significantly (2011, 2012, 2013) about the visual semiotics concerning the photographs proper of that exhibition as visual narrative; in this chapter, however, I refocus the lens of our attention to the narrative text used in constructing a scholarly personal narrative.

This type of research activity moves traditional disciplines out of their silos within a typical College of Arts & Letters, such as fine art, communication studies, and English literature (poetry), and allows for interdisciplinary collaboration to develop. Other disciplines that will use the ethnographic approach explicated further in this chapter include anthropology, sociology, and possibly psychology. Specifically, in this chapter, we will explore one particular textual methodology used to extract ideologies from narrative text that may accompany photographs or other forms of visual communication. First, however, we will briefly explore the more traditional approach to visual narrative typified within the photographic discipline. Next, within the qualitative researcher's toolbox, one has several methodological options available and often several are combined during the research process. One specific tool from that box will be examined in this chapter. The textual methodology known as ethnographic research poetry will be defined, along with examples given in previous literature. Following this review, the chapter will examine a case study involving the author's approach to analyzing a photographic art exhibition, along with associated qualitative methods used to build the research poems from narrative text. An overview of qualitative software used in creating the analysis will be offered. Finally, concluding thoughts regarding how the resultant research poems relate to a sense of personal identity and potential future applications for this interdisciplinary method will be considered.

Traditional Photographic Narratives

Oftentimes, narrative is defined as story. Stories are common and occupy numerous formats within society, such as literature, magazine articles, newspaper journalism, TV, and movies. Typically, stories or narrative arcs may contain common elements—a plot, set of characters, an environment, conflict/resolution—and serve some purpose such as informing the reader. In photography, especially photojournalism (news media or magazine editorial pieces), the photo story plays an important role in visual communication. W. Eugene Smith, a famous photojournalist for *Life* magazine during the mid-twentieth century, was the quintessential visual storyteller, and photographs were his primary medium. According to veteran photojournalist and author, Kenneth Kobré (2008, 244), *Life* magazine even developed a visual formula for their photographers to adhere to, thus ensuring they delivered good photo stories:

- Overall shot—wide angle or aerial to establish the setting
- Medium shot—one activity or group of people
- Close-up—show the details
- Portrait—environmental setting or tight head shot
- Signature shot—image that summarizes the story
- Sequence—beginning, middle, end; before/after; how-to

In the undergraduate courses that I teach at the University, we examine this aspect of visual storytelling extensively. But my discussion here takes us beyond the journalist's story and looks deeper into second-order narratives. Roland Barthes (1972, 1977), French philosopher and visual semiologist, wrote extensively about the interaction between photographs and text and how one informed the other. He also probed the deeper messages within photographs. Photographs traditionally were subordinate to text, especially within journalism. In other words, photographs helped to amplify the message of the written word. However, during the postmodern turn, when Barthes was writing, he had notions that text could influence how the audience interpreted a photograph. We find text influencing photographs not only in journalism through the use of stand-alone captions or extended texts within photo essays, but also with the text associated with contemporary advertisements. In Barthes's situation, he specifically examined the semiological relationship found between advertising photographs and their associated narrative text.

In his essay discussion of media photographs, *The Photographic Message*, Barthes stated, "the text loads the photograph"—in other words, the written word was amplifying the image's message (1977, 26). Through visual semiology (semiotics), he proposes the photograph's message moves from denotation to connotation through orders of signification, thus enabling the reader/viewer to reach the second-order narrative of myth or ideology. One method to help reach this understanding is the ethnographic research poem. Therefore, I show how visual narrative interacts when photographs and text are conjoined through poetry, which guides the reader to interpretations beyond a casual surface reading. Using a framework of visual semiology combined with the research poem, the reader moves the interpretation from simple denotation to higher orders of signification known as connotation. Deeper and broader personal and social issues of complex ideologies reside at Barthes's second order of signification, which he called *myth*. With this in mind, we can work with second-order visual narratives in ethnographic studies. Projects this type of narrative lends itself to would include the following:

- In-Depth Scholarly Personal Narratives (SPN), (Nash 2004)
- Ethnographies
- Autoethnographies
- Ethnographic Research Poems

In my research, I worked with second-order narratives to write a scholarly personal narrative about my self-identity acculturation journey of growing up in the South at the height of the American civil rights movement, to my current situation as a university professor. During the course of this research, the interpretation of photographs and text led to other forms of scholarly writing, specifically the ethnographic research poem.

The Research Poem Defined

Commonly, researchers are adept at combining research methods in order to provide some sense of reliability and validity to their research. My creative and research-based practice takes an interdisciplinary approach, which works well within the broader interplay between the humanities and the social sciences. As such, when I initially analyzed the *Wunderkammer* photographic art exhibition and its accompanying textual narrative panels,

I deployed a qualitative three-dimensional space approach involving the triangulation of interaction, continuity, and situation, as proffered by Clandinin and Connelly (2000; also see Ollerenshaw and Creswell 2002). Within their schema, "interaction" involves the personal and social; "continuity" considers the past, present, and future as the researcher moves through the text and other data; and, lastly, they combined the previous two aspects with "situation," which is the notion of geographical place. When considering this textual framework, therefore, research poetry can be one qualitative method among many and is used during the coding process and other qualitative analyses in order to recognize ideological themes and recurring patterns within the data (Ownby 2011). In this section, I examine that type of poetry as a research method for data analysis within visual ethnography.

Not unlike Fitzpatrick's (2012) recent discussion on poetry's purpose in critical ethnographic writing, I used the research poem (Furman, Lietz, and Langer 2006; Langer and Furman 2004; Poindexter 1998; Richardson 1992, 2000; Richardson and St. Pierre 2005) as a method to critically tease out meaning from the narrative text that accompanied the photographs in my *Wunderkammer* exhibition. This type of poetry may not conform to what might generally be considered as literary poetry. Conversely, within the context of this chapter, it serves as a method of data analysis. What I seek to demonstrate, therefore, is the research poem's ability to illuminate meaning as the "text loads the image" (Barthes 1977, 26), specifically by using the French Malaysian pantoum poetry style as "a powerful form that can create a haunting effect through the repetition of lines throughout the poem" (Furman et al. 2006, 5).

Originating in fifteenth-century Malaysia, the traditional oral poem that consisted of two couplets, which rhymed, was known as a pantun (Academy of American Poets 2004, 2015; Unst 2013). Later, during the nineteenth century, French poet Victor Hugo helped introduce Western society to the French pantoum, a modified variation grounded in Malaysian usages. I call this the French Malaysian pantoum. According to Furman et al. (2006), this poetry genre moved across the Atlantic and spread throughout poetry circles in the United States during the twentieth century. At this point in the pantoum's evolution, its structure changed, and today, it typically consists of four-line quatrains for "which the second and fourth lines of each stanza serve as the first and third lines of the next stanza. The last line of a pantoum is often the same as the first" (Academy of American Poets 2004, para. 1). This repetition effect between stanzas creates a rhythmic emphasis that the poet uses to highlight the narrative being told within the pantoum.

Poetry in ethnographic research and writing has endured back and forth arguments, similar to a Ping-Pong match, in regards to acceptance in qualitative research. From an anthropological viewpoint, some writers assert since the postmodern days of the 1990s' experimental writing approaches, poetry in ethnography commonly found its way into more scholarly settings (Maynard and Cahnmann-Taylor 2010). Conversely, health education ethnographer Katie Fitzpatrick (2012) indicated research poetry is "still marginal in academic writing" (8), yet she acknowledges its validity within qualitative research for some time. As such, nearly two decades ago Miles and Huberman (1994) showed poetry's usefulness as a data reduction device when working with large transcripts of narrative text. Similarly, Richardson (2000) employed the research poem in "Louisa May's Story of Her Life," to reduce thirty-six pages of transcribed notes from her interviews into five pages of focused, rich narrative poetry. Not only can poetry be used to reduce data to manageable pieces, according to Fitzpatrick, but also the poem lays bare the subjective nature of the writer's viewpoint and "doesn't pretend to be objective" (12). Likewise, she noted its ability to introduce ambiguity in scholarly writing along with the author's personal thoughts and attitudes as a means of making "research texts more interesting and readable" through their reflexive nature in our research (10). As such, I was able to maximize the data reduction capability of research poems, in concert with their subjectivity, as part of the three-dimensional space approach I utilized in textual analysis of narrative text.

A Case Study and Its Methods

Although my research was about understanding construction of self-identity within my childhood Southern cultural context through construction and deconstruction of a photographic exhibition, concurrently, it was about experimenting with an interdisciplinary approach to methodological design. I believe it is important when working within an academic environment of arts and letters to be open to research methods from other disciplines. This application of other methods can create richness within one's research practice and bring forth nuances previously missed. Certainly, this was the case when using research poetry within my own photographic discipline.

The primary data analyzed in this case study were composed of narrative text and photographic images, which resulted in a visual scholarly personal narrative. Research poetry was a component used in data reduction of the narrative text, which is the primary aspect of this chapter. Thus, in the scholarly personal narrative that explored my acculturation journey of self-identity construction, I set out on a twofold mission: First, I needed to examine my self-identity in relation to my Southern double vision through narrative text and photographs, and second, from an interdisciplinary perspective, I needed to apply seemingly disparate methodological approaches in order to paint a complete and holistic portrait of my acculturation journey. This latter aspect is something not typically done in my discipline, yet I found its application extremely rewarding in the final data analyses.

The data ($N=18$) collected for that study were purposeful in that I wrote a scholarly personal narrative about myself in relation to my *Wunderkammer* photography exhibit and how I constructed a sense of my self-identity through photographic artifacts in relation to my Southern cultural history.

Primary data for the visual semiotic analysis consisted of photographic images (*n* = 9), which were designed studio still-life compositions of personal artifacts that chronicled my life over half a century. Specifically, the nine photographs presented memorabilia and artifacts that narrated my life's story from roughly age six when I entered first grade in elementary school and then throughout the various life stages including adolescence, military life, graduate studies, midlife changes, and culminating at my present stage as university professor. Thus the nine photographs within the *Wunderkammer* series were grouped into three sections corresponding to my life stages: (1) *First Impressions of My Normal World* encompassed my elementary school years, (2) *Passage to Maturity* spanned my coming-of-age years and then into graduate school and military service, and (3) *Getting Comfortable* traced midlife transitions after career and military service to my current moment. The primary section of concern at the moment would be *First Impression of My Normal World*, as the story panels for those three photographs became the data for the research poems under consideration in this chapter.

The first three Wunderkammers in this series visually depict my elementary school days while growing up in the South. In order of appearance at my gallery showing, their titles work in concert with their content: *Little League*, *Scouting*, and *Space-Age*. Temporally, these three images span the decade of the 1960s. My age ranged from six to twelve during this period, which began at first grade and through my first semester of seventh grade at the local junior high school. The *Little League* and the *Scouting* photographs contained artifacts and objects that could broadly describe many Baby Boomer boys of that era, regardless of geographic region. Pocketknives and baseball gear, toy airplanes, snapshots of fishing trips and other outdoor Scouting activities, rock and stamp collections populate both photographs; these were popular pursuits for many children across America to engage in during the 1950s and 1960s. Activities such as these and similar ones marked and established American childhood from a White perspective.

However, the third Wunderkammer titled *Space-Age* presents a different situation. While many American children of the 1960s were probably exposed through mass media news to our nation's race for space against the former Soviet Union, only a limited number of children lived close enough to physically engage this scientific and technological marvel. Those were the children who lived in close proximity to Cape Canaveral and NASA's (National Aeronautics and Space Administration) Launch Operations Center (Ryba 2008) on Merritt Island, Florida, and I was one of those children.

Nearly every artifact in this Wunderkammer speaks to America's early space program. The 8"x10" black-and-white glossy photographs are unique in that they are originals taken by NASA and US Air Force photographers and were given to my father because of his job in that particular environment. The photograph of men standing and kneeling on a rocket launch tarmac includes my father, along with three of the original seven astronauts of Project Mercury (Gordon Cooper [Faith 7], John Glenn [Friendship 7], and

Gus Grissom [Liberty Bell 7 and Apollo 1, in which he was killed during an onboard fire]). The collection of three badges in the specimen display case in the upper-right corner was my father's, which gave him access to the various rocket launch facilities where he worked. Hand-written papers along the bottom of the photograph were various elementary school assignments I had written specifically about the space program.

Thus, these particular artifacts move this specific image out of the ordinary and into the extraordinary compared to other American boys and girls who lived outside the rural Atlantic coast of east-central Florida. Other artifacts in this particular image are not directly related to the space program, but were objects collected during this time frame and represent childhood mementos, such as the display case of pop culture trinkets known as Rat Finks, often traded among boys playing on the school yard or during our bus ride to and from school. The upper-left corner holds hand-painted clay figurines of American Indians around a campfire (toys passed on from my uncle's childhood), and interspersed throughout the remaining areas of the photograph are other simple childhood toys and good-luck charms.

In addition to the photographs, and of principal concern in this chapter, were corresponding narrative texts ($n = 9$) that I called story panels. An individual story panel accompanied each photograph. These narrative texts were treated in the same manner as ethnographic interviews (Spradley 1979) in regards to coding, other ethnographic analytic methods, and data reduction through research poems. Each story panel was devised as an intricate part of the overall aesthetic design of the exhibition and their purpose was to provide the gallery patron with a backstory for each photograph. The panels were designed to aesthetically mimic college-ruled notebook paper, while the text utilized a type font reminiscent of an old typewriter. Each panel floated on the wall next to their corresponding photograph. The narrative of each story panel was the primary data of the scholarly personal narrative itself, while secondary data became retrospective field notes (Burke 2007; Ellis 2004) in the form of my reflexive journaling during a one-year period that encompassed pre- and post-exhibit activities. Further, I combined my field notes, story panels, and research poems in an effort to frame the narrative components of the exhibit within the three-dimensional space approach mentioned earlier in order to write my scholarly personal narrative. I would also note, additional family snapshots, documents, personal journals, memos, and artifacts not contained within the *Wunderkammers* became tertiary data. Thus, these three data sources created a trio of validation, which Miles and Huberman (1994) refer to as triangulation.

Textual Narrative Analysis and Qualitative Software

For a moment, I will return to the first group of photos: *First Impression of My Normal World*. In order to write the scholarly personal narrative and the ethnographic research poems, I needed to analyze the data contained within the photographs and their accompanying story panels. To facilitate this process, I used qualitative analysis software for non-numerical or unstructured data. There are several excellent programs available, such as NVivo, Atlas/ti, and HyperRESEARCH, among others. Thus, the software used in my data analyses allowed for traditional ethnographic procedures, such as the following:

- Open and focused analytical coding
- Cultural domain analysis
- Creation of codebooks, memos, coding within photos and text

Portions of the photographs and the narrative text panels were coded using the traditional codebook method. For example, the software allows the researcher to select a portion of a photograph and assign a code(s) to that area of the image. It also allows for memos, or notes, to be added for future reference. Likewise, when dealing with large bodies of text, the researcher can highlight singular or multiple passages and assign either open or focused codes. Thus when I used traditional ethnographic methods combined with visual semiotic analysis, second-level narratives emerged. This is the connotation of the photographs functioning at the ideological level. In order to help make sense of the data, ethnographic research poems were constructed from the narrative text panels based on the aforementioned coding process conducted with the software.

Before moving directly into the modified pantoum poems and their analyses, I will provide a brief overview of the scholarly personal narrative study to delineate the underlying backstory. At the beginning of this chapter, I opened with one quatrain from my poem *Southern Baseball*, which in part addressed one of my research questions: What was it like growing up as a privileged White male Baby Boomer in the South in relation to development of my self-identity? To answer that question, I chose the qualitative analytical method of poetry, specifically the research poem, to answer this question most vividly. Research poems are an excellent analytical technique for making sense of certain data; they can be "a very involving way to present an analysis of your work," according to visual culture scholar James Banning's e-mail to the author on December 14, 2009. In this particular case, the first three Wunderkammer photographs, their narrative story panels, and their associated field notes, specifically addressed my childhood in the South during the civil rights movement era of the 1960s and offered rich descriptive data that addressed what it was like for me growing up during that historical moment.

Following Furman et al.'s (2006) advice for constructing a research poem based on the French Malaysian pantoum style discussed earlier in this chapter, I deconstructed and reduced the data of my narrative story panels through qualitative coding to write the poems about the perceived normality of my Southern childhood. The technique of data reduction through this analytical method distills the data to their essence. In referencing Laurel Richardson's (1992, 2000) observations on qualitative writing genres, including poems, Miles and Huberman (1994) noted this analytical reduction emphasizes one's lived experience and how it could emotionally engage the reader by illuminating the core of the case under investigation. Thus, just as Richardson cut and pasted original excerpts from field notes to write her poem "Louisa May's Story of Her Life," I followed her example in writing my pantoums. The notion of *normality* from a Southern child's perspective also crystallized while analyzing sports and civic involvement in Little League baseball and the Boy Scouts of America. This form of analysis revealed not only blindness to White privilege and racism in regards to others but also blindness to a male-dominated, patriarchal cultural hierarchy of that particular existing social order in the American South. The repetition of the phrase "all was normal back then" builds that haunting effect noted by Furman et al. (2006) in portraying my male-dominated White Southern world. Likewise, the repeated phrase "Within this Wunderkammer" serves as a discursive link for the reader/observer between the written narrative story panels and their associated photographs containing denotative representations of objects that form the underlying connotative ideological notions of that historical moment. Since I have been discussing the poems relating to baseball and scouting, I provide them here in their entirety for you to understand their full context. Keep in mind, the words comprising these research poems come directly from the text of each narrative story panel. During the coding process with the qualitative research software, these phrases were tagged with an appropriate code. While isolating the codes, these phrases were highlighted in the software and patterns became apparent. Then, while extracting these phrases based on those codes and arranging them somewhat in accordance to the pantoum principles, the following poems revealed themselves.

Little League Wunderkammer

Within this *Wunderkammer*
typical for any kid
of that era
provided they were White

all was normal
there were no girls
on our teams back then
Within this *Wunderkammer*

all of my teammates and opponents alike were White
typical for any kid
of that era
all was normal back then

Within this *Wunderkammer*
all of my teammates and opponents alike were White

I had no concept of race
It was just the way things were then

I was going to segregated public schools
I had no concept of race
racism, or racial stereotyping

that age of innocence
a sense of wonder
an overall silence in our home
all was normal back then

Within this *Wunderkammer*

Scouting Wunderkammer

It was the normal thing to do
It was American. I joined the Cub Scouts
No Blacks, Asian, Latinos, or *Indians* allowed!
all was normal back then

All my buddies at school were Scouts
I became a Scout as well
as so typical throughout the 1960s
was in "pack" #312 and "den" #3

3rd grade in 1963
mother had become the den mother
my father never took much interest
Within this *Wunderkammer*

Within this *Wunderkammer*
innocuous artifacts: the arrowhead collection
so typical of that era
Euro-Americans had effectively rendered Native Americans invisible

I joined a "Webelos" den
my father's job kept us moving

I never made it into the ranks of the Boy Scouts
Within this *Wunderkammer*

Understanding the Narrative

As with all empirical research, there needs to be appropriate research questions to guide the project at hand, regardless of whether that project is quantitative or qualitative in nature. Within qualitative research, such as that presented in this chapter, there should be a central question followed by appropriate sub-questions. However, as my particular research project progressed with the writing of my scholarly personal narrative, some questions proved to be irrelevant while others collapsed into new questions. This is not surprising since Creswell (2005), among others (Maxwell 1996; McCaskill 2008; Spradley 1980; Willis 2007), has stated qualitative research is an emerging process and oftentimes inductively the questions may change or be eliminated. Such was the case with my scholarly personal narrative. While my question regarding the construction of self-identity through photographic artifacts in relation to my Southern cultural history remained constant, the sub-questions became imbricated with one another as the data were analyzed and the results emerged. Thus, questions presented that needed answering. What was it like growing up as a privileged White male Baby Boomer in the South in relation to development of my self-identity? What experiences and defining moments during my acculturation journey of self-identity development turned the direction of my life story concerning racial issues and shaped my cultural perspective? As my self-identity construction progressed, how had my perception of racial representations changed temporally? How did this affect my professional craft as a photographic media educator? In this chapter, I am not going to attempt to address all the questions just posed, as many of them were answered through other analytical methods beyond the scope of our current topic (Ownby 2011, 2012). However, the notion of the ethnographic research poem undoubtedly revealed an underlying subtext of racial and patriarchal tensions within the geo-temporal dimension addressed earlier through the three-dimensional space model.

Through the use of ethnographic analysis techniques, in addition to the research poems, themes and patterns emerged that I had not anticipated when I began researching and writing this scholarly personal narrative. Returning to the three-dimensional space model (Clandinin and Connelly 2000; Ollerenshaw and Creswell 2002) and its application, I was able to chronologically narrate my acculturation journey of self-identity construction as a scholarly personal narrative. Once the narrative story panel texts and field notes had been thoroughly interrogated, I found myself staring at chunks of disheveled data as though they were randomly strewn puzzle pieces on a card table. The use of the research poem method allowed me to make sense of various aspects of this data and thus it allowed me to recognize the underlying racial tensions developed during that phase of my self-identity development and how that identity changed within the chronological flow of my acculturation journey. In his last work, *Identity, Culture and the Postmodern World*, before his untimely death, Madan Sarup (1996) addressed this issue of place and time as how individuals apprehend the identities they construct for themselves. Thus, with Sarup in mind, as I considered my different racial encounters over the course of my life within differing geographical locales, I constructed my identity, in part, through my narrative story: "We construct our identity at the same time as we tell our life-story" (Sarup 1996, 15). He goes on to clarify one's identity apprehension is always a relationship between time and place, or when framed within Clandinin and Connelly's (2000) paradigm, it is the situation in relation to the continuity of events. Thus, as my narrative story developed from the research poems, event listings, and cultural domain analyses, it served as an exemplar of the notions proffered by Sarup or Clandinin and Connelly.

Final Thoughts

In this chapter, I have examined one particular analytic method for developing narrative from the data within photography and text that is not typically used within my photographic discipline. This particular case, therefore, required I reach out beyond my discipline and embrace methods from other academic units. This interdisciplinary method of working with ethnographic research poems added incredible richness to my personal identity narrative. I would encourage other researchers to not shy away from utilizing such an interdisciplinary approach. This can be an effective way of adding both breadth and depth to one's research. But more importantly, if you find yourself working within a diverse college of arts and letters (or sciences for that matter) such as mine, you may find rewarding relationships develop as colleagues come together outside their defined disciplinary silos.

Within the broader view of the research project presented here, the use of visual semiotics and textual discourse analyses are common research tools used in many communication and media studies departments. The use of poetry, however, is not. At first blush, one might associate the terms "poetry" or "poems" with a typical language or literature department. However, the type of poetry I presented in this chapter falls more in the purview of anthropology, sociology, cultural studies, and even education departments. For instance, in my own personal academic journey, I studied ethnography within a school of education at a Research One university. Thus during my graduate studies I was encouraged to look beyond my particular discipline and to explore how other methods could enrich and expand my research efforts. Now at Idaho State University and the College of Arts & Letters that I call my academic home, I find myself very comfortable reaching across disciplinary lines in several of my research activities. This interdisciplinary interaction not only augments and expands my research methods toolbox but also helps me see my own narrative develop as I continue the arc of my personal identity acculturation journey.

As professional researchers, we oftentimes relate our identities directly to our methodologies. Some scholars may consider themselves to be quantitative researchers, or statisticians, if you will. Others may identify more with the qualitative vein of research and thus consider themselves as scholarly personal narrative writers or autoethnographers. Yet again, some may take an interdisciplinary approach and view themselves as some type of hybrid mixed-methods scholar. Regardless, as a community of researchers and academics within our particular college, I believe many of us imbricate our identities within our research methods. This interdisciplinary approach extends both my professional and personal identity narratives beyond the silo of communication studies and into those of my colleagues in anthropology, English, history, and art here in the College of Arts & Letters at Idaho State University. There are numerous rich methods across multiple disciplines that can certainly be applied outside their particular domain of existence—their silos. In other words, we should not practice our research as the satirical cartoon illustrates the professor working away at his desk in isolation surrounded by a medieval moat, crocodiles, and drawbridge, while fellow academics stand to the side questioning among themselves as to what really happens beyond the drawbridge.

References

Academy of American Poets. 2004. "Poetic Form: Pantoum." Accessed November 25, 2013. https://www.poets.org/poetsorg/text/poetic-form-pantoum.
———. 2015. "From a Poet's Glossary: Pantoum." Accessed October 30, 2015. https://www.poets.org/poetsorg/text/poets-glossary-pantoum.
Barthes, Roland. 1972. *Mythologies*. Translated by Annette Lavers. New York: Hill and Wang.
———. 1977. *Image, Music, Text*. Translated by Stephen Heath. New York: Hill and Wang.
Burke, Deborah. 2007. "An Autoethnography of Whiteness." PhD diss., Oregon State University. ProQuest (AAT 3268278).
Clandinin, D. Jean, and F. Michael Connelly. 2000. *Narrative Inquiry: Experience and Story in Qualitative Research*. San Francisco: Jossey-Bass.
Creswell, John W. 2005. *Educational Research: Planning, Conducting, and Evaluating Quantitative and Qualitative Research*, 2nd ed. Upper Saddle River, NJ: Pearson Education.
Daniels, Lee. 2013. *Lee Daniels' The Butler*. Directed by Lee Daniels. New Orleans, LA: Follow Through Productions.
Ellis, Carolyn. 2004. *The Ethnographic I: A Methodological Novel about Autoethnography*. Walnut Creek, CA: Altamira Press.
Fitzpatrick, Katie. 2012. "'That's How the Light Gets In': Poetry, Self, and Representation in Ethnographic Research." *Cultural Studies <=> Critical Methodologies* 12: 8–14.
Furman, Rich, Cynthia Lietz, and Carol L. Langer. 2006. "The Research Poem in International Social Work: Innovations in Qualitative Methodology." *International Journal of Qualitative Methods* 5 (3): 1–8.
Isachenkov, Vladimir. 2014. "Russian Envoy: Ferguson Shows US Racial Problems." News.yahoo.com. Accessed November 25, 2014. https://www.yahoo.com/news/russian-envoy-ferguson-shows-us-discrimination-162146459.html?ref=gs.
King, Martin Luther, Jr. 1963. *I Have a Dream*. National Archives and Records Administration. Accessed November 17, 2013. http://www.archives.gov/exhibits/featured_documents/mlk_speech/index.html.
Kobré, Kenneth. 2008. *Photojournalism: The Professionals' Approach*, 6th ed. New York: Taylor & Francis Group.
Langer, Carol L., and Rich Furman. 2004. "Exploring Identity and Assimilation: Research and Interpretive Poems." *Forum: Qualitative Social Research* 5(2), Single Contributions, Article 5. Accessed December 4, 2010. http://www.qualitative-research.net/index.php/fqs/issue/view/15.

Maxwell, Joseph A. 1996. *Qualitative Research Design: An Interactive Approach*. Thousand Oaks, CA: Sage.

Maynard, Kent, and Melisa Cahnmann-Taylor. 2010. "Anthropology at the Edge of Words: Where Poetry and Ethnography Meet." *Anthropology and Humanism* 35: 2–19. Accessed September 26, 2013. doi: 10.1111/j.1548-1409.2010.01049.x.

McCaskill, Terri A. 2008. "Exploring Personal Transformation through Autoethnography." EdD diss., Pepperdine University. ProQuest (1459924531).

Miles, Matthew B., and A. Michael. Huberman. 1994. *Qualitative Data Analysis: An Expanded Sourcebook*, 2nd ed. Thousand Oaks, CA: Sage.

Nash, Robert J. 2004. *Liberating Scholarly Writing: The Power of Personal Narrative*. New York: Teachers College Press.

Ollerenshaw, Jo Anne, and John W. Creswell. 2002. "Narrative Research: A Comparison of Two Restorying Data Analysis Approaches." *Qualitative Inquiry* 8 (3): 329–347. Accessed May 13, 2010. doi: 10.1177/10778004008003008.

Ownby, Terry. 2011. "Wunderkammers, Photographs, and Growing Up Southern: A Visual Semiotic Analysis of Self-Identity through Autoethnography." PhD diss., Colorado State University. ProQuest (UMI No. 3454625).

———. 2012. "Construction of Self-Identity through Photographs and Narrative Text in the Form of an Autoethnography." In *Conference Proceedings for the International Conference on Communication, Media, Technology, and Design*, edited by Agah Gumus, 95–99. Istanbul, Turkey: Eastern Mediterranean University.

———. 2013. "Critical Visual Methodology: Photographs and Narrative Text as a Visual Autoethnography." *Online Journal of Communication and Media Technologies* 2 (Special Issue—January). Accessed November 16, 2014. http://www.ojcmt.net/.

Poindexter, Cynthia Cannon. 1998. "Poetry as Data Analysis: Honoring the Words of Research Participants." *Reflections: Narratives of Professional Helping* 3 (4): 22–25.

Richardson, Laurel. 1992. "The Consequences of Poetic Representation: Writing the Other, Rewriting the Self." In *Investigating Subjectivity: Research on Lived Experience*, edited by Carolyn Ellis and Michael G. Flaherty, 125–140. Newbury Park, CA: Sage.

———. 2000. "Writing: A Method of Inquiry." In *Handbook of Qualitative Research*, edited by Norman K. Denzin and Yvonna S. Lincoln, 2nd ed., 733–768. Thousand Oaks, CA: Sage.

Richardson, Laurel, and St. Pierre, Elizabeth Adams. 2005. "Writing: A Method of Inquiry." In *Handbook of Qualitative Research*, edited by Norman K. Denzin and Yvonna S. Lincoln, 3rd ed., 959–978. Thousand Oaks, CA: Sage.

Ryba, Jeanne. 2008. "Kennedy Space Center Story: Origins." Accessed August 25, 2010. http://www.nasa.gov/centers/ kennedy/about/history/story/ch1.html.

Sarup, Madan. 1996. *Identity, Culture and the Postmodern World*. Athens, GA: University of Georgia Press.

Spradley, James P. 1979. *The Ethnographic Interview*. Orlando, FL: Holt, Rinehart, and Winston.

———. 1980. *Participant Observation*. Belmont, CA: Wadsworth.

Unst, Ariadne. 2013. "The Pantoum Verse Form." Accessed November 21, 2011. http://www.baymoon.com/~ariadne/form/pantoum.htm.

Willis, Jerry W. 2007. *Foundations of Qualitative Research: Interpretive and Critical Approaches*. Thousand Oaks, CA: Sage.

Section I Summary: An Author Conversation

Raphael Chijioke Njoku, Thomas Klein, Terry Ownby, and Alan Johnson

Raphael: In my opinion, I think the title "Interrogating and Framing Reality" for this section of the book captures very well the various themes explored by us as chapter authors. We all explored how groups and individuals construct "reality" as a product of cultural perceptions of their identity. Of course, we know that this sense of "reality" changes over time as perceptions change, too. In other words, realities are culturally invented within a given socioeconomic and political milieu. In relation to the theme of this book overall, it becomes clear that who tells the story and how it was presented has the power to influence the audience, the people.

Thomas: Yes, Raphael. And perhaps we could add that, in addition to context and culture, reality is "framed" by the medium that attempts to depict it. I'm struck by the way each of us has addressed distinctive narrative frames—Alan especially with film, Terry with photography, Raphael with market literature, and me with text messaging and letter-tablets. It seems that we've all noticed the particular effects of these distinct media on the message, to borrow from McLuhan.

Terry: I agree, Tom, that our disparate media (market literature, film, old and new tablets, and photography) impact the construction of our various cultural realities and, in turn, our identities. I'm not sure how "media" or "medium" gets worked into the title without it sounding like something from media studies. However, as I think about this and the fact all our chapters incorporate these disparate media, maybe if it were changed, it could read something like "Interrogating and Framing Reality Through Media: Identity and Cultural Perceptions."

Thomas: The addition of that little prepositional phrase, Terry, makes a great deal of sense to me; somehow, it really expresses the dynamism of the processes we're interested in.

Alan: A belated comment on reconsidering the title of our cluster: I like it, but (to defer to the pedant in me) wonder if "interrogating" logically comes before "framing." How about "Framing Reality?" (intentionally with the question mark)? Of course, this kind of a change might simply beg more questions!

Thomas: I think I must give a nod to the book's editorial team. It seems to me that, in this particular grouping of essays, we are largely operating with a similar sense of what both "narrative" and "identity" are (even as we recognize that these are quite capacious terms). I suspect that we might find the definitions becoming less similar in some of the other section groupings.

Speaking superficially, I for one noticed themes of cultural and postcolonial ideologies and representation—so that there is a certain resonance between Alan's description of the formation of Indian identity through film, Terry's exploration of the blindnesses of White culture in the American South, Raphael's analysis of gender and identity in African literary collections, and in my essay the fact that the texts come from a foreign occupation (by people who were themselves recently occupied). Of course, the themes do not always play out in the same ways, but the connections seem interesting.

Alan: I agree with Tom's points about the interconnections among our chapters. Our chapters also provide different angles on modernity, including various types of literacy, such as visual. Since we're concerned with current and future understandings of how our various disciplines interact, I think the visual is key, and it also, at least implicitly, relates to the pedagogical features of our disciplines.

Terry: I think it's an excellent observation that ideology and representation surface throughout the four chapters within this section. Since both ideology and representation are cultural constructs, it makes sense in turn that individual identity would be imbricated within these overarching notions. It seems to me, then, that as an individual transits their personal acculturation journey in life (which in and of itself becomes a narrative), their formative identity emerges from these themes. However, that identity is not static. As people move through their lives, cultures change within the moment, which, in my opinion, would also impact the overarching ideologies of representation (both of ourselves and of others). In essence then, what is really being discussed here is a narrative of cultural evolution.

Alan: Thanks, Terry. When we say "culture" (a notoriously broad and diffuse term, of course), I wonder if we all use it in the same sense. We have workplace cultures and national cultures, of course, but even these are not self-contained and vary in both

Section I Summary 85

              practice and perception. Also, again implied by Terry's post and no doubt self-evident, these cultures all constantly merge with and shape one another. So how these groups tell their own stories is the crux of the matter. Many ostensibly self-defining and all-encompassing cultural narratives contradict one another, as we see in all countries at the national level. Same for college departments, etc. That's why I like the topic of "cross-cultural" narratives!

Thomas: I agree with Alan that we're all studying how reality gets "framed" more than interrogating it. Perhaps none of us is in a position to say what reality "really" is, but we can use our different approaches to narrative to see how it can get delineated and demarcated.

Raphael: Among other things, I have come to realize fully that as scholars we occupy a very important position in the scheme of public influence. The ideas we put forth, whether they are found as books (fictions and nonfictions) or in artistic representations and presentations (as such films, paintings, and so on), they tend to travel far and wide. Most of these ideas are timeless and they will remain with society forever. Then there is the realization that the liberal arts disciplines not only complement one another but also impact the sciences, the world of business, and the professions.

Thomas: For myself, I now realize that I had myopically assumed that narrative was more or less the domain of departments of English and literature; I'm struck by what I see now as the multiple parallels between my work and that of Raphael and Terry, as well as Alan's. I've also been accustomed to working independently—single authorship tends to be the most common approach in my field—but this project has demonstrated that collaboration is entirely possible.

Terry: Tom, I'm glad to hear you were surprised how fields outside of your domain engage with "narrative." As a photographer, I also tended to view my work with a singular lens for a long time and I felt that all other disciplines remained in their appropriate silo. There seems to have always been a "visual" narrative, as such, central to images of all visual media, but as I explored ways of engaging an image to interpret its ideological underpinnings, I was surprised to find that a form of poetry could be used in that analysis. Moreover, to learn that poetry could be used ethnographically to help understand cultural dynamics was a true revelation to me. So this project has certainly engaged my creative mental wheels as I ponder the tremendous opportunities to collaborate with scholars outside of my particular silo.

Thomas: Terry, it strikes me that your approach in particular has the potential for quite innovative collaboration—crossing disciplines and deploying one creative form (poetry) in what seems to me a wholly unusual context (ethnographic research).

Terry: Yes, Tom, you're right. It was a rather experimental cross-discipline methodology. During my graduate studies in visual communication and higher education, we were encouraged to explore working with methods outside our traditional disciplines. I was actually studying qualitative methods from anthropology (ethnography) when I came across literature from the health sciences where researchers were working with research poetry to analyze interview transcript notes. I found the whole idea of cross-discipline methods fascinating. So I approached my advisor and methodologist about the notion of using this method with my work on images and narrative text. In turn, they found the idea to be novel and encouraged pursuing this line of inquiry. Needless to say, they approved this approach, and it's been received well from other scholars. As a result, I've given a couple of international conference presentations on this topic.

From my perspective, the more scholars climb out of their silos within the College of Arts & Letters and give attention to other narrative methods, they may find their research and academic lives more fulfilling.

Thomas: That makes sense. I will say that I don't find my particular work (which tends to address a fairly narrow group of scholars) unfulfilling, but I do find it stimulating to explain my work and its appeal to broader audiences!

Raphael: I think we have a wonderful piece of ideas here. As I review all of your comments, it comes to me that realities are framed through *three* critical channels: what we see (visual), what we read (literature), and how we interpret these through the lenses of culture (ideology *or mind-set*). Of course cultures are wired. They command certain volts of electricity that lights up our emotions, motives, values, identity, and sense of belonging or lack of it. It is out of this mind-set that narratives are born.

Alan: I like Raphael's comparison of culture to electricity and the observation that narratives emerge from the various points of our identity that this cultural voltage "lights up." This reminds me of Erving Goffman's idea of how conceptual frames, which are in a sense cultural lenses, shape our perspectives. And I think all of our essays here practice the "thick description" Clifford Geertz advocated, or in other words the attempt to situate a given text or activity in its social-historical context, including the author's own. What I find particularly interesting is that both Goffman and Geertz independently conclude that, as symbolic animals, our societies are all essentially theatrical.

Also interesting to me is how our essays move back and forth between objective and self-reflexive analysis. In other words, we are all acutely aware of how our examination of a text entails our particular biases. I think we in the humanities are more self-aware in this way than our science colleagues and that we need more of this self-critique in our world than ever before. Contra the conventional wisdom that scholarship should make one "more certain" of something, I believe it's precisely our embrace of uncertainty, of ambiguity, that should be celebrated.

I know these broad comments beg more questions. For example, to what degree are we all enculturated, and can we act independently of this enculturation? Are we all caught up in the conceptual frame of commodity culture, where everything, including education, is monetized? As teachers and scholars, can we resist the web of ideologies that condition us? These kinds of questions are obviously important, but often miss the forest for the trees. They, or rather their presumptions, undervalue the kind of individual agency we want our students to develop, and which we believe they can. Such questions also don't account for the huge variety of narrative expression that we in the humanities are fortunate enough to study and share, and that these essays exemplify.

Section II

Narratives at the Intersection of the Public and Private

5 Finding Story in Unexpected Places
Branding and the Role of Narrative in the Study of Communication

*John Gribas, Zac Gershberg,
James R. DiSanza, and Nancy J. Legge*

Narrative is story, and story is inherently communicative. And though many may automatically associate the idea of story with the written word (i.e., with story "books"), the truth is we are not far removed from our oral culture roots. For much of our time as social beings, our stories were shared and passed on primarily, and sometimes exclusively, by spoken word. So it should not be a surprise that narrative has an important and recognized role in the formal study of human communication.

We, the four coauthors of this chapter, share in being part of the "communication" discipline or field. We are members of a single college department and, therefore, have a sense of unity in subject, focus, and mission. We are part of a not-overly-large and exceptionally collegial program. Despite that, we each have our own academic specialties that can separate us and keep us, as is so often the case in academia, siloed in our areas of specialization. On the other hand, our department is somewhat unique in that virtually every faculty member has some background in classical rhetorical theory and views classical rhetoric as the foundation of our field. That helps unite us. But simply claiming that we all share an academic heritage tracing to Aristotle may not be enough to provide a real sense of connection or unity.

When the ISU College of Arts & Letters put out a call for chapter proposals focused on narrative, we met to discuss the possibility. In considering our various specializations—rhetorical theory, journalism, media studies, leadership, organizational culture, crisis communication—we realized that narrative could indeed offer a point of connection and a synthesizing dynamic. Demonstrating that dynamic is a large part of the motivation for this book. Yet these chapters are designed to do more than simply demonstrate that there are, in any university college unit, individuals across departments who have in some way an interest in narrative, broadly defined. This book project is also intended to show how narrative can provide a localizing and community-building place across departmental and disciplinary divisions.

Now, those of us in the field of communication typically have a rather easy time finding commonality with colleagues from a broad range of disciplinary homes. The history of communication is long, and even a brief look into that history demonstrates the inherently interdisciplinary nature of the modern field of communication. As Pearce and Foss's (1990) disciplinary history makes clear, we communication scholars draw theoretically and methodologically from the behavioral sciences, the social sciences, the humanities, and the arts. However, as academics, we exist in a college community with many for whom cross-disciplinary connection may not come so naturally. And we must admit that, even for communication folk, a general awareness of some distant methodological or theoretical shared genealogy is most often trumped by the realities of disciplinary teaching and research specializations, curricular uniquenesses, and terribly unfortunate departmental turf protection fostered by budget and resource limitations.

So, in response to the call for chapter proposals, we enthusiastically joined as departmental colleagues and with our Arts & Letters family to produce something collectively that demonstrates the powerful unifying force of narrative.

In this chapter, we review the historically important role of narrative in the communication field, from classical rhetorical theory to the work of Fisher (1985, 1987) and his identification of the person as "homo narran" (storytelling person). Then we explore applications of narrative in work related to organizational culture and leader communication, uncovering the generally unrecognized and even surprising foundational place that narrative holds in other well-established organizational communication perspectives such as crisis communication and organizational image repair. Finally, we argue that corporate identity is grounded in narrative; that is, organizations are primarily known and recognized by stories (histories) in which they are the main character. Additionally, Kenneth Burke's (1945, 1950) ideas can be used to show how "branding" is ultimately a process of inviting individuals into that corporate story. By extension, we show that, through the power of identification, organizational narrative becomes a powerful force in the construction and maintenance of personal identity. Through all of this, we hope to illustrate how narrative can be a unifying force, thus helping to connect academics and academic units as well as the phenomena they study.

The Important Role of Narrative in the Communication Field

A brief exploration of the ideas of early rhetoricians, founders of the modern communication field, can demonstrate the vital importance of narrative. Narrative is considered an essential element of rhetoric. And rhetoric is considered an essential aspect of democratic society, since citizens are required to develop rhetorical skills to speak persuasively on important matters, to listen critically to ideas, and to make decisions based on those arguments.

Ancient Greece was the first society to reflect this central connection between democracy and rhetoric. In 467 BCE, the Sicilians overthrew King Hieton and established democratic rule, where "free males over the age of eighteen constituted the government, judges decided cases, and the people determined their own destiny" (Ryan 1992, 5), requiring citizens to be "competent in public presentation, deliberation, and debate, decision making, adjudication, and critical judgment" (Poulakos 2001, 732). Teachers called sophists emerged to fill the increasing demand for teaching rhetorical skills. "The sophists were soon to dominate the public scene in Athens to the point that training in rhetoric was deemed an essential part of every citizen's education" (Murphy and Katula 2003, 24).

The first theory of rhetoric that was developed and taught emphasized the role of narrative in persuasion. Corax outlined a model for courtroom speeches in a handbook called the *Techne* (Ryan 1992), suggesting that, since it is difficult to prove any case absolutely, an arguer must construct a story—a narrative—that is more probable and reasonable than the other's story. Corax's theory outlines five steps a citizen should follow when preparing a speech, with narrative as a vital aspect to the structure: (1) the introduction to gain the favorable attention of the audience; (2) the narrative to explain the facts of the case and describe the events in a light that is favorable to the speaker, providing the storyteller's perspective of what happened; (3) the arguments, listing reasons for the case and utilizing evidence and reasoning to support claims; (4) the refutation to attack the opponent's claims and/or respond to the opponent's attacks; and (5) the conclusion to summarize and urge the audience for a favorable verdict.

For Corax, the narrative is not a detached, objective report of the events but, instead, the speaker's opportunity to emphasize his or her perspective of the events and communicate them in a way to present the speaker as "a just and honest person" who explains what happened. Though it may be tempting to focus on the arguments as the primary force of persuasion, this model demonstrates how narratives function as both foundation and support for the arguments themselves. Ultimately, for Corax, influence happens when a speaker's story is seen as the most plausible.

In *On Rhetoric*, Aristotle (1991) challenged the sophistic model and provided the foundation for the study of speech, and interestingly ignored narrative at the expense of devising basic categories for effective communication. For Aristotle, rhetoric relies on a speaker who assesses the situation and skillfully applies speaker credibility, emotional appeals, and logic to persuade the audience. Though Aristotle avoids an explicit consideration of narrative in *On Rhetoric*, it features prominently in his work on aesthetics, *Poetics* (1984), which emphasized, among other things, different genres of drama and the importance of providing very clear beginnings, middles, and ends.

This relegation of narrative only to the structures of aesthetics remained firm in theories of rhetoric until the twentieth century, when narrative gained attention in the study of communication. Narrative figured prominently in the mass communication areas of journalism and screenwriting, and it also became a key feature to the work of influential rhetoricians such as Kenneth Burke and Walter Fisher. Theoretically, these thinkers helped collapse the division between rhetoric and narrative in order to evaluate what constitutes effective communication better.

Burke challenged two key characteristics of Aristotelian rhetoric. First, he suggested that rhetoric operates in art, fiction, and poetry as much as in traditional public speaking situations. For Burke, the interplay between any source of communication and an audience constitutes a rhetorical transaction. Second, Burke challenged Aristotle's notion that rhetoric relies exclusively on the persuasive use of logic. According to Burke ([1950] 1969), identification is the dominant concept of rhetoric; audiences gravitate toward speakers with whom they share some sense of familiarity.

Under the umbrella term "dramatism," Burke ([1945] 1969) also examined how narratives are effectively deployed as a cycle of guilt, purification, and redemption. Guilt, for Burke ([1935] 1965), represents an audience's feelings of tension or ambivalence. This does not assume that an audience sees itself as responsible for a particular state of affairs, but simply that the audience recognizes a problem that causes strain. In response to this recognition and strain (guilt), effective acts of rhetoric employ identification to engage such an audience in required cleansing for purification (285). Communicators purge feelings of guilt through some act of redemption. As Burke describes it, redemption marks a call to action for the audience to achieve "perfection." Unfortunately, as Burke ([1941] 1967) would later point out, correcting guilt through purification and redemption often requires victimage, as witnessed in the Nazi rhetorical narrative to root out economic and social ills by scapegoating Jewish persons as the cause of societal ills. As David Bobbit (2004) noted, the Burkean guilt/purification/redemption narrative cycle can be enacted for positive change too. Dr. Martin Luther King Jr. accomplished such change in his "I Have a Dream" speech, where guilt signals the United States' history of racism, purification is the return to the "promissory note" of the Declaration of Independence, and the public audience is redeemed through the passage of the Civil Rights Act.

Burke was an unorthodox thinker who explored myriad concepts, including narrative, to understand the interplay of discourse. Walter Fisher (1987) was more focused in his case for narrative as the essential issue defining human experience and for the aesthetic power of narrative as a challenge to a more rationalist focus on the power of argument. By viewing all human discourse as the product of storytelling persons, or *homo narrans* (62), Fisher sought to synthesize rhetorical and persuasive discourse with literary and aesthetic values (58). Within this paradigm, effective rhetoric requires the achieving of narrative probability by suturing two interlocking components: coherence and fidelity. Coherence refers to whether the structure of the story makes sense to the audience, from the credibility of the characters to the style of delivery (64). Narrative fidelity speaks to whether the values of the story are consistent with the experience of the audience and the degree to which the narrative transcends mere story and persuades the audience to exercise judgment (105).

To demonstrate the power of the narrative paradigm, Fisher analyzed the rhetorical success of President Ronald Reagan. According to Fisher, former President Jimmy Carter applied instrumental logic in an attempt to reason with the public while Reagan infused his rhetoric with the mytho-poetic qualities of the Western hero to win the election of 1980 (147–150). Using words like recapture, rebirth, renew, restore, reaffirm, and redeem, Reagan presented a narrative of past glory and encouraged identification with the voting public (151). Fisher also highlights how speechwriter, Ted Sorensen, filled President John F. Kennedy's rhetoric with a different narrative—one of a new frontier pitching forward into the future (152–153). Both Reagan and Kennedy convinced publics of coherence and fidelity through narratives that people could both identify with and participate in.

The work of Burke and Fisher thus combine to recover the emphasis on narrative in rhetoric established by the sophists, and while Aristotle's legacy has not been erased within communication studies, it is nonetheless evident that our understandings of rhetoric, and narrative's role in rhetoric, have expanded immensely to cover a wide range of communicative phenomena.

Narrative Goes Beyond the Rhetorical Borders

Narrative has been embraced as a theoretical and methodological emphasis by scholars broadly, even in areas not customarily associated with the rhetorical tradition. In particular, the study of organizational communication has benefited from application of a narrative lens. Specifically, narratives/stories have been considered an important element of corporate culture research: an anthropological approach to examining communication in organizational settings that became established through the 1980s and that continues today. Additionally, recent writings that explore leadership as a primarily communicative phenomena often highlight the power of narrative or storytelling as a critical leader language tool.

For the field of organizational communication, "culture" research dominated the 1980s. There were serious questions posed about the overall value of the traditional functionalist assumptions and positivist: social scientific approaches to understanding communication in organizational contexts that had dominated academic research throughout the twentieth century. Innovative communication scholars borrowed methods—less scientific, less quantitative, more interpretive—from the world of cultural anthropology and began looking at organizations as "tribes" (Wilcock 1984), social groups with distinct collective identities and unique ways of living together.

Following the influential cultural anthropologist Clifford Geertz (1973), an organization's culture was understood as "a system of inherited conceptions expressed in symbolic forms by means of which [organizational members] communicate, perpetuate, and develop their knowledge about and attitudes toward life" (89). The "symbolic forms" that have been of interest to organizational culture researchers over the years are many, but in virtually all lists stories/narratives are directly or indirectly included.

Charles Bantz's (1993) comprehensive approach to analyzing organizational communication culture included attention to metaphors, stories, and fantasy themes. Popular business literature authors, Deal and Kennedy (1982), acknowledged the important role of stories, via the storyteller, in the corporate cultural network.

> Storytellers are in a powerful position because they can change reality... [They] preserve institutions and their values by imparting legends of the company to new employees. They also carry stories about the visionary heroes or the latent outlaw over in the manufacturing plant. Storytellers will also reveal much about what it takes to get ahead in the organization.
>
> (87)

Noted social psychologist Edgar Schein saw culture as highly complex, difficult at best to observe, and, contrary to authors such as Deal and Kennedy, impossible to "manage." Still, Schein (1988) acknowledged the role of narrative in organizational culture, particularly in culture dissemination and socialization.

> Stories often communicate the values and beliefs of founders or other central characters in the organization who have become symbolic role models. The stories are often prescriptive and can thus become direct vehicles of indoctrination. On the other hand, in an organization with many subcultures or conflicting coalitions, stories can become a means of spreading a counterculture or revealing inconsistencies or absurdities in the main culture.
>
> (125–126)

The variety of organizational culture work that dominated much of the 1980s' organizational communication research agenda often gave serious attention to narrative. Examples include Kelly's (1985) use of story to look into the Silicon Valley culture and implications for high tech innovation, Myrsiades's (1987) argument for closer consideration of narrative dimensions and attention to the oral tradition in examining organizational culture, Deetz's (1987) exploration of the relationship between story and university culture reflected in chairperson power and influence, and Brown's (1990) demonstration of the value of nursing home resident stories for revealing organizational culture.

So we see explicit recognition of narrative's role in exploration of organizational culture. We can see similar recognition in approaches to the study of leadership, an important topic in the field of organizational communication, as well as in related fields such as business management, educational administration, public administration, and social and organizational psychology. Scholars in each field have their own unique take on exploring leadership, and it should be no surprise that those in the field of organizational communication emphasize the importance of "messaging" as a critical element of leadership and leader effectiveness. Some pay particular attention to narrative messaging.

Mai and Akerson (2003) wrote,

> The concept of storytelling and narrative communication takes on special significance for leadership communications. It represents both a means for leaders to convey meaning and directions and the way employees may best remember and make sense of their own role in an organization and where the organization is headed.
>
> (4)

Their book, *The Leader as Communicator: Strategies and Tactics to Build Loyalty, Focus Effort, and Spark Creativity*, is only one of many similar recent publications. Some are in line with Mai and Akerson in presenting narrative as one element of or tool for strategic leader communication. For example, in *The Power of Framing: Creating the Language of Leadership*, Fairhurst (2011) lists narrative as one among many language forms that are useful to leader-communicators for a variety of framing purposes.

While some scholars and practitioners recognize narrative as one of a number of important leadership communication tools, others give narrative a more central and pivotal role. This is illustrated well by the titles of two books by leadership guru Stephen Denning: *The Secret Language of Leadership: How Leaders Inspire Action through Narrative* (2007) and *The Leader's Guide to Storytelling: Mastering the Art and Discipline of Business Narrative* (2011). Some would go so far as to claim that narrative and leadership are inseparable, indeed possibly synonymous. "Leadership is Narrative" is a chapter title in a 2012 book by Albert Mohler in which he claims, "The leader draws followers into a story that frames all of life" (37). Apparently, for Mohler, narrative framing is the essential, defining element of leadership.

Denning may not go as far as Mohler, but the fact that he puts narrative center stage for a solo performance in multiple extended works suggests strongly that narrative is more than just one of many leader-messaging tools for him. And he is not alone. *Hooked: How Leaders Connect, Engage, and Inspire with Storytelling* (Dolan and Naidu 2013) and *Whoever Tells the Best Story Wins: How to Use Your Own Stories to Communicate with Power and Impact* (Simmons 2007) are more examples of recent and popular business titles bolstering the claim that, in today's world of leadership studies, narrative is worth serious attention. It is so because "stories about reality completely change perceptions of what is true, important, and thus, real. Stories interpret raw facts and proofs to create reality" (Simmons 2007, 3).

This power to impact people's shared sense of reality has attracted the attention of individuals interested in leadership outside of traditional corporate settings too. Mohler (2012), mentioned earlier, expressed the fundamental link between leadership and narrative broadly; however, his primary attention was to those who, like himself, have allegiance to religious organizations, Christian seminaries and churches specifically. *Teaching Our Story: Narrative Leadership and Pastoral Formation* (Goleman 2010) and *Intuitive Leadership: Embracing a Paradigm of Narrative, Metaphor, and Chaos* (Keel 2007) are more of the same.

So in the exploration of organizational culture and in recent work to understand leader communication in various organizational contexts, contemporary scholars have embraced narrative principles. Of course, culture and leadership are not the only topics relevant to the field of organizational communication where we can see narrative applications. Clearly, Ernest Bormann's (1985) development of symbolic convergence theory as a framework for understanding group communication is grounded in narrative. As Winslade and Monk (2000) demonstrate, the communicative processes of mediation and conflict management, not exclusive to but certainly highly relevant to the organizational context, can also be approached from a narrative perspective. All of this work serves to demonstrate recognition, within and beyond the rhetorical tradition, of the power and pervasiveness of narrative.

Finding Narrative in Unexpected Places

Perhaps the real power and pervasiveness of narrative as a fundamental issue in human communication behavior is demonstrated best in how narrative can be seen underlying theory and practice in facets of the communication field not considered part of the narrative paradigm. Even where it is not recognized as such, narrative provides a valuable framework for understanding.

One important area of strategic communication exploration focuses on responses that organizations must make following crisis situations. In such situations, important audiences (e.g., customers, investors, suppliers, community members) often hold the organization responsible for crises, and the situation can leave lasting corporate image damage. Researchers have worked to identify common corporate image restoration strategies used in such situations and to consider the relative effectiveness of these strategies. Though this work is not considered part of the narrative paradigm, we argue that story is at the heart of corporate image management. In other words, though not typically framed as such by researchers, crisis responses are ultimately strategic tellings of events leading up to and following the crisis event. Thus crisis management can be understood as corporate narrative management.

Organizations invest extensive resources in creating and managing a positive organizational narrative. For example, the story of Apple is the story of Steve

Jobs ("Once upon a time, there was a very smart and ambitious man . . ."), who helped revolutionize computing with the Apple II and the Macintosh. However, as with any Greek tragedy, Jobs was brought down by his own character flaws. He redeemed, or purified, himself by starting NeXT Computers and purchasing the struggling Pixar, which led to his eventual redemption when he returned to Apple and created the iPod, iPhone, and iPad ("And everyone lived happily ever after!"). Apple's image of itself is intricately tied to Jobs's narrative. Although most public relations narratives may be far less dramatic, organizations do create attractive narratives about their benefits and accomplishments. Therefore, it is useful and even rather intuitive to understand crisis communication as managing interruptions to the carefully cultivated public relations narrative, forcing the organization to construct a new story while responding to attacks from various accusers.

Most crisis communication literature is based on a typology of tactics developed by Benoit (1995). Some see Benoit's typology as encouraging a reductionist approach that can distract from broader observations of the larger, unified narrative underlying crisis responses. On the other hand, rather than focusing on specific crisis communication tactics, Burke suggests that audiences will experience an organization's crisis as a complete narrative involving guilt, purification, and redemption. To illustrate the possibilities of taking a narrative approach to crisis communication, we will apply Fisher's (1985) concepts of coherence and fidelity, discussed earlier, to the case of the NFL's image repair narrative during Ray Rice's domestic abuse incident.

The Baltimore Ravens running back, Ray Rice, and his then-fiancée, Janay Palmer, made headlines when a video surfaced in February of 2014 showing Rice dragging Palmer's unconscious body out of an Atlantic City hotel elevator after he assaulted her. The NFL commissioner, Roger Goodell, suspended Rice for two games—a penalty that was heavily criticized for its leniency. In September, the online celebrity news source, TMZ, released the in-elevator video that showed Rice knocking Palmer out with a vicious punch to the face. The NFL, still reeling from public criticism, was forced out of its preferred narratives about heroes and victories. In order to craft a new narrative, Goodell suspended Rice indefinitely and did several interviews and press conferences.

In the first interview with CBS News on September 9 (CBS News 2014), Norah O'Donnell opened by asking whether anyone at the NFL had seen the in-elevator video prior to the TMZ release.

Goodell said, "No."

O'Donnell reiterated, asking, "No one in the NFL?"

Goodell replied, "No one in the NFL, to my knowledge, and I had been asked that same question and the answer to that is no. We were not granted that. We were told that was not something we would have access to. On multiple occasions, we asked for it. And on multiple occasions we were told no."

O'Donnell continued to press, asking how a website like TMZ could get hold of it when the NFL couldn't.

Goodell said, "Well, I don't know how TMZ or any other website gets their information. We are particularly reliant on law enforcement. That's the most reliable. It's the most credible. And we don't seek to get that information from sources that are not credible."

Goodell said that he wished he had seen the tape because, when he met with Ray Rice and his representatives, "it was ambiguous about what actually happened."

O'Donnell then asked what was ambiguous about an unconscious woman being dragged out of an elevator by her feet. Goodell replied,

> There was nothing ambiguous about that. That was the result that we saw. We did not know what led up to that. We did not know the details of that. We asked for that on several occasions. It was unacceptable in and of itself what we saw on the first tape. And that's why we took action, albeit insufficient action. And we acknowledge that, we took responsibility for that—I did personally—and I take responsibility for that now. But what we saw yesterday was extremely clear and graphic and was absolutely necessary for us to take the action we did . . . It was extremely graphic, and it was sickening.

When asked if the NFL had a larger problem with domestic abuse, Goodell began to highlight the NFL's plan for response—a commitment to purification and redemption.

"What we have is young men that are going to be unfortunately involved in this if we don't provide the right resources . . . We have to change our training and our education to try and eliminate that issue." Goodell went on to say,

> We're saying we have a problem. We have one incident, that's a problem. And what we want do is by the policy that we implemented two weeks ago and say, "We haven't done this right." We have had lots of conversations, lots of listening and learning right here in this room with experts not just in the last two weeks or three weeks or month, but over the last couple of years to say, "How can we deal with this issue better? How can we prevent the cases from happening?". . . People expect a lot from the NFL. We accept that. We embrace that. That's our opportunity to make a difference not just in the NFL, but in society in general. We have that ability. We have that influence. And we have to do that. And every day, that's what we're going to strive to do.

Goodall's narrative revolves almost entirely around the in-elevator video: how they tried to get it, failed, and how that failure led to their poor decision making. But his story goes on to explain how the NFL will purify and redeem itself in the eyes of the public.

First, consider Goodell's narrative by focusing on coherence. According to Hart and Daughton (2004), narrative coherence involves an evaluation of the qualities of a story, including completeness, believability, followability, and the degree to which the story's structure and characters hang together. From this point of view, Goodell's narrative fails in almost every way. The opening tale about the NFL's failure to get the tape is told poorly and lacks detail, specificity, and character development. We are not told who tried to get the video, how they tried to get the video, how many times they tried to get the video, who they contacted in law enforcement, and little about why these persons refused the request. The lack of development does not help the story's credibility, especially given that the planet's most powerful sports organization could not get the video, while TMZ, a paparazzi-style blog, got the video simply by asking the hotel. Because the story of the NFL's efforts are poorly structured, developed, and told, it is less than believable.

In contrast to Goodell's narrative, Baltimore Ravens owner, Steve Biscotti, told a much more coherent story regarding his team's attempts to get the video.

> We contacted the casino management and asked if there was video of the incident from inside the elevator that we could see. The casino would not share such video. We asked the local New Jersey police and the police refused as well. We asked the prosecutor's office and that office refused. It was our understanding at that time that Ray's attorney had not yet seen the video. NFL officials had been informed, and we know they were also trying to retrieve and/or see the video.
> (Gatto 2014, para. 9)

It is easy to see that this narrative is more fleshed out, telling, perhaps even in order, and reveals the specific agents from whom they sought the video and that each time they were rebuffed. The structure, detail, and consistency of this narrative make it much more believable.

Goodell's narrative moves to an important second act, wherein he blames Rice's earlier suspension on limited information. O'Donnell appears to recognize incoherence in this story and asks Goodell why he needed anything more than the outside-elevator video of Rice dragging the unconscious Palmer to make the right decision. Goodell's only response is that the first video was the reason he took action. Even his attempts to accept responsibility are denied by other elements of the narrative where he scapegoats law enforcement for failing to provide the video and Rice for not being honest. His narrative remains seriously incoherent, and when Goodell begins to describe the solutions to the problem, one gets the distinct impression that his actions are cynical rather than truly redemptive.

Second, consider Goodell's story in light of narrative fidelity with attention to narrative truthfulness—how well it captures what is known and how well it reflects the audience's morals and values (Hart and Daughton 2004). Goodell repeatedly emphasizes the necessity of having all the information, including the in-elevator video, to make a correct decision. Although "having all the facts" is certainly a value of American jurisprudence, appealing to this value is tenuous at best when justifying delayed discipline of apparent spousal abuse by an employee in a professional sports league where participation is a privilege. O'Donnell calls Goodell out for this contradiction by asking, "But what changed? I mean, on the first tape she was lying unconscious on the ground, being dragged out by her feet. Did you really need to see a videotape of Ray Rice punching her in the face to make this decision?" In asking this, O'Donnell is proposing a second, more important value: concern for the victim of this abuse and the safety for women everywhere if a popular figure such as Rice gets off with a minor penalty on the excuse that there was no clear evidence of the actual beating. O'Donnell interrogates the values Goodell expressed in his narrative and prioritizes the safety of women over Goodell's abstract formulation.

Even worse, Goodell implies that, in order to act, he needed to know what happened prior to the assault that might explain it. "That was the result of what we saw, but we did not know what led up to that. We did not know the details of that." Here Goodell's narrative continues to focus on the value of full discovery, apparently including what Palmer may have done to cause the assault. To his credit, he quickly pulls back from this "victim blaming" inference, but he suggests that Ray Rice was only partly responsible for the attack. Obviously, suggesting that the victim may have done something to cause the beating is unfaithful to most people's understanding of domestic violence and is not consistent with our cultural moral system.

This analysis suggests that Goodell's crisis narrative lacked coherence and fidelity and would do little to convince people of the NFL's sincerity. Indeed, Goodell faced significant pushback from various sources, including the National Organization for Women (O'Neill 2014) and several ESPN analysts. Of his performance during the interview, noted sports columnist Mike Lupica said, "When you looked at him Tuesday night with Norah O'Donnell, you really did start to imagine the NFL commissioner bleeding from both eyes in the late rounds of a fight he lost on points long ago" (Lupica 2014, para. 13).

In this brief case analysis, we see how organizational crisis management is inherently an act of narrative management. Not surprisingly, then, a narrative framework lent valuable insight into the failure of Goodell's crisis communication in ways that a dissection and catalog of distinct image restoration strategies could not. With the exceptions of some such as Hartman (2014, 2015), scholars exploring crisis communication and image restoration are not typically grounding their work in narrative. It seems evident to us that more of them should be.

Narrative's Role in Branding and Identification

We now extend the impact of narrative from the world of corporate image management to the world of brand identity and identification. Up until the twentieth century, advertising and marketing centered around rational descriptions of product uniqueness, quality, or cost, but offering a brand narrative to connect to and with consumer publics is now standard (Postman [1985] 2005, 59). As noted, Burke ([1950] 1969) considered identification as the primary force of rhetoric; therefore, his work serves as a lens through which to consider branding. Specifically, Burke argues that the symbols of discourse can be used to make persons feel consubstantial—of the same substance—with others: "For substance, in the old philosophies, was an *act*; and a way of life is an *acting together*; and in acting together, [people] have common sensations, concepts, images, ideas, attitudes that make them *consubstantial*" (21; emphasis in the original). As symbols of discourse, narratives can draw persons closer together in a sense of community.

Through this lens, then, branding is the telling of an organization's underlying story to foster identification with public audiences. These stories are not only an organizational communication option but also the very basis of a brand's rhetorical transaction. By responding to narrative in identification, consumers share the substance of the brand. Brand loyalty is achieved when individuals respond by editing themselves into the narrative. Therefore, the power of these branding narratives is fundamental to corporate identity, and its influence can be seen as trickling down into personal identity: I'm a Chevy driver! I'm a Mac user! I'm a Pepper, you're a Pepper! The branding narrative calculus is twofold, then: narratives are constructed to encourage identification, and they only succeed insofar as consumers adopt attitudes and behaviors allowing them to inhabit a personal identity associated with the brand.

The evolution of the Apple corporation exemplifies this. Its Macintosh personal computer was introduced through a television advertisement aired during the 1984 Super Bowl. The spot played on the dystopian novel *1984*, written by George Orwell. Awash in gray, drab uniforms, people in the ad march in lockstep toward a giant screen as a totalitarian figure lectures them about achieving "a garden of pure ideology." Then a brightly clothed female track-and-field athlete, chased by authorities in riot gear, runs forward and hurls a hammer into the screen. Following the implosion, a simple text appears, read aloud as voice-over: "On January 24th, Apple Computer will introduce Macintosh. And you'll see why 1984 won't be like '1984.' " The advertisement concludes with the iconic company logo, still in use today: an apple with a chunk bitten out of it.

The branding of Apple transcends its logo, however. As a producer of technologies from computers and phones to tablets and iPods, Apple embeds consumers within a narrative of individualistic authenticity. The message is that people can exercise a distinctive lifestyle by becoming an Apple user. In doing so, they become consubstantial with both the brand and other consumers. The "1984" ad is not some cautionary tale about resisting totalitarian government but, instead, a protest against the competition of the time, IBM, whose nickname, Big Blue, connoted a conservative, monolithic corporate structure. The Apple narrative presented a fresh alternative to IBM's unthinking, dated corporate establishment. The ad does not even specify that Macintosh is a computer; it is but a narrative inviting a following of those consumers who wish to distinguish themselves from others.

So to spur audience identification, Apple strategically branded itself in a narrative of division within the personal computing market. In his theorizing of identification, Burke observed that it "is compensatory to division" ([1950] 1969, 22). So by clearly demarcating inclusion and exclusion, identification is hastened. According to Burke, "a specialized activity makes one a participant in some social or economic class. 'Belonging' in this sense is rhetorical" (28). Apple offers a participatory narrative through which persons can both act and think differently, thus creating its own class of consumers who consubstantiate the brand. Its later slogan from the 1990s, "Think Different," illustrates this as well, as it was a direct challenge to IBM whose motto, from the time of its founding, was "Think."

Apple continued in the mid-2000s with its "I'm a Mac, I'm a PC" campaign (Benoit and Delbert 2010), contesting dominance of Windows-based systems. The narrative in this series of ads is personified through a young, disaffected guy in casual clothes, who represents Mac, while a bespectacled older man, clad in a saggy brown suit, represents PC. With whom, the spots ask through implication, would you prefer to identify? This ad series is not simply a story, but a public invitation for the consumer to embrace and enact an identity.

Before his passing in 2011, Apple cofounder and CEO, Steve Jobs, personified this narrative subtext. Before large crowds and dressed in jeans, white sneakers, and a sleek black turtleneck, Jobs hyped new product launches with a clear narrative message: join us and inhabit the personage of a cool Apple user, like me. The branding is thus facilitated, not with attention to the sum of its products, but through the promise of participation in an ongoing narrative that provides a desirable identity to loyal followers who can share a similar substance of cool authenticity. As Fisher (1987) argued, the human aptitude for identifying with and within narratives precedes reason itself. Therefore, the inherent contradiction of joining others so as to exhibit uniqueness is smoothed over by the power of Apple's narrative fidelity.

Apple is one company out of many that could be explored as a case study for the use of narrative in corporate brand identity. However, a focus on narrative branding can also offer insight into other discourses, such as politics and sport/celebrity. The 2008 presidential campaign of Barack Obama, for example, indicates the efficacy of constructing a branding narrative. Trailing frontrunner Hillary Clinton in the polls during the primary season, the Obama campaign marshaled branding to promote its candidate. Both the iconic "Hope" poster, designed by street artist Shepard Fairey, and "Yes We Can," the viral social media video produced by rapper will.i.am, contributed to a narrative of enthusiasm that emphasized change and, importantly for politics, established brand loyalty. Each artifact employed an antiquated, minimalist aesthetic to construct the Obama brand as new and different. Fairey's poster used washed-out blues and reds to render Obama's portrait, below which rested the single word, "Hope," and the Obama campaign symbol. Obama looks wistfully past the viewer's sightline, projected out and above and, presumably, into the future. The video, which took advantage of the nascent surge in social media sharing, via YouTube, is shot in black-and-white and features famous personages whispering to dubbed Obama speeches word-for-word, accompanied by a background beat and chorus. It is an effective branding device insofar as it embeds the viewer in an ongoing narrative, driven by the notably vague goal, "Yes We Can." But this represents its chief rhetorical power: the public is invited to join an affirming ("Yes"), participatory ("We"), optimistic ("Can") brand.

The career of NBA superstar LeBron James provides another example of how branding narratives have expanded out from the corporate world and rely on identification. Born and raised in Akron, Ohio, James was drafted by the local Cleveland Cavaliers of the National Basketball Association (NBA) in 2003. He won accolades as Rookie of the Year and then, in 2008 and 2009, Most Valuable Player. James's interest went beyond just basketball, however, as he would later create a branding firm and announce, in interviews, that he hoped to be seen as a "global icon." His narrative was supported by his mission to win a championship for his hometown Cavaliers, who had never won the NBA title. The fans of Cleveland became, by narrative inclusion, consubstantial with their superstar. The sports apparel company, Nike, who sponsored James at the time, created popular T-shirts and a billboard in downtown Cleveland with text reading, "We Are All Witnesses."

Yet when James entered free agency after the 2010 season, he opted to play for the Miami Heat. In fact, the sports cable network ESPN hyped what amounted to a prime-time product launch, called "The Decision," which aired live. "This fall I'm going to take my talents to South Beach," James announced on the air, adding, "I feel like I can compete down there." Though James would go on to win two NBA championships with Miami, the reaction to the superstar's method of handling "The Decision" was critical. In spurning his hometown—the rust-belt city of Cleveland, which was intimately connected with his brand—for the exotic and lush paradise of "South Beach," James lost control of his narrative and, significantly, his audience who felt consubstantial with him. That this was done on live television, combined with reports that he failed to notify his team of the choice in advance, came off to the public and the media as callous. As one sportswriter reflected at the time:

> In a few moments, he burned [his] image down. Gone is the loyal teammate. Gone is the hometown hero. Gone is the devotion to lifelong friendships. Gone is the feeling that LeBron James knows how to market himself. Gone is the happy-go-lucky kid James who could sell millions of product with a smile.
>
> (Jones 2010, para. 11)

Yet if James assumed the role of sports-villain in his time in Miami, he regained the initial promise of his branding narrative when opting to return to the Cavaliers during the free agency period of 2014. Avoiding live television, James (2014) announced his intention to return to Cleveland by writing a story for the website of *Sports Illustrated* magazine. "I feel my calling here goes above basketball," he wrote, adding,

> I have a responsibility to lead, in more ways than one, and I take that very seriously. My presence can make a difference in Miami, but I think it can mean more where I'm from. I want kids in Northeast Ohio, like the hundreds of Akron third-graders I sponsor through my foundation, to realize that there's no better place to grow up. Maybe some of them will come home after college and start a family or open a business. That would make me smile. Our community, which has struggled so much, needs all the talent it can get.
>
> (para. 10)

James thus recognized that his branding narrative was rooted in place: home. As such, he effectively enacted the narrative of Burke's guilt-purification-redemption cycle. James sought forgiveness through the humility of his second announcement and wound up redeemed by the community who would embrace him once more.

Despite winning championships in Miami, he was just another great athlete. By returning to Cleveland, James created a narrative of "symbolic resurrection" for both the city and himself, ascending to the status of a folk hero (Zirin 2013, para. 2). James now literally embodies the public he plays for since Cavalier fans are once again consubstantial with him in his quest to win a title for his hometown. Marketers, for their part, have not only a great athlete but also an ambassador for humble roots and authentic values to associate with their brands. And, sure enough, the Cavaliers won the 2016 NBA championship series in dramatic fashion. It was the first ever comeback for a team down three games to one in a final series and resulted in a celebration parade attended by 1.3 million people in downtown Cleveland (Mazzeo 2016, para. 2). The championship completed the perfect redemption story of a brand wrapped in a coherent, hi-fidelity narrative that invites collective identification and transcendence.

Conclusions and Caveats

The examples of corporate, political, and sports branding are admittedly high profile and by no means provide an exhaustive account of the ways in which branding narratives function. However, in these examples, as well as in our demonstration of narrative's presence and power throughout the history and field of communication studies, we show how considering narrative means more than identifying elements of story, like characters and plot, and assessing their aesthetic worth and consistency. For communication studies scholars, to examine narrative is to consider "the effect[s] of the discourse" (Wichelns [1925] 1993, 29). Those effects are substantial. The power of narrative fidelity and coherence (Fisher 1985, 1987) can draw us, as active participants, into stories. Those stories are more than narratives "about" corporations, politicians, and sports celebrities. As we present branding, the narratives "constitute" those corporations, politicians, and sports celebrities. Through identification (Burke [1950] 1969), we become consubstantial with—having the same symbolic substance as—those entities, those narratives, those brands.

Because the prevalence and power of narrative is so evident, we need to pause to acknowledge that it entails some potential dangers. Specifically, some have argued that the very allure of narrative, inviting us to get caught up in the story, can discourage critical thinking. Hart and Daughton (2004) suggest that "recent studies have shown that people reason differently in the presence of narrative" (88). That is, we can become disarmed of our critical eye and instead get caught up in the story line, listening for details about characters, the plot line, the sequence of events, and other details. We tend to be more forgiving if the logic is not evident because we think that "stories don't argue." Thus when hearing narratives, audiences may be more willing to let facts slide and allow unsubstantiated arguments to go unchallenged because "it's just a story." Edwin Black (1992) argues that narratives are "extraordinarily powerful" because listeners are distracted by the story line and avoid thinking about the arguments embedded within the story. Hart and Daughton contend that this is "ample reason to keep an eye on" narratives (91). As listeners and consumers, it is imperative to maintain a critical stance when confronted with narratives, and to hold narrators accountable for the reasoning in their stories just as we hold arguers responsible for the reasoning in their positions. To return to Fisher's (1985, 1987) language, we must make sure that narrative coherence and overall aesthetic appeal do not blind us to concern for narrative fidelity.

With serious attention to these cautions, we still submit that narrative has much value to offer, especially to the diverse members of universities in general and liberal arts colleges in particular, and especially in times of serious upheaval and challenge when members of those institutions are looking for something that can provide a sense of identity, unity, community. We have shown that, at least in the communication field, narrative is powerful and maybe even inescapable. Our efforts in producing this chapter have shown us that narrative can offer very different individuals in one department a greater sense of shared focus and mission. We believe it can do the same for very different individuals across college departments. Our academic mission—our sense of what we are all doing each day when we engage as faculty in a liberal arts college unit—is central to our individual identities. And when narrative provides a shared focus and a sense of being part of a collective mission, then much has been accomplished in the development of unified community. The relationship between narrative and branding, too, seems highly relevant, particularly today as universities become more and more market driven. Often, efforts to develop a competitive brand to draw and retain students is, perhaps rightfully, viewed with cynicism as distasteful, slick, gimmicky, even deceptive salesmanship, designed only to capture enough market share (i.e., students and tuition) to keep the institution financially sound. We suggest that, instead, academic branding can be productively approached as an effort to recognize, take ownership of, and invite others into our collective story—a story with coherence and fidelity. The same story that offers identity and community for the diverse academic faculty can be the narrative brand into which students are invited to be active participants and characters essential to the story line. For the members of the Idaho State University College of Arts & Letters, a big part of our story is narrative itself. All the work that is part of our narrative project has become part of our brand, part of our story—a story that helps bridge specializations and break down the academic silos that so often reinforce departmental and disciplinary divisions.

References

Aristotle. 1984. *The Poetics of Aristotle*. Translated by Ingram Bywater. New York: Modern College Edition.

———. 1991. *On Rhetoric*. Translated by George Kennedy. New York: Oxford University Press.

Bantz, Charles R. 1993. *Understanding Organizations: Interpreting Organizational Communication Cultures*. Columbia, SC: University of South Carolina.

Benoit, William L. 1995. *Accounts, Excuses, and Apologies: A Theory of Image Restoration Strategies*. Albany, NY: University of New York Press.

Benoit, William L., and Jeffrey Delbert. 2010. "'Get a Mac': Mac versus PC TV Spots." *Relevant Rhetoric: A New Journal of Rhetorical Studies* 1: http://relevantrhetoric.com/Get%20A%20Mac.pdf.

Black, Edwin. 1992. *Rhetorical Questions: Studies of Public Discourse*. Chicago: University of Chicago Press.

Bobbit, David. 2004. *The Rhetoric of Redemption: Kenneth Burke's Redemption Drama and Martin Luther King, Jr.'s "I Have a Dream" Speech*. Lanham, MD: Rowman & Littlefield Publishers.

Bormann, Ernest G. 1985. "Symbolic Convergence Theory: A Communication Formulation." *Journal of Communication* 35: 128–138.

Brown, Mary Helen. 1990. "'Reading' an Organization's Culture: An Examination of Stories in Nursing Homes." *Journal of Applied Communication Research* 18: 64–75.

Burke, Kenneth. [1935] 1965. *Permanence and Change*. Indianapolis: Bobbs-Merrill Company.

———. [1941] 1967. *The Philosophy of Literary Form*. Baton Rouge: Louisiana State University Press.

———. [1945] 1969. *A Grammar of Motives*. Berkeley: University of California Press.

———. [1950] 1969. *A Rhetoric of Motives*. Berkeley: University of California Press.

CBS News. 2014. "Roger Goodell: We Didn't See Full Ray Rice Video." CBS This Morning (blog). Accessed September 10, 2014. http://www.cbsnews.com/news/ray-rice-controversy-commissioner-roger-goodell-defends-nfl-says-league-didnt-see-second-video/.

Deal, Terrence E., and Allen A. Kennedy. 1982. *Corporate Cultures: The Rites and Rituals of Corporate Life*. Reading, MA: Addison-Wesley.

Deetz, Stanley. 1987. "Stories, Accounts, and Organizational Power." *Association for Communication Administration Bulletin* 61: 36–41.

Denning, Stephen. 2007. The Secret Language of Leadership: How Leaders Inspire Action through Narrative. San Francisco: Jossey-Bass.

Denning, Stephen. 2011. *The Leader's Guide to Storytelling: Mastering the Art and Discipline of Business Narrative*. San Francisco: Jossey-Bass.

Dolan, Gabrielle, and Yamini Naidu. 2013. *Hooked: How Leaders Connect, Engage, and Inspire with Storytelling*. Milton, Australia: John Wiley & Sons.

Fairhurst, Gail T. 2011. *The Power of Framing: Creating the Language of Leadership*. San Francisco: Jossey-Bass.

Fisher, Walter R. 1985. "The Narrative Paradigm: An Elaboration." *Communication Monographs* 52: 347–367.

———. 1987. *Human Communication as Narration: Toward a Philosophy of Reason, Value, and Action*. Columbia, SC: University of South Carolina Press.

Gatto, Tom. 2014. "Roger Goodell Interview: I Didn't See Video of Rice Punch until Monday." *Sporting News*. Accessed September 10, 2014. http://www.sportingnews.com/nfl/story/2014-09-09/roger-goodell-interview-cbs-ray-rice-video-norah-o-donnell.

Geertz, Clifford. 1973. *The Interpretation of Cultures: Selected Essays*. New York: Basic Books.

Goleman, Larry A., ed. 2010. *Teaching Our Story: Narrative Leadership and Pastoral Formation*. Herndon, VA: Albon Institute.

Hart, Roderick P., and Suzanne M. Daughton. 2004. *Modern Rhetorical Criticism*. Boston, MA: Allyn & Bacon.

Hartman, Karen L. 2014. "Fields of Dreams and Gods of the Gridiron: The Trinity of Myth, Sport and the Hero." In *Myth in the Modern World: Essays on Intersections with Ideology and Culture*, edited by David Whitt and John Perlich, 165–184. Jefferson, NC: McFarland & Company.

James, LeBron. "I'm Coming Back to Cleveland." Sports Illustrated. Accessed July 11, 2014. http://www.si.com/nba/2014/07/11/lebron-james-cleveland-cavaliers.

Jones, Mike. "Congratulations LeBron James, You Just Destroyed Your Brand!" Bleacher Report. July 10, 2010. http://bleacherreport.com/articles/418392-congratulations-lebron-james-you-just-destroyed-your-brand.

Keel, Tim. 2007. *Intuitive Leadership: Embracing a Paradigm of Narrative, Metaphor, and Chaos*. Grand Rapids, MI: Baker.

Kelly, Jan W. 1985. "Storytelling in High Tech Organizations: A Medium for Sharing Culture." *Journal of Applied Communication Research* 13: 45–58.

Lupica, Mike. 2014. "In His TV Defense of NFL's Handling of Ray Rice, Commissioner Roger Goodell Looks Like He's Guilty." *New York Daily News*. Accessed September 9, 2014. http://www.nydailynews.com/sports/football/lupica-television-interview-roger-goodell-guilty-defense-article-1.1934271.

Mai, Robert, and Alan Akerson. 1989. *Human Communication as Narration: Toward a Philosophy of Reason, Value, and Action*. Columbia, SC: University of South Carolina Press.

———. 2003. *The Leader as Communicator: Strategies and Tactics to Build Loyalty, Focus Effort, and Spark Creativity*. New York: Amacom.

Mazzeo, Mike. "Crowd of 1.3 Million Celebrates Cavs Title at Downtown Parade." ESPN. Accessed June 22, 2016. http://www.espn.com/nba/playoffs/2016/story/_/id/16408697/fans-toast-cleveland-cavaliers-downtown-parade.

Mohler, Albert. 2012. *The Conviction to Lead: 25 Principles for Leadership That Matters*. Bloomington, MN: Bethany House.

Murphy, James J., and Richard A. Katula. 2003. "The Sophists and Rhetorical Consciousness." In *A Synoptic History of Classical Rhetoric*, 3rd ed.), edited by James J. Murphy and Richard A. Katula, 21–58. Mahwah, NJ: Lawrence Erlbaum Associates.

Myrsiades, Linda Suny. 1987. "Corporate Stories as Cultural Communications in the Organizational Setting." *Management Communication Quarterly* 1: 84.

O'Neill, Terry. 2014. "NOW Calls for Roger Goodell's Resignation, Appointment of Independent Investigator." *NOW* website, September 9, 2014. http://now.org/media-center/press-release/now-calls-for-roger-goodells-resignation-appointment-of-independent-investigator.

Pearce, W. Barnett, and Karen A. Foss. 1990. "The Historical Context of Communication as a Science." In *Human Communication: Theory and Research*, edited by Gordon L. Dahnke and Glen W. Clatterbuck, 1–19. Belmont, CA: Wadsworth.

Postman, Neil. [1985] 2005. *Amusing Ourselves to Death*. New York: Penguin Books.

Poulakos, John. 2001. "Sophists." In *Encyclopedia of Rhetoric*, edited by Thomas O. Sloane, 732–733. Oxford: Oxford University Press.

Ryan, Halford R. 1992. *Classical Communication for the Contemporary Communicator*. Mountain View, CA: Mayfield.

Schein, Edgar. 1988. *Organizational Culture and Leadership*. San Francisco: Jossey-Bass.

Simmons, Anette. 2007. *Whoever Tells the Best Story Wins: How to Use Your Own Stories to Communicate with Power and Impact*. New York: AMACOM.

Wichelns, Herbert. 1993. "The Literary Criticism of Oratory." In *Landmark Essays on Rhetorical Criticism*, edited by Thomas W. Benson, 1–32. Davis, CA: Hermagoras Press.

Winslade, John, and Gerald Monk. 2000. *Narrative Mediation: A New Approach to Conflict Resolution*. San Francisco, CA: Jossey-Bass.

Wilcock, Keith D. 1984. *The Corporate Tribe*. New York: Warner Books.

Zirin, Dave. 2013. "The Aspiring Folk Hero: Why LeBron James Will Return to the Cleveland Cavaliers." The Nation. Accessed March 25, 2013. https://www.thenation.com/article/aspiring-folk--hero-why-lebron-james-will-return-cleveland-cavaliers/.

6 The "Not Yet Pregnant"
The Impact of Narratives on Infertility Identity and Reproductive Policy

Kellee J. Kirkpatrick

My Journey to Narrative

My journey to narrative began on November 6, 2013, at 4:21 p.m. when I received an e-mail from Dr. Jeffrey Callen, a professor in the Political Science Department at Idaho State University. Dr. Callen was contacting me to schedule a phone interview for an assistant professor position in the department. After carefully crafting a professional response to his inquiry that conveyed my interest and hopefully masked my profound giddiness, I immediately launched an investigation of my potential future colleagues. While I had some familiarity with the program at ISU, when submitting nearly one hundred job applications, there is only so much pre-research one can do.

As I combed through the CVs and research of the current faculty, my attention was immediately captured by the work of Dr. Mark K. McBeth. Dr. McBeth's CV indicated that he shared my love of public policy theory, and I was particularly intrigued by a new policy theory that he and his coauthors had recently developed, the Narrative Policy Framework (NPF). I also learned that the new theory was going to be included in an upcoming edition of *Theories of the Policy Process*, or what my graduate school colleagues and I referred to as "The Policy Bible." Knowing that other policy theory scholars had to lobby the editor for years to include their theories, I knew the NPF was something I needed to learn more about. Thus began my journey down the path of narrative.

Clearly, I am still new to the study of narrative. However, narrative inquiry is a research tool that makes intuitive sense and nicely complements many of the concepts and theories that we have been studying in political science for years. Oxford Dictionaries defines political science as, "the branch of knowledge that deals with systems of government; the analysis of political activity and behavior." Not only can narratives provide a better way for us to understand how and why governments act, but they also allow us to understand and perhaps predict how these actions will affect the response of the governed. For instance, scholars of public policy have long suggested that the way in which we define and frame public problems influences policy design and the nature of government action. In other words, the narratives we attach to problems directly shape public perceptions and, consequently, public policy.

One side effect of studying narrative that I have noticed is that you begin to think of everything in terms of narrative, and that is how I came to this current project. I have been studying policy surrounding the use of assisted reproductive technologies (ART) for quite some time, but only recently have I begun to examine how the narratives of family, femininity, and motherhood affect those facing infertility and ultimately shape the policy landscape. Narratives help individuals to make sense of the world around them, and it seems apparent that narratives influence the identities of those facing the difficult situation of infertility.

The "Not Yet Pregnant"

Scholarship is increasingly acknowledging the role that narratives play in how individuals and groups construct their identities and make sense of their lives (Phinney 2000). For example, narrative analysis has been used to better understand constructed identities of women (Stewart and Malley 2004), immigrants (De Fina 2003), Holocaust survivors (Carney 2004), and even social movements (Davis 2002). Despite the growth of this interdisciplinary exploration, the narratives and constructed identities of those facing infertility is deserving of further exploration. While some scholarship in this area does exist (i.e., Riessman 2002), advancements in medical technology necessitate further examination of the ever-changing landscape that those diagnosed as infertile must navigate.

According to the Centers for Disease Control and Prevention (CDC) (2012a), approximately 10.8 percent of women and 7.5 percent of men in the United States have sought infertility treatment. Although this data provides us with some insight, these numbers do not necessarily give us the full picture of how many individuals or couples are facing the issue of infertility because there are still individuals who do not seek out treatment for a variety of reasons including health and financial concerns. Advances in medical technology have created new pathways to parenthood, and treatment options range from drug therapy, to in vitro fertilization, to surrogate parenthood. These new technologies—often referred to as assisted reproductive technologies (ART)—appear to present a solution to the heartache of infertility, but they have also evoked debates about the role of women, the definition of family, parental rights, gay parenting, and even eugenics.

The classification of infertility as a disease, rather than a personal and private issue, has added to the intense pressure for women and couples to seek out and submit to any and all available forms of infertility treatments (Inhorn and Biernbaum-Carmeli 2008). The personal desire, and perhaps biological drive to have children, is strong, and many women and men go to great lengths to grow their families. This intense desire to bear children is reinforced by the medical community which frames ART as the "only choice" or "last hope" for becoming pregnant (Boden 2013; Lasker and Borg 1987, 17). There are also cultural pressures to seek medical intervention. Society has created and normalized narratives of what it means to be female, and for women, "the cultural ideal is almost always focused on motherhood" (Lasker and Borg, 13). Those who are unable to have children or who do not take extreme measures to conceive are often stigmatized and viewed "in some way diminished, failed, subjects for pity or even disapproval" (Edwards 1989, 25; Sternke and Abrahamson 2014). Their intense personal desires, coupled with medical and societal pressures, drive women to undergo years of treatments. With an ever-increasing number of treatment options, individuals undergoing treatment remain hopeful, sometimes developing unrealistic expectations about outcomes. Interestingly, as Whiteford and Gonzalez (1995, 27) observed, many individuals undergoing infertility treatment have begun to "define themselves not as childless, but as 'not yet pregnant.'" In this chapter, I explore the development of this narrative of hope, the resulting identity of the "not yet pregnant," and how infertility narratives are reinforced by public policy and the associated reproductive politics. To do this, I begin with a brief discussion of the history of infertility, its treatments, and the regulation of the fertility industry in the United States. Next, I explore the anatomy and origins of the narratives that influence infertility identities. Then I examine two cases where infertility narratives seem to have had an influence on reproductive policies. Finally, I discuss the implications of public policy for creating and contributing to lasting narratives which influence and structure individual choices and behaviors regarding becoming a parent.

The History of Infertility and the Regulation of Treatment in the United States

As previously noted, the CDC estimates that 6.1 million women and 4.7 million men have sought out fertility treatment in the United States. These numbers only capture those who have sought treatment and do not necessarily reflect the true number of those who are unable to conceive. As of 2013, there were 497 fertility clinics in the United States, offering a variety of treatment options to those wanting assistance to become parents. Treatment options can range from drug therapy, to artificial insemination, to in vitro fertilization, to contracting with a surrogate to carry the child through gestation (CDC 2012a; Markens 2007).

Although Louise Brown, the first baby conceived using in vitro fertilization, was not born until 1978 in England, humans have been exploring the possibilities of assisted reproduction since the fourteenth century. Assisted reproduction was first used in the fourteenth century to assist in the breeding of animals—namely, highly prized Arabian horses (Herman 1981, 2; Mamo 2007)—and those methods slowly began to spread to human reproduction. In the sixteenth century, several low-technology methods were recommended and used to assist with human conception. In 1550, Eustachius, a well-known physician at the time, claimed to have successfully assisted a couple with reproduction by recommending that the husband use his fingers to direct the sperm toward the cervix after intercourse (Cusine 1988).

Despite these few early documentations of assisted reproduction, prior to the late nineteenth century, women generally did not seek out medical solutions for infertility. They instead turned to religion and clergy to understand childlessness (Mamo 2007).

Beginning in the late eighteenth and early nineteenth centuries, issues of women's health and reproduction moved out of the private realm and began to become dominated by the medical community (Gordon 2002; Mamo 2007). Infertility and reproductive issues became medicalized. In other words, this once private issue came to be viewed as a public health issue labeled as an "illness" or "disease" and thus came under the jurisdiction of medicine. Medical knowledge about reproduction became privileged and women's knowledge of their own bodies and the knowledge of midwives and "wise women" was downplayed and delegitimized (Gordon 2002; Woliver 2002).

Increased medical knowledge and scientific discoveries introduced new "solutions" to the medicalized disease of infertility. In 1909, artificial insemination was used as the first reported "cure" for human infertility. Despite the success of this treatment, using donor sperm was still considered unnatural, immoral, and even labeled by some as adultery (Hard 1909; Mamo 2007; Pfeffer 1993). By the 1960s, multiple forms of treatments to assist ovulation were developed and began to be extensively used by the 1970s (Chen and Wallach 1994; Mamo 2007).

The 1970s saw the introduction of new methods to treat infertility. As previously mentioned, in 1978, Louise Brown became the first "test tube" baby born as a result of in vitro fertilization outside the womb. Although this scientific breakthrough occurred in England, scientists in the United States were also working toward achieving conception outside the womb, or in vitro, literally meaning "in glass" (Henig 2010). In fact, in 1973, several New York doctors attempted to assist John and Doris Del-Zio by performing fertilization outside the womb. At that time, in vitro fertilization in the United States was in its early stages and had only been practiced on lab mice. Dr. Landrum Shettles, without authorization or hospital privileges, collected gametes from the Del-Zio's, fertilized the egg, and then placed the fertilized egg in an incubator. The egg was to be implanted into Mrs. Del-Zio four days later. Authorities at Columbia Presbyterian Medical Center soon discovered the test tube in the incubator and discarded it. Several years later, the Del-Zio's filed suit against the hospital. In August 1978, one month after the birth of Louise Brown, the Del-Zio's won their case, but received only $50,000 in damages (Henig 2010; Test Tube Babies 2006).

Louise Brown and the Del-Zio's opened the door to other reproductive options including the use of donor sperm, donor eggs, and even donor wombs, also known as surrogate parenting. Use of such assisted reproductive technologies has since exploded with a significant number of fertility clinics opening in the 1980s. Today, nearly 500 fertility clinics exist in the United States, and the CDC estimates that in 2010, more than 47,000 babies in the United States were born using some form of ART (CDC 2012b, 2013).

These new methods of achieving pregnancy and their increased acceptance have prompted the federal government and state governments to regulate the use of fertility treatments, but to a limited extent. Only one federal law, the Fertility Clinic Success Rate and Certification Act of 1992 (FCSRCA), exists. This law requires the CDC to collect data on fertility clinics across the United States and report on fertility treatment use and success rates. It also required the CDC to establish guidelines and fertility lab standards. However, states are allowed to adopt and enforce their own lab guidelines and standards (Lal 1997).

States have approached the regulation of ART in varying ways. Some states have adopted legislation that limits the use of these technologies by restricting access to certain populations or even criminalizing the use of surrogate contracts. Other states have passed legislation that increases access to fertility treatments by requiring insurance companies to cover treatments or by recognizing the legality of surrogate contracts. Although state regulation of the fertility industry does exist, there are still a number of states that have no legislation concerning the use of assisted reproduction. In these instances, state courts have been left to determine the outcomes of complex, and sometimes bitter, disputes. This patchwork of legislation and case law within the states has created fifty unique environments concerning the use and availability of infertility treatments.

The history of infertility and assisted reproduction makes it clear that this issue is complex and multifaceted. It spans areas of health, medical technology, economics, regulation of the body, and social constructions of family, class, sexuality, and gender. Although the issue itself is quite complex and reaches into many arenas, it can also be boiled down into simple and easily accessible concepts, and in the simplest of terms, assisted reproductive technologies are viewed as the solution to childlessness.

The Origins of Infertility Narratives and Identities

While the history of narrative analysis is rich and complex, simply put, narratives are the stories people tell, and an examination of these stories offers us a way to understand how individuals make sense of their realities. As the chapters in this book illustrate, disciplines within the humanities and social sciences approach the study of narrative in a variety of ways, but one thread that seems to run through these methods is the understanding that narratives themselves are a form of knowledge and the study of narrative can tell us much about a given society and its cultural values, human behavior, and construction of individual and collective identities (Kim 2016; Patterson and Monroe 1998).

Somers and Gibson (1994) specifically speak to the influence that narratives can have on the construction of identity. They provide a taxonomy of four types of narratives that is particularly useful in understanding how narratives have contributed to the birth of the "not yet pregnant" identity. They contend that "public narratives" are the narratives of social institutions. In political science, we often think of institutions as physical entities such as Congress or the Supreme Court. However, scholars such as Ostrom (2007) and March and Olsen (1984) remind us that institutions are more than just physical entities, and that the term institution can apply to any commonly accepted set of rules or norms that structure human behavior such as the institution of marriage. Somers and Gibson (1994) also define "ontological narratives" as narratives that individuals use to maneuver through society. These ontological narratives are made up of our own personal stories, which are built on public narratives. As the next section attempts to demonstrate, these two types of narratives can help us to understand the sources of the identity of the "not yet pregnant."

There are a variety of narratives that are pervasive in current American culture that shape our perceptions and understandings about what it means to be a woman, a mother, and an ideal family. Together, these narratives have contributed to the identity of the "not yet pregnant" and their ontological narrative of hope. Narrative scholars argue that there are several characteristics that are fundamental to a narrative including a setting, a plot, a cast of characters containing victims, villains and heroes, and a moral (Kim 2016; McBeth, Jones, and Shanahan 2014). In the sections to follow, I outline several public narratives that inspire the narrative of hope and thus the "not yet pregnant" identity. I argue that these public narratives, which include the social construction of motherhood and family and the medicalization of infertility have worked in tandem to define the setting, the victims, the heroes, the plot, and the moral of the narrative of hope.

The Social Construction of Motherhood and the Ideal Family: Defining the Setting and Casting the Victims

Body politics refers to the ways in which human bodies are socially constructed. A social construction, or a social ideal, is "a cognitive categorization comprising normative judgment, created by actors to make sense of a situation and to communicate this sense through discourse" (Montpetit, Rothmayr, and Varone 2005). These constructions are often enduring and difficult to change (Ingram, Schneider, and DeLeon 2007). These constructions govern what functions and behaviors of the body are deemed normal or deviant by society and also what information and understandings about the body are privileged (Scott and Morgan 1993).

Body politics and the social construction of motherhood and family have contributed to a public narrative that places significant pressure on couples to seek solutions to infertility. Society has created normalized ideas of what it means to be female, and for women, "the cultural ideal is almost always focused on motherhood" (Greil, McQuillan, and Slauson-Blevins 2011; Lasker and Borg 1987, 13). Several scholars have argued that society imposes a "motherhood mandate" on women to have and raise at least two children (Hays 1996; Russo 2010). While the force of this "mandate" may have lessened somewhat in the United States due in part to the increase of voluntary childlessness, the "social identity of women has remained strongly linked to their status as mothers" (McQuillan et al. 2012, 1167; Park 2002). Those who are unable to have children or who do not take extreme measures to conceive are "in some way diminished, failed, subjects for pity or even disapproval" (Edwards 1989, 25). Not wanting to deviate from the accepted narrative of womanhood, some women facing infertility undergo years of treatments, subjecting their bodies to drug regimens that cause mood swings and induce superovulation, or they submit to invasive treatments to harvest gametes and re-implant embryos (Inhorn and Biernbaum-Carmeli 2008). These treatments can put them at risk for health complications, can derail careers, and can jeopardize their financial stability (Cousineau and Domar 2007). As we can see, the social construction of womanhood and motherhood characterize those facing infertility as the victims of our narrative of hope.

In addition to constructing the meaning of womanhood and motherhood, society has also defined the ideal family. These normative ideals of family consist of the "normal," nuclear family, which are based in the ties of biology and heteronormativity (Kitzinger 2005). In other words, public narratives reinforce the idea that the model family consists of a middle-class, married, heterosexual couple who reside with their dependent biological children. Assisted reproductive technologies that allow individuals to conceive children outside the traditional family unit challenge culturally held ideas about family. These new technologies open the door for non-traditional families to be formed, and while ART is "acclaimed for enabling the creation of enduring, affectionate families; equally it can be, and is, condemned for manipulating the dimension of human reproduction and thereby contributing to the breakdown of traditional family life" (Dolgin 1997, 31). These culturally constructed images define the boundaries of who should become parents, and those who deviate from this prescribed image are viewed negatively or are seen as deviants. The social constructions of family contribute to the narrative of the "not yet pregnant" as they lay out the socially preferred qualities of those who should have the privilege of becoming parents and prescribe that couples should take all measures to reach this ideal. Thus the social construction of family clearly outlines the setting, or the "agreed-on norms" that are "taken for granted" in this narrative of hope (McBeth et al. 2014, 228).

The Medicalization of Infertility: Laying Out the Plot, Crowning the Heroes, and Imparting the Moral

While the social constructions of motherhood and family establish the victims and setting of the narrative of hope, the medicalization of infertility provides the plot of the narrative, defines the heroes, and instills the moral of the story. The narrative of the "not yet pregnant" has roots in the medicalization of the once private issue of infertility. Through the history of medicalization, we can see how this individual, private problem became a public issue that is now dominated by the medical community and thus a target for governmental intervention and regulation. As the history of medicalization shows, the narrative of the "not yet pregnant" portrays those dealing with infertility as victims of circumstance and fertility doctors as the heroes who hold the key to ending their suffering. This narrative also conveys the moral that if you want a child enough, you will seek out any and all treatment, and if you do, you will become a parent. While the medicalization of infertility has already been briefly discussed in earlier sections, I want to revisit certain aspects of this history to demonstrate how medicalization has played a role in establishing the heroes, plot, and moral of the narrative of hope.

Medicalization of reproductive issues began in the late eighteenth to early nineteenth century, but prior to this time period, reproduction and infertility was viewed as a private issue. Although men can also be infertile, women often bore the sole responsibility for infertility, and they turned to their clergy for advice and counsel. The inability to bear a child was viewed as an act of God, and seeking treatment was perceived as an act of defiance to God's will (O'Dowd 2001). Even so, women often sought out home remedies such as special potions or herbal teas to try to treat infertility.

The medicalization of infertility was prompted by the growth of the medical profession. In an effort to build confidence in the medical field, doctors began to discredit the practical knowledge of midwives and downplay a woman's knowledge of her own body. This served to elevate or privilege medical knowledge, taking the authority over female bodies away from women and placing it in the hands of the male-dominated medical field (Marsh and Ronner 1996). This process was aided by the invention of the speculum, which opened a window to female anatomy. During this time period, infertility became defined as a "medical condition" rather than a "social state" or act of God (Cusine 1988; Marsh and Ronner 1996, 2). By 1850, doctors had developed surgical techniques to treat infertility and women subjected themselves to these invasive and often ineffective procedures (McGregor 1990; O'Sullivan and Brandon-Christie 2004).

The treatment of infertility continued to evolve and options continued to expand. In the 1920s, infertility treatments centered on the role hormones played in impeding pregnancy. Although low technological forms of artificial insemination had been around for some time, it became a popular method for assisting in conception in the 1930s (Cusine 1988). In the 1960s, doctors began prescribing fertility-enhancing drug regimens, and in 1978, the first child conceived through in vitro fertilization was born (Marsh and Ronner 1996). In 1993, the World Health Organization classified infertility as a disease and categorized it as a condition "requiring medical intervention" (Mamo 2007, 30). This classification further bestowed the medical community with privileged knowledge and increased medical authority over a woman's body, and women's bodies became "viewed as flawed machines requiring expert intervention" (Greil 2002, 102). Researchers have hypothesized that the medicalization of reproduction has led to the loss of women's control over their own bodies, as medicine began to "take on the role of social regulation traditionally performed by religion and the law" (Freidson 1970; Greil et al. 2011; Lupton 1997, 95; Zola 1972). The medical field was able to classify and define natural body function, and any activity that deviated from this definition was labeled as a pathology or disease.

The history of medicalization clearly shows how medical professionals, and specifically fertility doctors, have emerged as heroes, battling the villain of infertility and bringing hope to its victims. With the victims, villains, and heroes in place, the plot and the moral of the story naturally emerge. The plot of a narrative refers to the temporal nature of the story or, in other words, the beginning, middle, and end (McBeth, Jones, and Shanahan 2014). In the case of the narrative of hope, the plot begins with a childless couple striving to grow their family. Facing an uphill battle, they seek help from our heroes, the fertility doctors who hold in their hands the "only choice" or "last hope" for becoming pregnant (Lasker and Borg 1987, 17). With strength, perseverance, and the help of medical technology, the plot ends with the new life they have created. This plot also reveals to us the moral of the story. If a couple wants a child enough, they will place their lives and bodies in the hands of the experts, submit to any and all treatment, and if they do, their efforts will be rewarded with a healthy, happy baby.

As Somers (1994) points out, narrative and identity are inherently linked, and while individual and collective identities have many ingredients, it seems clear that narratives are major components. In the case of the "not yet pregnant," there are a variety of culturally pervasive public narratives or stories about womanhood, the infallibility of doctors, and the ideal family that drive couples to embrace and adopt a new personal, or ontological, narrative of hope, even when data show the odds of becoming pregnant and giving birth to a healthy baby are not in their favor. As mandated by the FCSRCA of 1992, the CDC compiles and reports the success rates of fertility clinics across the United States. The most recently available data indicate that the likelihood of becoming pregnant per ART cycle ranges between 14 percent for women over the age of forty and 55 percent for women less than thirty-five. The chances of having a full-term healthy baby, however, are much lower with success rates ranging from 6 percent for women over forty to 27 percent for women under thirty-five (CDC 2013). The presence of public narratives help to explain why the "not yet pregnant" adopt and cling to this identity throughout the course of their infertility treatments, even when their own personal experience denies their continued hope.

As Patterson and Monroe (1998, 320) point out, narratives "are profoundly influenced by what is possible and what is valued in our culture." With a constant flow of public narratives that present the ideal woman as a mother, that portray the perfect family as consisting of a mother, a father, 2.5 children, and a loyal golden retriever, and that elevate doctors to the level of miracle workers, is it any wonder that those not living up to these "standards" find a way to make sense of their perceived "failure" in reaching this ideal? Indeed, we see that "when narratives of culturally acceptable success are not available or are beyond the imagination for a particular group, subcultures provide alternative ways to make sense of one's place in the world," (Patterson and Monroe 1998, 320). In the case of those undergoing infertility treatments, this alternative presents itself in the form of a new identity, the "not yet pregnant," whose only way to make sense of their reality is not to provide a counter-narrative, but to simply claim that their story is not yet complete.

The Influence of Infertility Narratives on Reproductive Policy: Two Cases

Knowing the makeup and the source of infertility narratives allows us to observe further how these narratives intermingle to influence public perceptions and reactions to the political world. As Patterson and Monroe (1998, 315–316) point out, because "narratives affect our perceptions of political reality, which in turn affect our actions in response or in anticipation of political events, narrative plays a critical role in the construction of political behavior." Thus we can see that narratives shape political behavior and therefore policy making at a variety of levels including the individual and collective level (micro), the group and coalition level (meso), and at a variety of governmental levels (macro) (McBeth, Jones, and Shanahan 2014).

In recent years, political science scholars have begun to give more attention to the role that narrative can play in shaping public policy. This line of research led to the development of the Narrative Policy Framework (NPF). This framework, which borrows from deep literatures in social construction and causal stories, contends that the way in which a policy is presented is just as important as the substantive content of the policy. The authors contend that policy narratives have several defining characteristics such as a setting, a cast of characters including victims and heroes, a temporal plot, an overarching moral, and a narrator (McBeth, Jones, and Shanahan 2014).

While this framework provides a useful tool for understanding how policy entrepreneurs can construct and utilize narratives to influence public opinion and policy making, it does not yet fully address how long-standing cultural and public narratives shape political behavior, especially in the absence of a strong policy entrepreneur serving as a narrator. The following two brief case studies demonstrate how the narrative of hope, which has borne the identity of the "not yet pregnant," has had an influence on policies addressing two areas of reproductive politics.

Case One: State Mandates on Coverage of Fertility Treatments

The high costs associated with fertility treatments serve as a significant barrier to access, and very few insurance programs offer coverage of treatments.

Costs can range anywhere from $10,000 to more than $100,000 per cycle depending on the treatment options chosen, and most individuals require multiple cycles of treatment in order to achieve pregnancy (Goodwin 2010; Spar 2006). Only seventeen states have addressed the issue of insurance coverage of ART through state legislation, and their approaches are quite diverse.

Twelve[1] states require some form of insurance coverage, and each of these states varies on what type of treatments must be covered. For instance, Arkansas requires insurance coverage for only in vitro treatments; New York requires coverage of infertility drug treatment but not in vitro, and the other states require multiple treatment options. California and Texas do not mandate coverage of infertility treatments, but they do require that insurance companies offer optional coverage, which individuals may purchase if they desire. California's mandate requires that insurance companies specifically provide information to consumers about their fertility treatment coverage options. The presence of such mandates increases access to fertility treatments, but, obviously, only to those who have health insurance. While these mandates do not prevent insurance companies from covering infertility treatments, they do set the minimum coverage requirements of the state.

These insurance coverage statutes, however, come with strings attached. Several states have imposed limitations and exemptions to their coverage mandates, and some of these limitations exclude individuals from having access to insurance coverage based on their age, marital status, and socioeconomic status. Four states impose age restrictions on coverage. Connecticut,[2] for instance, sets its age limit at less than forty. New Jersey's[3] limit is forty-six. New York[4] restricts coverage to those between twenty-one and forty-four, and Rhode Island[5] only mandates coverage for those between twenty-five and forty-two. Rhode Island's statute is even more targeted than the others, as its age restriction applies to women, but not to men.

Other state laws exclude from coverage those who are single, or those whose marriages were not legally recognized until the recent Supreme Court case (*Obergefell v. Hodges* 2015) brought marriage equality to all fifty states in June 2015. These states include Arkansas,[6] Hawaii,[7] Maryland,[8] Rhode Island,[9] and Texas.[10] Other states only require coverage if individuals use their own gametes. In these states, including Arkansas,[11] Hawaii,[12] Maryland,[13] and Texas,[14] those who wish to use donor gametes or embryos are excluded from coverage. While this could impact a variety of individuals, it directly excludes same-sex couples who require the use of one or more donor gametes to create families through the use of ART.

While not necessarily exclusionary in nature, states have included several other types of exemptions from coverage mandates. California,[15] Connecticut,[16] Illinois,[17] Maryland,[18] Massachusetts,[19] New Jersey,[20] and Texas[21] provide a religious exemption for employers who offer insurance. Two of these exemptions carry special caveats. For instance, the Massachusetts exemption only applies to diocese employers and the New Jersey exemption only applies to certain treatments. Furthermore, eight states[22] have passed legislation that exempts certain government insurance programs, including Medicaid, from having to cover infertility treatments.

These myriad approaches to regulating insurance coverage of infertility treatments seem to reflect several themes that underlie the narratives of those facing infertility. State regulation of insurance treatments reinforce the narrative of the "ideal" nuclear family. First, states that provide exemptions from coverage mandates based on age reinforce the narrative that there is an ideal age for parents. Four of the twelve states that have coverage mandates allow insurance companies to refuse coverage to those who fall outside of the acceptable age range. Four out of twelve states also mandate that couples be married in order to be covered, adding support for the narrative that the ideal mother is not single. Another four states require that couples must use their own gametes in order for coverage mandates to apply to them. This effectively eliminates coverage for same-sex couples who must use donor gametes in order to achieve pregnancy. Again, these state policies reinforce the narrative that ideal families are nuclear and heterosexual. Finally, states that exempt certain state-run insurance programs reinforce the idea that those who rely on public assistance do not fit the model of the ideal parent. While states that provide any insurance coverage mandates are rare, the exemptions attached to these mandates suggest that states wish to restrict this privilege to those who are married, heterosexual, and of a certain age and socioeconomic class. This suggests that the narrative of the ideal family influences and then is reinforced by insurance coverage statutes.

Case Two: Personhood Bills and Proposed Constitutional Amendment in Mississippi

Several states have also recently considered legislation and even constitutional amendments that would grant "personhood" status to embryos. Many of these initiatives have been supported by pro-life groups such as Personhood USA based in Colorado. The goal of such initiatives is to define that life begins at conception by granting personhood status to embryos and thus preventing abortions by making the destruction of an embryo legally the same as murder. Despite being a strongly pro-life state, the initiative failed in Mississippi due in part to a local grassroots organization that feared that the proposed amendment to the Mississippi constitution would restrict access to fertility treatments such as in vitro fertilization (Grady 2011). Infertility treatments often involve the creation of multiple embryos. If a woman achieves pregnancy on the first cycle, there is then a question of what should be done with excess embryos. The current options are to cryogenically freeze and store them, destroy them, or even donate them. Some individuals have worried that fertility industries would either not want to expand expensive storage facilities or take the risk of accidental destruction, thus subjecting them to criminal charges, therefore potentially reducing options for women wanting to obtain fertility treatments (Grady 2011).

Atlee Breland, who describes herself as a Christian and conceived her daughters through in vitro fertilization, mobilized the anti-personhood effort in Mississippi. She began her campaign as a Facebook page and then a website titled, "Parents against Personhood," reaching "tens of thousands" of Mississippi voters (Grady 2011, para. 2). Ms. Breland, despite her faith, opposed these bills in part because she "saw the amendment as likely to restrict in vitro fertilization and threaten the ability of women like her to have children" (Grady 2011, para. 3). Since the defeat of the personhood amendment (Initiative 26) in Mississippi, Ms. Breland's website has expanded to address similar bills and amendments being considered in fourteen additional states.[23]

The grassroots efforts to block the passage of a constitutional amendment in Mississippi appear to be influenced by the narratives surrounding those facing infertility. Those fighting against the bill specifically noted that this initiative could prevent individuals facing infertility from accessing treatment that would allow them to become parents. It is particularly interesting that this anti-personhood/pro-fertility industry narrative was more effective than the pro-life narrative that accompanied the personhood initiative. This reaction has not been isolated to Mississippi, as a number of these bills and amendments have been defeated in several states for similar reasons (Culp-Ressler 2014). The narrative of the "not yet pregnant" seems to suggest that becoming a parent is within reach as long as these personhood bills do not stand in the way.

Advancing the Story of Narrative and Public Policy

As these two cases demonstrate, narratives not only influence the identities of those seeking infertility treatment but also have the power to shape governmental approaches to the regulation of reproductive health. The "moral" of the narratives surrounding motherhood and family serve as a mechanism to construct who the public sees as deserving of infertility treatments and ultimately who is worthy of becoming a parent. Consequently, this "moral" becomes the foundation for policy approaches, which in turn can either open or close pathways to parenthood for those who rely on ARTs.

As Lowi (1972) contended, "policy predicts politics." In other words, as policy solutions are proposed and adopted, a new politics can emerge. The two cases presented in this study exemplify this idea. First, state insurance coverage mandates served to reinforce the narrative that infertility treatments are a legitimate way to "solve" infertility. At the same time, the restrictions placed on access strengthened the narrative that some are more worthy and deserving of becoming parents than others, primarily those who are married, heterosexual, and within a certain age range and socioeconomic class standing. Second, the anti-personhood movement that blocked the passage of personhood bills and amendments in multiple states provided support for the narrative that infertility treatments are the "solution" to the heartache of infertility.

In these cases, narrative and public policy are engaged in a self-reinforcing relationship, and I contend that this is not unique to this policy domain. Public policy and political science scholars have only scratched the surface in terms of understanding the explanatory power of narrative analysis. As a scholar who is new to narrative myself, I humbly suggest that future research dig deeper into the role that public narratives play in policy formation. As the two very brief cases suggest, narratives beget public opinion. Public opinion begets public policy. Public policy either reinforces current narratives or yields counternarratives. These new narratives are either embraced or rejected, and the cycle begins again.

And this is how I will end my maiden voyage as a narrative scholar, with a mission to continue this line of work and to contribute to the advancement of narrative scholarship within political science. On this self-given mission, I know that I will have many supporters and partners among my colleagues. Going back to the words of Patterson and Monroe (1998, 320), our stories are "profoundly influenced by what is possible and what is valued in our culture," and clearly, narrative analysis is valued in the College of Arts & Letters at Idaho State University. As I begin to internalize this narrative, I am pondering whether I, like those undergoing infertility treatment, will use this narrative to make sense of my reality and adopt a new identity as a full-fledged narrative scholar. For now, I am comfortable saying that my story isn't complete, and I fully embrace the identity of "not yet a narrative scholar."

Notes

1 Arkansas, Connecticut, Hawaii, Illinois, Maryland, Massachusetts, Montana, New Jersey, New York, Ohio, Rhode Island, and West Virginia.
2 CT Gen Stat § 38a-536 (2014)
3 NJ Rev Stat § 17B:27-46.1x (2015)
4 NY Ins L § 3321 (2015)
5 RI Gen L § 27-41-33 (2015)
6 AR Code § 23-85-137 (2015), AR Code § 23-86-118 (2015), Arkansas Insurance Department Rule and Regulation 1: In Vitro Fertilization 054.00
7 HI Rev Stat § 432:1-604 (2015)
8 MD Ins Code § 15-810 (2015)
9 RI Gen L § 27-41-33 (2015)
10 Tex Ins Code Ann §§ 1366.001-.007 (2015)
11 AR Code § 23-85-137 (2015), AR Code § 23-86-118 (2015), Arkansas Insurance Department Rule and Regulation 1: In Vitro Fertilization 054.00
12 HI Rev Stat § 432:1-604 (2015)
13 MD Ins Code § 15-810 (2015)
14 Tex Ins Code Ann §§ 1366.001-.007 (2015)
15 CA Health & Safety Code§ 1374.55 (through 2012 Leg Sess)
16 CT Gen Stat § 38a-536 (2014)
17 215 Ill Comp Stat 5/356m
18 MD Ins Code § 15-810 (2015)
19 MA Gen L ch 175 § 47H (2015)
20 NJ Rev Stat § 17B:27-46.1x (2015)

21 Tex Ins Code Ann §§ 1366.006 (2015)
22 Arkansas, Minnesota, Montana, New Jersey, Ohio, Oklahoma, Pennsylvania, and Rhode Island.
23 Alabama, Arkansas, California, Colorado, Georgia, Iowa, Montana, Nevada, North Dakota, Ohio, Oklahoma, Oregon, Virginia, and Washington.

References

Boden, Jane. 2013. "The Ending of Treatment: The Ending of Hope?" *Human Fertility* 16 (1): 22–25.
Carney, Sarah K. 2004. "Transcendent Stories and Counternarratives in Holocaust Survivor Life Histories: Searching for Meaning in Video-Testimony Archives." In *Narrative Analysis: Studying the Development of Individuals in Society*, edited by Colette Daiute and Cynthia Lightfoot. 201–221. Thousand Oaks, CA: Sage.
Centers for Disease Control and Prevention (CDC). 2012a. "Infertility FAQ's." Centers for Disease Control and Prevention. Accessed October 1, 2012. http://www.cdc.gov/reproductivehealth/Infertility/index.htm.
———. 2012b. "What Is Assisted Reproductive Technology?" Centers for Disease Control and Prevention. Accessed October 1, 2012. http://www.cdc.gov/ART/.
———. 2013. "Assisted Reproductive Technology: Fertility Clinic Success Rates Report." Centers for Disease Control and Prevention. Accessed October 1, 2015. ftp://ftp.cdc.gov/pub/Publications/art/ART-2013-Clinic-Report-Full.pdf.
Chen, Serena H., and Edward E. Wallach. 1994. "Five Decades of Progress in Management of the Infertile Couple." *Fertility and Sterility* 64 (4): 665–685.
Cousineau, Tara M., and Alice D. Domar. 2007. "Psychological Impact of Infertility." *Best Practice & Research Clinical Obstetrics and Gynaecolocy* 21 (2): 293–308.
Culp-Ressler, Tara. 2014. "Even in Deep Red States, Voters Reject Radical 'Personhood' Measures." Think Progress. November 5, 2014. Accessed February 16, 2013. https://thinkprogress.org/even-in-deep-red-states-voters-reject-radical-personhood-measures-73eb041da7af#.daz46f6nw.
Cusine, Douglas J. 1988. *New Reproductive Techniques: A Legal Perspective*. Brookfield, VT: Gower.
Davis, Joseph E. 2002. "Narrative and Social Movements: The Power of Stories." In *Stories of Change: Narrative and Social Movements*, edited by Joseph E. Davis, 3–29. Albany, NY: State University of New York Press.
De Fina, Anna. 2003. *Identity in Narrative: A Study of Immigrant Discourse*. Amsterdam: John Benjamins Publishing Co.
Dolgin, Janet L. 1997. *Defining the Family: Law, Technology, and Reproduction in an Uneasy Age*. New York: New York University Press.
Edwards, Robert. 1989. *Life before Birth: Reflections on the Embryo Debate*. New York: Basic Books.
Freidson, Eliot. 1970. *Professional Dominance: The Social Structure of Medical Care*. Chicago, IL: Aldine.
Goodwin, Michele Bratcher. 2010. "Baby Markets." In *Baby Markets: Money and the New Politics of Creating Families*, edited by Michele Bratcher Goodwin, 2–22. Cambridge: Cambridge University Press.
Gordon, Linda. 2002. *The Moral Property of Women: A History of Birth Control Politics in America*. Urbana, IL: University of Illinois Press.

Grady, Denise. "Medical Nuances Drove 'No' Vote in Mississippi." New York Times, November 14, 2011. Accessed March 5, 2013. http://www.nytimes.com/2011/11/15/health/policy/no-vote-in-mississippi-hinged-on-issues-beyond-abortion.html.

Greil, Arthur L. 2002. "Infertile Bodies: Medicalization, Metaphor, and Agency." In *Infertility around the Globe: New Thinking on Childlessness, Gender, and Reproductive Technologies*, edited by Marcia C. Inhorn and Frank Van Balen, 101–118. Berkeley, CA: University of California Press.

Greil, Arthur L., Julia McQuillan, and Kathleen Slauson-Blevins. 2011. "The Social Construction of Infertility." *Sociology Compass* 5 (8): 736–746.

Hard, Addison Davis. 1909. "Artificial Impregnation." *Medical World* (April): 163–164.

Hays, Sharon. 1996. *The Cultural Contradictions of Motherhood*. New Haven, CT: Yale University Press.

Henig, Robin Marantz. 2010. "In Vitro Revelation." *New York Times* October 5. 31.

Herman, Harry A. 1981. *Improving Cattle by the Millions: NAAB and the Development and Worldwide Application of Artificial Insemination*. Columbia: University of Missouri Press.

Ingram, Helen, Anne L. Schneider, and Peter DeLeon. 2007. "Social Construction and Policy Design." In *Theories of the Policy Process*, 2nd ed., edited by Paul A. Sabatier, 93–126. Boulder, CO: Westview Press.

Inhorn, Marcia C., and Daphna Biernbaum-Carmeli. 2008. "Assisted Reproductive Technologies and Culture Change." *Annual Review of Anthropology* 37: 177–196.

Kim, Jeong-Hee. 2016. *Understanding Narrative Inquiry*. Los Angeles: Sage.

Kitzinger, Celia. 2005. "Heteronormativity in Action: Reproducing the Heterosexual Nuclear Family in After-Hours Medical Calls." *Social Problems* 52 (4): 447–498.

Lal, Meena. 1997. "The Role of the Federal Government in Assisted Reproductive Technologies." *Santa Clara Computer & High Technology Law Journal* 13 (2): 516–543.

Lasker, Judith N., and Susan Borg. 1987. *In Search of Parenthood*. Boston: Beacon.

Lowi, Theodore J. 1972. "Four Systems of Policies, Politics, and Choice." *Public Administration Review* 32 (4): 298–310.

Lupton, Deborah. 1997. "Foucault and the Medicalisation Critique." In *Foucault: Health and Medicine*, edited by Alan Petersen and Robin Bunton, 94–110. London, UK: Routledge.

Mamo, Laura. 2007. *Queering Reproduction: Achieving Pregnancy in the Age of Technoscience*. Durham, NC: Duke University Press.

March, James G., and Johan P. Olsen. 1984. "The New Institutionalism: Organizational Factors in Political Life." *American Political Science Review* 78 (3): 734–749.

Markens, Susan. 2007. *Surrogate Motherhood and the Politics of Reproduction*. Berkeley, CA: University of California Press.

Marsh, Margaret, and Wanda Ronner. 1996. *The Empty Cradle: Infertility in America from Colonial Times to the Present*. Baltimore: Johns Hopkins University Press.

McBeth, Mark K., Michael D. Jones, and Elizabeth A. Shanahan. 2014. "The Narrative Policy Framework." In *Theories of the Policy Process*, 3rd ed., edited by Paul A. Sabatier and Christopher M. Weible, 225–226. Boulder, CO: Westview Press.

McGregor, Deborah Kuhn. 1990. *Sexual Surgery and the Origins of Gynecology: J. Marion Sims, His Hospital, and His Patients*. New York: Garland.

McQuillan, Julia, Arthur L. Greil, Karina M. Shreffler, Patricia A. Wonch-Hill, Kari C. Gentzler, and John D. Hathcoat. 2012. "Does the Reason Matter? Variations in Childlessness Concerns among U.S. Women." *Journal of Marriage and Family* 74 (5): 1166–1181.

Montpetit, Éric, Christine Rothmayr, and Frédéric Varone. 2005. "Institutional Vulnerability to Social Constructions: Federalism, Target Populations, and Policy Design for Assisted Reproductive Technology in Six Democracies." *Comparative Political Studies* 38 (2): 119–142.

Obergefell v. Hodges. 2015. 135 S.Ct. 1039.

O'Dowd, Michael J. 2001. *The History of Medications for Women*. New York: Parthenon Publishing.

O'Sullivan, Colleen, and Jennifer Brandon-Christie. 2004. "Approaches to Infertility through the Ages: You've Come a Long Way Baby!" In *Proceedings of the 13th Annual History of Medicine Days*, edited by W.A. Whitelaw, 378–395. Calgary, AB: Health Sciences Centre.

Ostrom, Elinor. 2007. "Institutional Rational Choice: An Assessment of the Institutional Analysis and Development Framework." In *Theories of the Policy Process*, 2nd ed., edited by Paul A. Sabatier, 21–64. Boulder, CO: Westview Press.

Park, Kristin. 2002. "Stigma Management among the Voluntarily Childless." *Sociological Perspectives* 45 (1): 21–45.

Patterson, Molly, and Kristen Renwick Monroe. 1998. "Narrative in Political Science." *Annual Review of Political Science* 1: 315–331.

Pfeffer, Naomi. 1993. *The Stork and the Syringe: A Political History of Reproductive Medicine*. Cambridge, UK: Polity.

Phinney, Jean S. 2000. "Identity Formation across Cultures: The Interaction of Personal, Societal, and Historical Change." *Human Development* 43 (1): 27–31.

Riessman, Catherine Kohler. 2002. "Positioning Gender Identity in Narratives of Infertility: South Indian Women's Lives in Context." In *Infertility around the Globe: New Thinking on Childlessness, Gender, and Reproductive Technologies*, edited by Marcia C. Inhorn and Frank Van Balen, 152–170. Berkeley, CA: University of California Press.

Russo, Nancy Felipe. 2010. "The Motherhood Mandate." *Journal of Social Issues* 32 (3): 143–153.

Scott, Sue, and David Morgan. 1993. "Introduction." In *Body Matters: Essays on the Sociology of the Body*, edited by Sue Scott and David Morgan, vii–x. London, UK: Falmer Press.

Somers, Margaret R. 1994. "The Narrative Constitution of Identity." *Theory and Society* 23 (5): 605–649.

Somers, Margaret R. and Gloria D. Gibson. 1994. "Reclaiming the Epistemological 'Other': Narrative and the Social Constitution of Identity." In *Social Theory and the Politics of Identity*, edited by Craig Calhoun, 37-99. Oxford UK & Cambridge USA: Blackwell.

Spar, Debora L. 2006. *The Baby Business: How Money, Science and Politics Drive the Commerce of Conception*. Boston: Harvard Business School Press.

Sternke, Elizabeth A., and Kathleen Abrahamson. 2014. "Perceptions of Women with Infertility on Stigma and Disability." *Sexuality and Disability* 33 (1): 3–17.

Stewart, Abigail J., and Janet E. Malley. 2004. "Women of 'The Greatest Generation': Feeling on the Margin of Social History." In *Narrative Analysis: Studying the Development of Individuals in Society*, edited by Colette Daiute and Cynthia Lightfoot. Thousand Oaks, CA: Sage.

Test Tube Babies. 2006. Directed by Chana Gazit and Hilary Klotz Steinman. Boston: Public Broadcasting Service. DVD.

Whiteford, Linda M., and Lois Gonzalez. 1995. "Stigma: The Hidden Burden of Infertility." *Social Science & Medicine* 40 (1): 27–36.

Woliver, Laura R. 2002. *The Political Geographies of Pregnancy*. Urbana, IL: University of Illinois Press.

Zola, Irving. 1972. "Medicine as an Institution of Social Control." *Sociological Review* 20: 487–503.

7 Letter-Writing and the Eighteenth-Century Scientific Community
Constructing Narratives and Identity

Paul Sivitz

As a historian, I know that narrative plays a crucial role in my field. A large part of what we do in history is tell stories, both in our teaching and our writing. Interdisciplinary methodology permeates my own work, allowing narratives to become more complex, addressing "the facts," as well as how particular societies saw themselves and their relationship to others (whether socially constructed or not) in the past. This chapter examines the narratives constructed by the exchange of letters in the eighteenth-century scientific community, and how that community placed just as much emphasis on the *continuity* of communication as they did the scientific content. Indeed, this conversational quality mimicked what best can be described as "dialogue." Although the writing style of the eighteenth century might seem theatrical to the modern reader (written British English of the period being somewhat more formal, but not always), the tone of much of the correspondence was one of familiarity.

The relationship between narrative and the "conversations" of the eighteenth-century scientific community illuminates how authors, characters, and plots were intertwined. Each letter-writer served as an author of the narrative. At the same time, each author was also a character in the narrative. Each participant contributed to the plot, but such contributions were not limited to only those who were authors. Indeed, many who actively engaged in the pursuit of science did not write letters, but instead had their work reported in the missives of others. Moreover, two distinct narratives are revealed: first, the conversations about science and communication contemporary to the historical actors themselves. And second, the historical narrative created by the entire corpus of letters, explicating the practice of science and scientific communication in the eighteenth century.

Commitment and Community

The narratives, or conversations, that members of the eighteenth-century scientific community created within their letters illuminate how scientific information moved through that community with great precision, as opposed to "whispering down the lane," where information changed from person to person. Furthermore, narratives of the process of engaging with the natural world that allowed (or did not allow) the observation and collection of information, demonstrated each practitioner's personal commitment to the community. In other words, simply reporting success or failure was crucial to communal perceptions of an individual. Since these were "open" letters—it was assumed that practitioners would show missives to others who resided nearby, or forward them to those who lived at a distance—the integrity of the letter-writer demanded honesty. Moreover, practitioners sent similar letters to multiple recipients, who, as it turned out, often compared notes. Indeed, it was much easier to keep one's story straight by being forthright. Thus individual identity was driven by narrative.

Narratives among scientific practitioners often had common elements, particularly during the Seven Years' War (1754–1763). Writers spent a great deal of page space discussing the war's effect on the safe and timely transmission of knowledge and specimens. This collective concern defined the identity of the group, not only during war but also throughout the period.

Writing a Narrative of Science and a Narrative of Communication

During the mid-eighteenth century, practitioners of science in Britain and America, as well as parts of continental Europe, formed a letter-writing, or epistolary, network in order to facilitate the communication of knowledge.[1] Furthermore, the dissemination of knowledge was not only confined to the scientific community but also aimed at a wider, literate public. Through the exchange of thousands of letters from the early 1730s to 1780s, these men of science created layers of narrative: the scientific conversations among the participants (and part of the larger story of science in the eighteenth century) and the parallel conversation of the process of the communication of knowledge itself. At the same time, the collective identity of scientific practitioners emerged. Most, but not all, members of the scientific community applied the contemporary maxim, "for the greatest benefit of mankind," to their work. It was not *primarily* about personal gain, but rather advancing the world's knowledge. Contributors relished the acknowledgments, compliments, and occasional financial benefits (not always in the form of cash, but as gifts), but saw their collaborative efforts to transmit knowledge as more important than the work of one individual.

While the phrase "paradigm shift" has been applied to many disciplines and situations, philosopher of science Thomas Kuhn originally intended the concept as a descriptor for dramatic changes in scientific practice (Kuhn 1996, 18–19). Here Kuhn's label appropriately defines dramatic changes in scientific communication. Prior to the 1730s, scientific exchanges were confined to individual pairs of correspondents. Within a decade, network membership reached sufficient size, and letter-writers routinely asked their recipients to share information with others, or even wrote missives containing the same content to several colleagues. Indeed, privacy as we know it today did not exist in the eighteenth century. Correspondents needed to request explicitly that a letter not be shared. This (mostly) uninterrupted flow of information directly contributed to the multiple narratives that were being created by the participants in the scientific community.

Part of the Kuhnian paradigm shift at play during the eighteenth century had to do with letter-writing etiquette itself. Letter-writing etiquette of the time instructed that one should never send another letter to a correspondent until a reply to a first missive had been received. The transmission of knowledge was far too important not to send a necessary follow-up, even if a letter had gone out the day before. Thus the conversations unfolded rapidly, particularly if multiple writers contributed to the same discussion. Continuity problems arose when writers did not reference the dates of their correspondents' letters in their own (most were careful to do so), or when a ship was delayed because of weather or piracy. But assuming a transatlantic letter reached the British or American shores, postal services could deliver quickly.[2] For scientific practitioners, such restrictions ran counter to their goals. Consequently, the rules of "polite" correspondence were ignored. Moreover, there is no evidence that any member of the scientific community ever even addressed the issue. In this case, the "silence" becomes part of the narrative: participants clearly had a shared, and what seems to be an a priori, understanding of their situation.

More Than a Hobby, Less Than a Career

The narrative of mid-eighteenth-century men of science shared little in common with that of the practitioners of the seventeenth—and early eighteenth century. They were not "men of leisure": a significant number had little formal education and most had what could be called "day jobs," practicing science in their spare time.[3] Among those at the center of scientific correspondence were a merchant, a farmer, and a printer. None of the three possessed a university degree, yet the nature of the eighteenth-century scientific community offered full participation to anyone who contributed information. The printer was Benjamin Franklin (1706–1790), who, as the publisher of the best-selling newspapers in the colonies, was already disseminating information to a broad audience. But it was Franklin's position as postmaster, beginning in 1737, which allowed the producers of scientific knowledge, whether in Britain, continental Europe, or the British colonies, to circulate their work in America among their peers at no cost. A perk of Franklin's office was the franking privilege, which allowed all mail that was sent via the postmaster to be forwarded to the final recipient postage-free.[4] Unlike today, all mail was sent postage due, and given the volume of letters that were exchanged, this saved every participant a significant amount of money. Franklin's administrative contribution allowed correspondents' conversations to continue unabated.

Educated members of the scientific community were, more often than not, physicians. Botany and chemistry were required for all medical students, thus giving them an advantage over their self-taught counterparts. In most cases, autodidacts received praise from those who had received an advanced education, but not always. The aforementioned farmer, John Bartram (1699–1777), who had to teach himself to read, was allegedly once described by the Swedish naturalist Linnaeus (1707–1778) as "the greatest natural botanist in the world."[5] By contrast, South Carolina physician and naturalist Alexander Garden (1730–1791) called Bartram "a man who can scarcely spell, much less make out the characters of any one genus of plants" (Smith 1821, I:538).[6] Despite Dr. Garden's criticism, people such as John Bartram were full-fledged members of the scientific community.[7]

All for One, One for All

Unlike the closed, secretive world of science in the seventeenth century, the egalitarian approach of eighteenth-century practitioners allowed all to contribute. While there were no formal written rules for participating, there were expectations. Most important was the willingness to accept critique of one's own work, offer critiques of others' contributions, and respond as promptly as possible (given the technological limitations of communication at the time) to messages from members of the scientific community. However, it was not always necessary to engage personally in the epistolary network: many practitioners, particularly in London, saw one another regularly, and it was not uncommon for one to write a letter incorporating messages from local colleagues. This was especially true if a writer was sending multiple copies of the same information to practitioners in disparate locations.

Participation in the epistolary network promoted a free exchange of ideas in much the same way that theorist Jürgen Habermas proposed the formation of a "*bourgeois* public sphere" in the eighteenth century (Habermas 1989). For Habermas, the public sphere relied heavily on face-to-face contact in coffeehouses, taverns, and other public spaces. The Habermasian model also restricted who could participate in such a sphere: literate white men. In Britain, only those with some wealth acquired literacy. This remained the case until later in the eighteenth century, but in New England and mid-Atlantic American colonies, literacy was nearly universal regardless of economic class or gender, except for unfree Africans and African Americans. In the southern colonies, the ability to read mirrored that of Britain, with wealthy, white men dominating the ranks of the educated.

Practitioners of science, often separated by great distances, developed what I term the "scientific public sphere" as a virtual community, whose existence was predicated on the remarkable efficiency of the epistolary web, allowing its members to transcend international geographic boundaries. Ironically, while participating in this virtual public sphere, John Bartram thought a corporeal one to be problematic. It would be better, Bartram wrote, to "exchange ye time that is spent in ye Club, Chess & Coffee House for ye Curious amusements of natural observations" (New-York Historical Society, 1919–1937, 3:160).[8] Bartram thus wrote between the lines, insisting that one's "natural observations" should be committed to paper and shared with the scientific community. Bartram practiced what he preached by disseminating seeds, plants, and scientific descriptions to his colleagues. However, as far as a broader audience was concerned, Bartram relied on other members of the scientific community to promote and publish what he sent.

London-based merchant, botanist, and naturalist Peter Collinson (1694–1768) provided the essential link to a wider reading public. Like Franklin and Bartram, Collinson was an autodidact, acquiring scientific knowledge by reading and observation, not through schooling. As a member of high standing in the Royal Society of London, his associations ran deep within the British scientific community, both at home and in the colonies. Collinson was well connected to leading politicians, as well as to King George II's court. Furthermore, Collinson maintained contacts with learned colleagues on the Continent, including Linnaeus. The Royal Society's *Philosophical Transactions* offered scientific knowledge to the educated community, and Collinson contributed his own work, along with that of other scientific practitioners. However, it was Collinson's connection to Edward Cave (1691–1754), publisher of the *Gentleman's Magazine* that provided the greatest dissemination of scientific knowledge to an English-speaking (and reading) audience.[9]

Published monthly, "The Magazine" (as it was usually referred to) functioned as the primary source of knowledge and learning for many literate Britons. It contained not only science but also literature, history, the arts, and a variety of other subjects. When Benjamin Franklin began his famous electrical experiments, he wrote detailed letters to Collinson explaining the process. Collinson passed shortened, edited versions on to Cave to print in the *Gentleman's Magazine*, which were used to "tease" Franklin's *Experiments and Observations on Electricity*, published in 1751 (Franklin 1751). Thus began the narrative of Franklin and electricity, which has had a life of its own since the mid-eighteenth century, and with its inception made Franklin into arguably the first international superstar.

Moving the Knowledge, Moving the Narrative

Collinson's position as a successful merchant in London also replicated much of what Franklin was doing as postmaster in America. The circulation of knowledge during the mid-eighteenth century relied on a combination of land-based postal services and merchant ships. While the British and American colonial post offices proved efficient, Britain did not institute a transatlantic postal service until 1755. "The packet," as it was called, sailed under navy escort and was designed to keep London government officials informed of events in America during the Seven Years' War.[10] Prior to 1755, the use of merchant vessels provided cost savings for correspondents. Merchants simply packed letters along with the goods being shipped. The added weight was minimal, and the frequency of departures insured timely delivery (with some notable exceptions discussed next) across the Atlantic. Average crossings took six-to-seven weeks from London to Philadelphia, but only four weeks in the other direction. Members of the scientific community used the system to great advantage. Once on land, letters were delivered cheaply (in Britain), or at no cost (in the colonies).

John Bartram and Peter Collinson corresponded without interruption from 1734 until Collinson's death in 1768. Their epistolary exchange grew out of the British fascination with gardening, which flourished during this period, particularly among the wealthy. This drove demand for plants and seeds from various parts of the world. Collinson secured well-to-do subscribers for Bartram, who supplied American specimens in exchange for payment. However, the Bartram-Collinson correspondence was far more than a series of business letters. The study of natural history dominated their conversations.

Although Collinson did not possess an advanced education, he, unlike his longtime correspondent, went to school as a child. As a teenager and young adult, Collinson clearly devoted time to understanding the natural world, as he was made a Fellow of the Royal Society at age thirty-two. While Bartram never achieved "F.R.S." status, his natural history observations were published several times in the Society's *Philosophical Transactions*. These pieces began as letters to Collinson. Likewise, Bartram benefited from Collinson's link to Edward Cave of the *Gentleman's Magazine*, which offered more of the Philadelphia botanist's natural history work. Like Collinson, Bartram continuously studied nature, particularly botanical productions, and his limited formal education rarely was at issue. Indeed, Bartram even taught himself Latin, although his working knowledge of the ancient language was limited. Bartram freely admitted his linguistic shortcomings when he sent a message to New York physician and botanist Cadwallader Colden (1688–1776) in early October of 1745 regarding a letter received from the Dutch physician and botanist Johann Frederick Gronovius (1690–1762). The missive contained, in Bartram's words, "curious remarks." Bartram wrote, "I wish thee could see them," his letter "is so mixed with Latin I cant read many of his words. altho I understand his English pretty well: if I could meet with safe conveyance I should be ready to send thee ye Original" (New-York Historical Society, 1919–1937, 3:158).[11] Colden, whose advanced learning in medicine included Latin study, was an obvious choice to translate for Bartram. This episode serves as one example of another Kuhnian shift in the eighteenth-century communication of scientific knowledge. Indeed, this subject was among the most widely discussed by practitioners of science, offering a long, complex narrative.

Speaking in the Vernacular

Members of the epistolary web wrote their letters predominantly in English. For scientific practitioners in Britain and America, this provided avenues for contributions by those who did not have the benefit of learning Latin as part of their education. Even practitioners of science on the Continent frequently added to the epistolary discourse in English when their correspondents were in Britain or America. Furthermore, with this move toward the use of English, science could ultimately reach a broader audience on both sides of the Atlantic. The movement toward English as the *lingua franca* of scientific communication had begun in the mid-seventeenth century. However, even by the beginning of the nineteenth century, English had not supplanted Latin as the international language of choice for communicating scientific knowledge.[12]

When the Royal Society began publishing *Philosophical Transactions* in English in 1665, the Society initiated the movement to make English the language of scientific knowledge in the Anglo-American world. The quarrel with Latin had little to do with *identifying* scientific specimens. Latin, of course, is still used for this purpose more than 340 years after the *Philosophical Transactions* first appeared. Instead of using Latin like their seventeenth-century predecessors, these new British practitioners of science wanted to communicate information and ideas more effectively to a larger (and growing) community. During the eighteenth century, people interested in science expressed through their words (especially their personal correspondence) and their actions (in publications) that English was the preferred language of science in both Britain and North America. Indeed, expansion of science from London and Edinburgh to the American colonies provided an inclusive atmosphere for scientific practitioners that furthered the use of English on *both* sides of the Atlantic. Moreover, since members of the scientific community in America increasingly saw themselves as provincial Britons during the forty-year period prior to the American Revolution, use of their native language reinforced their identity as British.[13]

Publishers, printers, and authors also needed to decide which language to employ for their books, articles, and journals, and while the shift to English was palpable in many facets of science, not every scientific field followed this trend. Changes in medical vernacular were much more tentative.[14] Some practitioners of science from the European mainland who traveled to Britain and America during the eighteenth century adopted English as their working language, but such adoption was by no means universal. This influence of English on mainland Europeans was not always long lasting, but it supported the efforts of those who wished it to be so.

In the seventeenth century, scientific letters, even those exchanged among native English speakers, were often written in Latin. John Ray[15] (1627–1705), whose natural classification system was replaced during the much of the eighteenth century (and into the nineteenth) by Linnaeus's sexually based system, corresponded regularly with physician, naturalist, and fellow

Englishman Martin Lister (1639–1712). Their correspondence was necessitated by geography: Ray lived in Essex (about forty miles from London), and Lister resided first in Cambridge (as a student), then in York (after taking his medical degree), and finally in London.

On November 15, 1669, Ray wrote to Lister, "Having now received a *second* letter from you in English, I look upon myself as licensed to answer you in your own language" (Lankester 1848, 43).[16] Ray wrote at least one letter to Lister prior to this in English. It was a response to a letter that Lister had written in Latin. Lister's reply to Ray was also in Latin and made no mention of the latter's use of English (Lankester 1848, 11–13, 13–14, 15).[17] It may be that since Ray's English missive contained *mostly* non-scientific information, he may have assumed that Latin was unnecessary. Lister's Latin reply indicates that if science was to be discussed at all, Latin should be the language of choice.

From that point, Ray, like Lister, wrote in Latin until the exchange that led Ray to point out Lister's use of English. The two men then corresponded predominantly in their mother tongue, although old habits apparently died hard. There are several instances of Latin letters after Ray's letter of November 15, 1669, but neither writer acknowledged a shift in language. It is unknown why Lister decided to begin writing to Ray in English, but it is possible that once Lister began his medical practice, he was often too busy to take the time to craft letters in Latin. Ray, whose other correspondents primarily utilized English, was likely quite pleased with this turn of events.

Many eighteenth-century practitioners of science, such as Peter Collinson, had a working knowledge of Latin, but his preference for correspondence was English, even when writing to Linnaeus, who almost exclusively (but not entirely) corresponded in Latin. However, it seems Collinson was a bit confused about the Swedish naturalist's linguistic capabilities. Along with a March 1747 letter to Linnaeus, Collinson sent "some tracts," which were obviously written in Latin. Collinson wanted to send others, but as he explained to Linnaeus, "if you did but read English, I should send you more" (Smith 1821, 1:17).[18] In another letter to Linnaeus in October of the same year, referring to "The treatise on gravitation, by our friend Dr. Colden of New York," Collinson wished that "it had been wrote in Latin, to have been more universally read." However, Collinson noted, since "a great many of your learned men [in Sweden] read English, I hope it will be acceptable to some of them" (Smith 1821, 1:19).[19] Perhaps Collinson knew that Linnaeus was fluent enough in written English for correspondence, but at the same time thought that something as detailed as a scientific publication was beyond the Swede's ability for swift comprehension.

Linnaeus wrote his own studies in Latin, but Collinson had "no doubt but they will be translated into English, for we are very fond of all branches of Natural History; they sell the best of any books in England" (Smith 1821, 1:18–19).[20] On the one hand, Collinson realized that (literate) English people were invested in the study of natural history and English translation of works in that field was commonplace and necessary. On the other hand, Collinson tacitly acknowledged, his was still not a common language in non-English-speaking countries; Latin remained the only viable alternative.

In his first letter to Linnaeus, London merchant and naturalist John Ellis (c1710–1776) wrote, "I wish I had begun a correspondence earlier with you," and now that it had "begun I hope you will continue it" (Smith 1821, 1:83).[21] Ellis learned, likely through his close friend Collinson, that Linnaeus preferred communicating in Latin, but read English well. Collinson, who wrote to Linnaeus in English, probably told Ellis that he could do the same, but should expect the Swede to write in Latin. Armed with this information, Ellis told Linnaeus, "I read latin familiarly, yet I cannot write it to please me" (Smith 1821, 1:83).[22] Here Ellis, who wanted to establish a regular correspondence, needed to be clear about *how* the exchange would have to proceed in order to be successful. Ellis carefully addressed the comfort of both himself and Linnaeus directly, implying that it was his own shortcomings that created the need for the use of two languages. As their long correspondence shows, each man writing in his mother tongue (Latin for Linnaeus here) clearly put both men at ease with all future interchanges.

"I am endeavouring as much as in me lies to establish your system [in Britain]," Ellis wrote to Linnaeus, concerning the Swedish naturalist's classification system. However, it seemed that Ellis's primary consideration was for "the public to have it in english." That said, Ellis was ambivalent as to the scope of the proposed translated publication. First, Ellis thought that the best course of action would be to provide enough of Linnaeus's "botanical system as would tempt young beginners to study this art," noting that "if there was too much to be learnt, few would attempt it." On the other hand, it seemed "a compendious description of your method in familiar english should be published, to understand your terms" (Smith 1821, 1:83–84).[23] While Ellis desired to disseminate the Linnaean System to a broader British readership, he did not seem surprised that an English translation was not yet available. Ellis proposed to have the book be a composite of Linnaeus's previous works, rather than simply a translation of *Species Plantarum*, the Swede's latest, and the first complete work of botany utilizing the Linnaean System (Smith 1821, 1:84).[24] Spurred on by the 1753 publication, Ellis saw botanists and gardeners as the target audience for his English-language compilation.

Cadwallader Colden of New York firmly believed in the use of English as the language of science; unlike Collinson, he was unequivocal in his position on the subject. However, Colden's overt support for English was evident well before translating the Linnaean System for his daughter Jane for her own botanical studies. In 1742, observing the need for a botanical text for American plants (and requesting Collinson's help in the matter), Colden argued that since there was "nothing in Botany tollerably well don in English," such a work would be "usefull in America where the learned languages are little understood" (New-York Historical Society, 1919–1937, 2:282).[25] Colden wanted the volume "to be in English" and acknowledged it would be "more difficult to do [in English] than in Latin" (New-York Historical Society, 1919–1937, 2:281–282).[26] Notable here is Colden's recognition of the potential problems with an English botanical text, but his insistence that the project should be undertaken regardless of the consequences. He was clearly concerned that the widest audience possible understood the work. The end of the decade saw the possibility of broadening this same audience further.

Jane Colden (1724–1766), who produced her botanical studies exclusively in English, was, by her own remarkable talent, able to enter a world dominated by men. As Collinson wrote to Linnaeus in 1756, "[Cadwallader Colden's] daughter is perhaps the first lady that has so perfectly studied your system. She deserves to be celebrated" (Smith 1821, 1:39).[27] Because of her gender, Jane Colden would have been completely shut out from the scientific correspondence network if not for her father's ties to the scientific community (Parrish 2006, 196).[28] Bartram, Gronovius, and Garden were among her correspondents. The men of the scientific community took Jane Colden's botanical work seriously. More important to the present discussion, however, is that Colden worked solely in English. Nowhere in the record is there an attempt to discredit her work because it was not in Latin. By acknowledging the quality of her work, members of the scientific community simultaneously (if only tacitly) endorsed the legitimacy of English as the working language of science.

For some, such as illustrator, painter, and naturalist Georg Dionysius Ehret, the conversion to English-language scientific communication was a function of geography. Ehret was born and raised in Germany, but from the mid-1730s spent most of his life in London. Ehret's field sketchbooks from 1746, 1747, and 1748 demonstrate that the artist was beginning to incorporate English into his scientific descriptions, although Latin remained his primary choice. While the names and the "characters" of the plants he sketched were notated in Latin, Ehret used English to describe *where* he was sketching (or where the specimen came from) as well as the date.[29] Furthermore, Ehret's descriptions of a specimen's color or other special characteristics were in English. "The fruit is here delineated of their proper Colour, as received by a dry specimen of Mr. P. Collinson" (Ehret 1748, Banksian MSS no. 109).[30] Ehret's choice of London as his home would certainly have forced him to communicate in English with members of the London scientific community. His English sketchbook notations further indicate this attempt to assimilate.

Ehret had illustrated an early work of Linnaeus, *Hortus Cliffortianus*, and maintained a sporadic correspondence with his Swedish collaborator. His eight letters to Linnaeus over a period of thirty-two years are valuable, not only for their content but also for their construction. Ehret's first seven letters, written between 1736 and 1762 are in German. The eighth, written in 1769, is in English, thus raising relevant issues. While Ehret favored Latin for at least a portion of his scientific writing, he was far less comfortable using it in correspondence, unlike Linnaeus, who, as was his custom, replied to all eight letters in Latin.[31] Ehret apparently did not feel comfortable corresponding with Linnaeus in English until nearly the end of his life. Why, after an association with Linnaeus of over three decades, did Ehret's decide to write in English in 1769? It seems that Ehret's assimilation into British culture was so complete by that date, it was simply second nature, although given the paucity of Ehret's correspondence, the question is likely to remain unanswered.

Books, pamphlets, and serializations in magazines were the three means of publication available in the eighteenth century. Each had its own advantages and shortcomings, but still ultimately communicated knowledge to a wider audience. As previously noted, the publication of scientific knowledge in English began in the seventeenth century with the founding of the Royal Society. Its *Philosophical Transactions* was the primary venue for printed scientific discourse. Although this continued to be the case in the eighteenth century, more choices became available. However, prestige accompanied inclusion in the *Transactions*, and publishing in book form had significant drawbacks. First, the author was responsible for all costs; subscriptions were a necessity for larger, multivolume works, as well as some single-volume editions. In addition, books were expensive and few could afford them. As a result, many scientific (as well as non-scientific) works were serialized in magazines. For those invested in promoting English as the language of science in Britain and America, serialization encouraged publication of work in English as opposed to Latin, which was far less accessible to the readership of periodicals. In the end, as far as English was concerned, this had the same effect as publication in the *Transactions*.

While English flourished as the preferred language of scientific communication in letters, the change in publications was more measured. Physician and botanist John Berkenhout (1730?–1791) produced a botanical lexicon in 1764, *Clavis Anglica Linguae Botanicae*. Despite its Latin title, the book aimed to provide English equivalents for Linnaean botanical terms. Berkenhout described a previous English translation of Linnaeus's *Philosophia Botanica* as "a very useless attempt." Similar to Colden's lament two decades earlier concerning the lack of an English-language botanical text of American plants, Berkenhout wrote, "there is hardly a single botanical book, of any repute, in the English language; Latin is the established language of Botany in all nations."[32] While Berkenhout's acknowledgment of Latin's continued international dominance is plain, he clearly thought that change was possible, as he surely would not have produced a book in English otherwise.

This narrative continued unabated until later in the nineteenth century. Once the United States established its dominance in science, English became universal for the field.

Conclusion: Collaboration and Community

The discussion in this chapter, while *intra*disciplinary, is reflected in the now-commonplace *inter*disciplinary work of academic community writ large. Narratives of scholarship—and the communication of that scholarship—are constructed through collaborative efforts with colleagues in multiple fields. Those stories provide future scholars with frameworks to build their own collaborations and then proceed to pass their own narratives to the next group, and so on. Lacking an ending, this process is clearly *not* a narrative itself, but as the scientific practitioners of the eighteenth century have demonstrated, it's not always the message, but the medium.

As the director for the College of Arts & Letters' Colloquium on Narrative, I have the opportunity to experience my colleagues' approaches to narrative during our monthly gatherings. In turn, my work is informed by my participation as the moderator, forcing me to think about narrative in different (and beneficial) ways. The post-colloquium conversations provide even more food (figurative and literal) for thought. Like our counterparts in the eighteenth century, we, the participants in the colloquium, create a narrative. Each presenter and each audience member is a character, and the presentations and the questions provide plot. Our goals in the College are identical to those of the eighteenth-century scientific practitioners: accumulate and disseminate knowledge both within the community and to a broader audience. While their narrative had a beginning, middle, and end, our own continues.

Notes

1 In this chapter, I intentionally avoid the word "scientist." First, it was not coined until the nineteenth century, and second, its use was frequently pejorative early on. The terms "practitioners of science," "scientific practitioners," and "men of science" are used instead. The last phrase, "men of science," reflects the highly gendered nature of scientific endeavor during the eighteenth century. Women were not completely absent from scientific discourse (and even made important contributions), but they were few and far between.
2 Here the southern colonies suffered. With few roads and trails, rural residents often had to wait weeks (or even months!) for delivery. A letter from Philadelphia to London often arrived at its final destination well before a letter from Philadelphia to Virginia.
3 There were no "professional" scientists until the nineteenth century.
4 Franklin also used the system to distribute his newspapers for free. Since they were not considered "mail," the sender paid the postage. This cost-savings contributed to Franklin's great wealth.
5 There is no extant proof that Linnaeus ever said this. However, Bartram's status as an autodidact, as well as his numerous contributions to botany and natural history are well documented.
6 Alexander Garden to John Ellis, July 15, 1765.
7 Garden had a penchant for leveling some of his harshest critiques against *dead* colleagues, who obviously had no opportunity to defend or revise their work. His scathing criticism of the very-much-alive Bartram was unusual, but no less heartfelt.
8 John Bartram to Cadwallader Colden, October 4, 1745.
9 The *Gentleman's Magazine* enjoyed an unusually long run. It was published from 1731 until 1868, then in various forms until 1922.
10 The war, known in America as the French and Indian War, lasted from 1754–1763. Observers will note that this is more than seven years. Despite the military

escort, many "packets" were seized. The best synthetic work on the Seven Years' War is Fred Anderson, *Crucible of War: The Seven Years' War and the Fate of Empire in British North America, 1754–1766* (New York: Alfred A. Knopf 2000). Anderson's compelling thesis is that the war was the first true world war, not simply a conflict between Britain and France in Europe or the colonists fighting the French and Indians in North America.
11 Bartram to Colden, October 4, 1745.
12 Indeed, French, not English, was more universally accepted for this purpose internationally.
13 This is the argument put forth in Ned C. Landsman, *From Colonials to Provincials: American Thought and Culture, 1680–1760* (Ithaca and London: Cornell University Press, 1997).
14 Science and medicine are now considered separate domains, but until near the end of the eighteenth century, all physicians were required to study botany. To that end, medical practice is considered part and parcel of science in the present study.
15 He spelled his name "Wray" until 1670. See Robert W.T. Gunther, ed., *Further Correspondence of John Ray* (London: Printed for The Ray Society, 1928), 16*n*.
16 My emphasis. John Wray to Martin Lister, November 15, 1669. Ray's choice of words here is rather amusing, since it implies that English was only *Lister's* mother tongue.
17 Lister to Wray, April 8, 1667; Wray to Lister, June 18, 1667; Lister to Wray, July 6, 1667.
18 Peter Collinson to Linnaeus, March 10, 1747.
19 Collinson to Linnaeus, October 26, 1747.
20 Collinson to Linnaeus, April 16, 1747.
21 Ellis to Linnaeus n.d. (Smith 1821).
22 *Ibid.*
23 *Ibid.*
24 *Ibid.* Ellis outlined his plan quite specifically.
25 Colden to Collinson, November 13, 1742. The "learned languages" are Latin and Greek, but Colden is specifically referring to Latin in this context. In seeking Collinson's assistance, Colden referred to his own "superficial knowledge" of botany, but severely underestimated his own talent for the subject. Colden's botanical prowess would surpass that of many other practitioners, and he emerges as one of the great botanists of the eighteenth century. The first comprehensive American botanical text in English was not produced until sixty years later, when Benjamin Smith Barton published *Elements of Botany* in 1802.
26 Colden to Collinson, November 13, 1742.
27 Collinson to Linnaeus, May 12, 1756. Collinson knew of Jane Colden's botanical exploits as early as 1753, but if he mentioned them to Linnaeus at that time, no record is extant. See Bartram to Collinson, [Fall 1753]. *COJB*, 360.
28 Parrish points out that Cadwallader Colden's wealth and status permitted daughter Jane to flourish in a situation typically untenable for women during this time period.
29 Four sketchbooks are housed in the Botany Library at the Natural History Museum-London. Note the Anglicizing of Ehret's name on the title information of two of the four sketchbooks. See Georg Dionysius Ehret, *Original drawings of rare plants delineated by George Dennis Ehret* (Natural History Museum-London, Botany Library, Banksian MSS no. 106, 1746); Ehret, *Original drawings of rare plants delineated by George Dennis Ehret* (Banksian MSS no. 107, 1747); Ehret, *Original drawings of rare plants collected and designed by George Dionysius Ehret* (Banksian MSS no. 108, 1748); Ehret, *Original drawings of*

rare plants collected and drawn by George Dionysius Ehret (Banksian MSS no. 109, 1748). While composed of drawings primarily from 1746, 1747, and 1748, the sketchbooks also contain some later material as well. Ehret, keenly aware of the cost of paper, clearly did not want to waste available space. Furthermore, the sketchbooks show that Ehret removed some pages (perhaps for perspective clients) and also pasted loose sheets into the books for safekeeping.

30 Georg Dionysius Ehret, *Original drawings of rare plants collected and drawn by George Dionysius Ehret* (Natural History Museum-London, Botany Library, Banksian MSS no. 109, 1748).

31 See *The Linnaean Correspondence*, an electronic edition prepared by the Swedish Linnaeus Society, Uppsala, and published by the Centre international d'étude du XVIIIe siècle, Ferney-Voltaire. This project will eventually make available, in English, all correspondence to and from Linnaeus, as well as other manuscripts. The website can be found at http://www.linnaeus.c18.net.

32 John Berkenhout, *Clavis Anglica Linguae Botanicae* (London: Printed for the Author, sold by T. Becket and A. De Hondt, in the *Strand*; and Mess. Hawes, Clarke, and Collins, in *Pater-noster-row*. 1764), x. Berkenhout has a somewhat bizarre connection to Linnaeus: Although it is often the Swede who gets the credit, it was Berkenhout who identified and named the infamous Norway rat.

References

Ehret, Georg Dionysius. 1748. Original drawings of rare plants collected and designed by G. D. Ehret, Banksian MSS no. 108.

Franklin, Benjamin. 1751. *Experiments and Observations on Electricity: Made at Philadelphia in America*. London: Printed and sold by E. Cave at St. John's Gate.

Habermas, Jürgen. 1989. *The Structural Transformation of the Public Sphere: An Inquiry into a Category of Bourgeois Society*. Translated by Thomas Burger. Cambridge, MA: MIT Press.

Kuhn, Thomas. 1996. *The Structure of Scientific Revolutions*, 3rd ed. Chicago and London: University of Chicago Press.

Lankester, Edwin, ed. 1848. *The Correspondence of John Ray: Consisting of Selections from the Philosophical Letters Published by Dr. Derham and Original Letters of John Ray in the Collection of the British Museum*. London: Printed for the Ray Society.

New-York Historical Society. 1919–1937. *The Letters and Papers of Cadwallader Colden*, 9 volumes. New York: New-York Historical Society.

Parrish, Susan Scott. 2006. *American Curiosity: Cultures of Natural History in the Colonial British Atlantic World*. Chapel Hill: University of North Carolina Press.

Smith, Sir James Edward, ed. 1821. *A Selection of the Correspondence of Linnaeus and Other Naturalists*, 2 volumes. London: Printed for Longman, Hurst, Rees, Orme, and Brown, Paternoster Row, 1821.

Section II Summary: An Author Conversation

Zac Gershberg, Paul Sivitz, and Kellee J. Kirkpatrick

Zac: The title of this section of this book [Narratives at the Intersection of the Public and Private] that includes our chapters makes me think about how narratives are more than just the characters and plot points of a story. They involve a communicative, if not otherwise rhetorical, relationship between the author (or sources) of a narrative and the target audience. Under this formula, how tension is created and, ultimately, relieved or transcended becomes the defining characteristic of public narratives, which are initiated at the behest of private individuals, corporations, movements, and/or campaigns. The objective of public narratives is to convince an intended or general audience to identify with the narrative source as it sees itself.

Paul: Yes, Zac, I agree. However, it seems to me it goes even further than you are suggesting. In my chapter, the authors of the narrative (the communication of scientific knowledge) are also the initial intended audience. Later, knowledge is communicated to a wider literate public, so the semi-public (or semi-private, depending on how you look at it) nature of the narrative in its creation stage must not only speak to the audience, but allow for changes to that narrative.

Zac: Interesting, Paul. It almost sounds like you've discovered what amounts to the collaborative genesis of a narrative. Just as eighteenth-century scientists were composing their own narrative arc through private discussion, so, too, it could be argued, do advertising executives when contemplating their products, brands, and target audiences. Of course, this is not to equate, or even conflate, the musings of, say, Benjamin Franklin and the folks behind the Dos Equis beer ad campaign featuring "The Most Interesting Man in the World." Rather, it shows how private contemplation, or discussion, is ultimately transformed into a public narrative.

Speaking to your work on scientific communication, Paul, we might even connect this to the broader themes of the Enlightenment. Expanded more, what, if anything, is postmodernism other than a public counter-narrative to the narratives of individualism and reason? Jean-Francois Lyotard, for example, is quite clear about the postmodern challenges to, and skepticism of, Enlightenment narratives that rely on a presumed understanding of meaning.

Paul: Well, Zac, if one goes back to the original concept behind Enlightenment thinking, it is that "the world is knowable." The paradox of course is that those who gathered this knowledge never presumed an understanding of anything.

Kellee: Zac and Paul, I think you both make good points. But if my brief dabbling with narrative has taught me anything, it is that narrative means something different to every discipline. I think this is the beauty of narrative analysis. It can be used in so many different contexts to understand the world around us and to see how individuals situate themselves in this world. Thinking about our chapters and the title of our section, I have a slightly different perspective. The human experience is complex, and narratives provide a way for individuals to make sense of their experiences. These private narratives help individuals to navigate difficult situations and give them a way to normalize their experiences. These private narratives are also influenced by public discourse. In the case of my chapter, the source of this public discourse is public policy and the infertility industry. Because the public discourse seems to support this personal, private narrative, it becomes even more solidified, and I argue that it then shapes identity.

Zac: Even in discussing the private internalization of narratives, Kellee employs an effective turn of phrase that speaks to how narratives can affect a rhetorical transaction—namely, that narratives help people "normalize their experiences." That process of normalization, for me, represents the power of narratives. If any source of communication can get an audience to absorb its attitudes or experiences as normal, it reflects a successful, perhaps hegemonic, relationship between the parties. This is the very stuff of ideology, in fact—rendering a narrative to be accepted as a norm. And this process plays out diffusely across a variety of contexts, whether science, politics, or branding. Identifying this tension between the public and private complicates matters, however. This is especially the case in Kellee's chapter on fertility. Is reproduction, from viability to abortion rights, a public issue or a private matter? I do not enter such charged and fraught matters lightly. My sense is simply that the narrative one adopts about these topics precedes the position one holds.

Paul: Yes, the blurred boundaries of public and private often make for strange bedfellows. Look at endorsements. We know that endorsers must avoid using (or even standing next to) competitors' products. Yet we also know that those same PUBLIC endorsers use competitors' products in the privacy of their own homes. So in your case Zac, has Company X successfully lured (through their narrative, of course, but MAYBE even through the quality of their product;

Section II Summary 145

	sorry for the cynicism, which is not usually my thing) the endorser of Company Y? Moreover, there are ethical concerns, sometimes. What many people don't know is that some endorsements come with no pecuniary reward. So if one endorses a product without any sort of monetary gain, should he or she be restricted to using ONLY that product?
Kellee:	I agree with what Paul seems to be suggesting—that narratives change over time. If we think of narratives as a mechanism for how individuals relate to and situate themselves in the world, how could we not see them as constantly evolving?
Paul:	Or revolving for that matter.
Kellee:	So, Paul, by "revolving," do you mean that we see the same narratives resurface over and over again? As we see in fashion, all things return (even bell-bottoms). Is this the same with narrative? Do we see similar themes resurface? I am not sure if I am willing to make that claim about infertility narratives just yet, but your comment is really making me think about this.
Zac:	I initially approached this project from a pretty broad, expansive view of narratives, which owes in large part to my experience as a journalist and education in media and rhetorical studies. Kenneth Burke was a favorite scholar of mine who challenged the early twentieth century art-for-art's-sake movement as well as the New Criticism methodology of close readings. For Burke, narratives must be considered through the prism of the relationship between authorship and audience; the task of the critic is in discovering how identification and affect are generated between the two. A major goal of our essay, then, is expanding how narratives function beyond just story to branding devices across politics, business, and celebrity entertainment. That said, I feel challenged by the other chapters insofar as narratives can take shape when they are not necessarily contrived. What's emerging, at least in my view of other scholarship on display here, is that public narratives can also arise organically from private communications between persons. The point at which such narratives become public is difficult to discern without lapsing into causal relationships, but it's fascinating to see other scholars chart how narratives form without a specific intention. A novelist, a campaign consultant, or an advertising exec is sensitive to the formal properties of narrative and will select among a variety of choices. What I've been forced to reckon with, however, is how narratives may emerge from various interests and discussions.
Kellee:	Zac took the words right out of my mouth when he said, "I feel challenged by the other chapters." Each of the authors in this section approaches narrative in a different way, and yet the thread of public and private narrative ties them all so neatly together. With this chapter being my first step into narrative scholarship,

my conception of narrative and utilization of narrative analysis is still in its infancy. However, reading the other chapters has challenged me to expand my understandings of narrative. As a social scientist, engaging with other narrative scholars in the humanities has pushed me out of my comfort zone, and this has allowed me to reflect on my research agenda as a whole.

Paul: I concur with Kellee (who concurred with you, Zac) on the "challenge." I want to take this in a slightly different direction though. This narrative project has given us the opportunity to develop "public" and "private" engagements (spheres, if you will) within our section of this book, as well as the book writ large. As an offshoot of the narrative colloquium we have all participated in over the last two years, the book has brought us together in ways that we as academic colleagues have not necessarily experienced before. The "public spirit" of the College is so very evident in this endeavor, but at the same time draws on the "private" (for lack of a better word) relationships among individual faculty members. Putting on my narrative book "editorial team" hat for a moment, this is unbelievably gratifying. We have all now come to understand narrative through MULTIPLE lenses. I think this speaks pretty directly to the relationship between narrative and "identity."

Zac: This is a terrific point, Paul. The collaborative scholarship on narrative really does help us move these discussions of narrative from the private domains of our respective fields out into the open as a broader, more public academic community. This, in fact, becomes a big challenge for academics and academic scholarship in general. If there exists a skeptical narrative about the Ivory Tower from audiences—whether the traditional news media or the public at large—it remains nevertheless our goal to address that and make what we do more relevant. To that end, a focus on narrative is both relevant and useful for scholars who span the disciplines. It provides a consistent prism through which to anchor the scope of thought and knowledge, whether located by the specifics of our research or the breadth of departments in the college. So given we feel narratives are significant and relevant to learning, how do we pivot and consider the ways in which narrative can be transformed into our teaching? Or should it? I guess what I'm getting at here is this—we've established that the study of narratives, far beyond the simplistic details of story, are both useful and relevant. What, if anything, might then be done at the college/university level to solidify this? Is there another "move," following the publication of this book, wherein the school can galvanize this interest in narrative—or do we, as scholars, retreat back into our silos and work on our narrative research in the tranquility of scholarly quiet? This is not, I promise, an antagonistic provocation, either. I am genuinely curious, if nothing else, whether this enthusiasm and motivation to focus

	on narrative can be sustained. This book project is admirable, but in terms of identity, how, if at all possible, might the study of narrative become one of the many public narratives of our institution?
Paul:	Zac, I don't think that, after this project, any of us will "retreat back into our silos and work on our narrative research in the tranquility of scholarly quiet." As far as how to move this forward, I think the momentum can continue at the College level without too much difficulty, but at the University level, I must admit I have some concerns. I tried to engage the sciences in our narrative colloquia, but, for this year at least, the attempt went nowhere. I have been assured by my contact in one of the science departments that next academic year will work for this "experiment" (pun intended). We'll have to see how that goes, of course. In terms of the "skeptical narrative about the Ivory Tower from audiences," I think my involvement with our local public library's Human Library Project, along with the College's Humanities Cafe, of course, has shown the Pocatello public (albeit a select portion of it) that we are aware of this particular narrative. Moreover, we are clearly demonstrating that we are out to shatter such skepticism. While I don't know how many of us will bring this into our teaching (consciously) on a regular basis, we all will do it intermittently.
Zac:	Right on, Paul! The college colloquia and Humanities Cafe, which each of us have contributed to, make the school and surrounding areas a really nice atmosphere for making connections in the community. It would be terrific if our colleagues in the sciences became more involved. The geologists and vulcanologists among us may be situated particularly effectively to engage narratives due to their relationship between changes to the earth and time. Evolution itself, it might be said, functions narratively. I'm afraid I might be heading out over my head into uncharted waters in which I have little expertise. But the way I see it, narratives take on different shapes in the trajectory of their arcs in how tension is both created and transcended. With respect to my colleagues across the disciplines, at least in the College of Arts & Letters, it appears that narratives are more than just a story line. They involve public discussion, identity, and a relationship between the sources of narrative and audiences. If we, as academics, serve to generate knowledge, it would appear that across the humanities and social sciences, narrative functions as cathexis, meaning it is a point of departure, if not a method in itself, to locate and understand phenomena.
Kellee:	You know, upon arriving at ISU, I was instantly immersed in the narrative scholars' community. So, in many ways, narrative provided an immediate connection to the College of Arts & Letters (CAL) community. Having been at several other universities in my academic career, I think that the CAL narrative colloquium

and book project provide a unique opportunity for scholars across campus to connect in ways they would not otherwise have done on their own. Narrative analysis provides a common language to facilitate conversations, collaborations, and even friendships. I suppose just as narratives help individuals to situate themselves in the world around them, so too have the narrative projects helped me to situate myself in the ISU community. Because it is fun to play devil's advocate, I would like to pose a question to the other authors. While I believe that the narrative project has given me a way to connect to the broader CAL community, do you think that it has the potential to exclude those who don't engage in narrative scholarship? Or, is narrative so ever present that it can draw in even those who do not use the approach in their own research?

Zac: It's a fair question, Kellee, concerning whether a focus on narrative is exclusive. However, a book proposal such as this one is also a very direct challenge: In what ways does our work, across a variety of disciplines, function narratively? Implied within this is an assumption—persuasive, in my mind, but not to everyone, I'm sure—that, yes, we all indeed do DO narrative. So how do we do it, then? What do narratives include? What are the implications—or the effects? Scholars may not feel they engage narrative explicitly in their work, of course, but I think it's worth heeding the stand articulated by the communication scholar, Walter Fisher, which is reflected in the book project itself: the defining characteristic of human communication is, ultimately, narrative. Not everyone will submit to such an undergirding assumption, mind you, yet adopting such a stance is, or might function as, a scholarly anchor point worth pursuing and one that can help facilitate interdisciplinary discussion and productivity.

Paul: Personally, Kellee and Zac, I really don't think "exclusion" applies here. My own sense is that, while only a limited number of people have presented at the narrative colloquium, the number of those attending (and participating during the Q&A) means that, while narrative might not necessarily be a part of their own work, the shared nature of the IDEA of narrative seems to be universal, insofar as our College is concerned. My own identity within CAL has been nurtured by the entire narrative project (not just the book). I have had the opportunity to meet and talk to colleagues that I might not have had a chance to otherwise. I can't tell you how many times I've been approached with the question, "You're the guy who does the narrative program each month, right?" Aside from the ego boost, it seems that I'm making a difference, and that in and of itself connects me even more with the entire College.

Section III

Performing Bodies, Creating Stories

8   Narratives of Pain

Gesine Hearn

Why use narrative to study pain? Loeser (2005) says this about both the assessment and the treatment of chronic pain: "In no other disease is the role of narrative so critical" (26). He reasons that to assess chronic pain and suffering requires knowledge of individuals and their cultures. Loeser defines pain as the detection of some tissue damage via nerves. Suffering is the "negative affective response in the brain by pain" (Loeser 2005, 19), and he agrees with the definition suggested by Eric Cassell (2004) who defined suffering as the perception of a threat to a person's physiological or psychological integrity. Both pain and suffering require consciousness. Thus "narratives are a resource, certainly underemployed for studying the pain beliefs and pain experiences of individuals and of social groups" (Carr, Loeser, and Morris 2005, 11).

Chronic pain has a tremendous impact on the daily life and the identity of those who experience it. It invades every aspect of life and unmakes and de-constructs the normal world of sufferers. Chronic illness and chronic pain are often interpreted as biographical disruptions and assaults upon self-identity. However, sufferers also reorganize their biographies and lives by searching for meaning through narratives. Narratives are contingent on the social context and have been recognized as organizing elements not only for identity but also for community. The experience of pain thus has the potential to connect the self, body, and society.

This chapter will describe the "pain narratives and practices" of college athletes and will contribute to theoretical discussions of embodied practices, narratives, and identities. The data for the chapter are derived from in-depth interviews with forty Division I college football players.

My Personal Journey to Narrative

How did I get involved in narrative research? Before I became a sociologist, I was a nurse—and there were a lot of stories: late-night stories told by patients who could not sleep, and stories told by relatives about hope, desperation, and grief. Doctors told stories about their quests and conquests and of the patients they helped and the patients they lost: the nice patients, the difficult patients, the patients they will never forget, and the patients they wanted to forget. And I told stories to doctors, to patients, and to relatives: to explain, to instruct, to ease the pain—theirs and mine. And I wondered about those stories: What was their meaning? Why did patients have all these different experiences? Why were doctors always the heroes in the stories? Why did patients from lower-income groups tell stories about enduring fate, while patients with a higher-class background told stories of overcoming challenges? I kept pondering these and similar questions.

So I became a sociology student and learned about social action, social interaction, social structure, and the meaning of experiences; I learned how to theorize about society and its components; I learned research methods and statistics. We conducted a large research survey about female students at our university that yielded "very interesting" results, so they said. But I always wondered. Wondered what was behind the numbers. What was the story behind the "data points?" What else would we know if we would just let them tell their stories? I came across Berger and Luckmann (1966) and their concept of social construction of reality. Then I came across Foucault (1978, 1982), and I learned a lot about narrative and discourse: narratives of history, knowledge, power, science; how and why particular narratives were generated; how discourses developed; and how to deconstruct discourses. My master's thesis was a critical evaluation of the existing discourse about the problems female students encounter in universities. I analyzed thirty years of survey research about the situation of female students in universities. I found that a discourse of lack, stereotypes, and marginality was the starting point of each research project and the findings always substantiated the existing discourse (Küspert 1992). What we needed instead was to listen to the stories of female students that would have conveyed the details of their lived experiences in their complexity, ambiguity, nuances, and shifts over time. None of those nuances of their lived experiences could be captured with "data points," frequencies, and correlations.

My sociology PhD thesis brought me back to the questions I had pondered while working as a nurse. My research now focused on health and illness and in particular on the experiences of patients with unexplained chronic pain syndromes. I discovered that, beyond the individual narratives, there were collective narratives those patients—or a subgroup of patients—"constructed." Online patient self-help groups shared experiences, searched for meaning, and made their stories heard. In the process, individual illness narratives were forged into *a* collective narrative of *a* disease. The many stories of these sufferers became one story. A major element in the illness narratives was the experience of chronic pain: the invisibility of the pain, the complex nature of this pain, the impact of chronic pain on daily life and identity, and the meaning of pain (Hearn 2006–2007; 2016).

The topic of chronic pain led to my next research endeavor. It again started with narratives. I had suffered a typical sports injury, an ACL tear. Despite being on crutches, then having surgery and a huge brace on my knee, I continued to work, right after the accident and a few days after surgery. This earned me the respect of the college football players in my classes. They started sharing their stories about their ACLs, their injuries, surgeries, pain, and rehab. I listened to their stories and noted many similarities with the stories told by patients with unexplained pain syndromes. Just like these patients, chronic pain had a tremendous impact on the daily life of the athletes. It invaded every aspect of life and unmade their world. And just like the patients with pain syndromes, the athletes searched for meaning. The particular social world of elite organized sports with its peculiar cultural narrative of pain provided meaning to their experiences. In addition, the narrative of sport and pain also served as an organizing element for identity and community. Their shared experiences of pain brought them together; it served as a rite of initiation, determined status within their community, maintained collective bonds by effectively isolating members from others who do not understand, and reinforced commitment to the community by repeated infliction of pain. The experience of pain connected self, body, and community through both narratives and practices (Hearn 2010).

Sociology and Narrative

In sociology, narratives are considered a social phenomenon and a method. Stories capture experiences, both of individuals and groups, and relate the meanings of those experiences. Sociologists ask, "What does this story mean?" and "What inferences can be made from these stories about the individuals and larger structures of society?" One of the founding fathers of sociology, Max Weber (1968), declared that sociology

> is a science which attempts the interpretive understanding of social action in order thereby to arrive at a causal explanation of its course and effects. In 'action' is included all human behaviour when and insofar as the acting individual attaches a subjective meaning to it.
>
> (4)

To understand meaning one has to know the intent and the context of the actors: "Thus for a science which is concerned with the subjective meaning of action, explanation requires a grasp of the complex of meaning in which an actual course of understandable action thus interpreted belongs" (Weber 1968, 9). Experiences derive their meanings from the circumstances surrounding them and a host of social, cultural, political, and economic influences. Sociologists explore the meaning of experiences and attempt to understand those meanings by placing experiences in context. As C. Wright Mills (1959) argued, the "sociological imagination" is the art of understanding private problems as public issues—how individual experiences are formed by large-scale phenomena. And narratives have played a critical role in this endeavor from the very beginning of our discipline. It was stories about the miserable living and working conditions of factory workers during early industrialization that triggered Karl Marx's analysis of modern capitalism; it was the Sunday sermons in Calvinist churches praising the virtue of work that led Max Weber to propose a connection between the protestant ethic and capitalism; after observing spiritual rituals, Emile Durkheim argued that morals are the basis of integration and thus society; Georg Simmel used his detailed observations of people in modern cities to argue that modernity led to increasingly rational behavior and interactions. Later, theorists such as Erving Goffman observed how individuals present themselves in front of others and analyzed stories told by patients, relatives, and health-care professionals to develop the concept of "moral careers" of patients (Goffman 1961, 1967). While narratives always played a pivotal role in sociology, in the 1970s, a conscious turn to "narrative sociology" took place. Social constructivism explicitly placed narratives at the center of their methodological and theoretical inquiry to capture how individuals and groups experience and construct their social worlds. They asserted that individual and group identities are fundamentally narrative. Postmodernism critically explored narratives. They deconstructed existing grand narratives to show that these mega-theories do not reflect the fragmented and ambivalent nature of contemporary social worlds. They also argued that narratives can be resisted and recasted (Edles and Appelrouth 2010a, 2010b).

As a method, narrative research is distinguished from other qualitative research approaches by focusing on the story in the data, gathering data in the form of stories, and presenting data in the form of stories. The researcher gathers actual stories using interviews, observations, or videos. These stories are then organized into pivotal events or epiphanies. The data analysis aims at determining the meaning in the stories and situating the stories within larger social structures to explain the meaning. The researcher thus becomes the re-interpreter of the story (Denzin 1989; Lichtman 2014).

Football and Narratives of Pain

In 2007–2008, I researched the experience of pain among elite athletes. I conducted interviews with forty college football players at a mid-major university and observed the team at practices and games over a period of six months. I analyzed data using a qualitative research approach. The interviews were coded, and I then placed codes into analytic categories. And here is where the trouble started: I found myself unable to fit the data nicely into categories. Rather, what I found were stories: a descriptive account of subjective experiences interpreted and reinterpreted by the respondents through telling a story. There were plots, characters, and a setting, but the stories were not always complete or coherent. These stories were not only about the experience of pain but also about identity and community. Respondents gave their experiences meaning by adopting existing cultural narratives, here a dominant sports narrative. However, their experiences did not always fit the existing cultural narrative. Many athletes were critical of the cultural narrative of sport and often struggled to corroborate the sports narrative with their experiences.

In our interviews, we purposefully naively asked if there is pain in football and often received a snickering response: "Pain in football? What kind of a question is that? (Laugh)"

"Football *is* pain," explains Farrell, a big guy who is in his fourth year of playing college football. He started playing football when he was six years old. He wanted to quit after his first practice in the peewee league because it "hurt so bad," but his dad made him go back. Pain from then on was his companion, the "sacrifice to football." Now in college, pain was major and constant. His teammates agree: "Again and again pain—there is no recovery" (Ira). "Pain is severe and recurrent, almost like you never want to do it again. But you know you gotta" (Jack). They accept that they have to live with constant pain, but they sure do not like it: "Pain is a bitch; it's frustrating and a sense of loss of control."

Pain is felt individually and collectively. The football players are submitted to the same physical regimen: the practices, the games, the conditioning, the running of stairs or extra laps as a punishment. They are told that this pain is positive, leading to individual as well as collective success. The athletes also were told that individually and collectively felt pain brings the team together. Jack quotes what he was told:

> And that's something the coaches say that kind of pain brings the team together. You know. Just if everyone is going through the same thing, like after a hard, like 5:30 a.m. workout or something you know, everybody's going through the same thing that brings everybody together, you know.

Omar also repeats what he heard:

> But also at the same time, football is a team sport you know. And they say if you can't do something for yourself, do it for the man next to you, in football. You know, give everything you can.

They know that in order to be successful, in order to maintain the team, they have to pay this price. And the better they want to be, the more they want to win, the higher the price. A way to measure self-improvement is how much pain one can withstand. Pain is a "means to an end"—to success, to winning. Feeling a lot of pain indicates that you "gave it your all," and if it all works out, it also means winning. If you do not feel pain or cannot take the pain, you and your team cannot be successful.

The pain during the competitive season worsened as the season went on, but the pain was also more tolerable. There was the excitement of the games and clearly, the pain was instrumental. Pain was endured for the collective, and was inflicted by an external force. On the other hand, pain during the off-season was harder to endure. The reward was not immediate, and the effort was more solitary. Lane points to the peculiar aspect of pain in the off-season: "The opponent is the self." The off-season is an important time in which "committed" members develop "mental toughness"—attitudes toward injury and pain in line with institutional norms. During this time, players work out to prepare their bodies for the next season, constantly seeking to get "bigger, faster, and stronger." According to Jack,

> In the off-season the most pain is . . . workouts. Pushing yourself as far as you can go. But you know your threshold before, you know. Some guys don't do it; some guys don't push themselves to that point but if you want to be good, then you pretty much put yourself in as much pain as you can handle before you pass out or throw up or whatever.

Even though this pain is obviously physical, most of the players stated that the pain in the off-season is mental. Jack states,

> In the off-season, the mental is the biggest thing, like, during a workout you're just, this sucks, you know, like you just want to quit and when is this going to be over. It's all just, ahu, you kinda maybe sometimes even over think yourself like I can't do this or this. I'm gonna die. I'm gonna throw up. I'm gonna pass out. You know it's a lot of mental pain more than anything I guess.

The lines between physical and mental pain are blurry. Ben says, "I know I am in pain, but it doesn't ring a bell." Patrick states that he was told that the pain is in his head or even "is his head":

> They just beat into you and you are just: Oh it's all in your head and like alright it's in my head and just keep running . . . . Basically, what they're saying is it's in you, *the pain is your head*. Oh, the pain is in your head so you, like, if you just don't think about it or if you just keep going through it, you just got to change your mentality about how, about how you see life, basically.

These statements point to a fusion of mind and body in the face of persistent and repeated pain. Similar experiences have been observed among chronic pain patients (Carr et al. 2005; Mailis-Gagnon and Israelson 2002).

Not everybody can take this pain, mental or physical. Karl and Gary suggest that one must have a special disposition to start with:

> It's just pain; it's just something that you have to be able to take.
>
> (Karl)

> There's always aches and pains. My back hurts right now, my knees hurt, my hip hurts, but pain, that's why we play football, because we can deal with it.
>
> (Gary)

Those who are not able or willing to tolerate pain quit the sport. They are a "failure," a "coper" who needs to step aside. Those who stick with the sport can overcome pain in order to be successful: no pain, no gain! Jack and Mark reiterate other sports adages when they assert that "to be good and excel, pain is necessary" and that "beyond pain is success . . . succumbing to pain is failure." These sport adages express the norms of the sports ethic, but practices targeting the body and the mind, such as "mental toughness" days, also socialize players into the subculture of football. Mental toughness days are designed to build a specific mental disposition by putting players through extreme workouts. According to Ted, players who cannot handle these days quit the team.

> It was mental toughness days and . . . I mean there's been guys that quit just after that, just cuz that day.

The ability to endure pain determines who joins the team and stays on the team, and thus can assume the identity of a football player.

The effect of the repeated practices and experiences of pain is a body and mind that is "used to pain." They say that, over time, they acquired an elevated pain threshold. Paul, for example, says, "You can handle more pain; it doesn't affect you anymore." Patrick even thinks this:

> I guess it, it helps build some serious character cuz, uh, like say someone got hit with like a bat or something, and they would be like a really hurt, but say like a hardcore football player got hit with a bat; he probably wouldn't feel it as much as the person that got hit with a bat that doesn't play any sports. Probably because they just know that, oh, it's just a little bit of pain; it'll go away.

Harold had a particularly interesting metaphor to describe his pain threshold:

> It became the norm. So, you know, you learn to live with it; if you live with dog shit all your life in your house, then you know . . . dog shit is nothing.

But even if you manage to endure the pain, it is a constant battle "within yourself." The mind battles matter, because the only way to overcome pain is to "tell yourself you can." The athletes believe that pain can be overcome because the mind has power over the body. Ira reports, "You can manipulate pain mentally." Mark says, "To get over pain, you need to think you can." Hank states,

> ... yah, mental pain it's, it's, it's something I'm starting to use to ... It's a push yourself beyond, you know, out of your comfort zone, you know. I've never been a person that really, really did get pushed in my comfort, you know, outside of my comfort zone very often. You know, I always once I got tired I quit or I would stop, you know? Or even during workouts and things like that but ... but here it's a little different, you know, I mean, we're, we're learning how ... to stay focused. When you're tired, you know, and uh, and just deal with that, you know, use that, use that mental, your mental power, you know, to look past physical pain, and things like that. Does that make any sense?

While pain is never liked, they say they get used to it. However, the senior players mentioned that enduring pain did not get easier over the years. They actually reported more pain than the freshman, which contradicts directly the notion that football players get used to pain. The players also qualified much of the pain they endured as "good pain." Good pain is instrumental; it leads to something else. But the notion of a *constructive pain* unravels when injury enters the picture. Pain as a result of injury amplifies and exacerbates pain. The collectively held beliefs about pain, the sports adages, are now proven wrong. The athletes feel a deep sense of betrayal. Pain did not lead to success. The "sacrifice" for the collective did not help the team. The loss of a player to an injury hurt the team's chances for success. This is "bad pain!" It does not "help in the long run" or "feels like you are doing something with your life." This pain separates a player from the rest of his team and threatens his identity.

When asked how they cope with pain, they again recite well-known sports adages such as "suck it up," "push through," "deal with it," or "get over it." One way of countering the impact of pain is to develop a "tunnel vision"—to focus on one aspect of life, sports, while neglecting other areas.

> Tunnel vision. All I'm thinking about is football. All I think about is, okay, what do I gotta do to get through. That's it. Everything else—I don't see anything else around me. Or above or below. The horizon is gone.
> (Farrell)

Yet overcoming pain is not a purely mental exercise. Ralph proclaimed, "Pain occurs when you don't take care of your body." The athletes also respond to pain with self-isolation. They "do not want to be bothered," "do not want to talk to anybody," or they "do not want to do anything social." Often, roommates are teammates. Farrell said, "Athletes, we all stick together. We know the whole routine."

The athletes characterized the relationship between football and pain by repeating common sports adages: pain is an integral part of football; pain has a purpose in football; pain serves as a selection tool; pain unifies the team; pain signifies improvement; pain can be countered with mental and physical efforts. These often repeated common sports adages are emblematic of the "sports ethic" (Hughes and Coakley 1991). However, statements such as "they say" or "coaches say" indicate that the athletes distance themselves from these beliefs. The frequent use of "we" and "us football players" reflects collective rather than authentic personal experiences. Respondents recited the specific expectations and beliefs about pain within the subculture of football. However, they also had not fully internalized this pain model. Many of the beliefs and expectations directly contradicted their experiences. Leder (1990) has argued that, when in pain, the body arises as alien, and we feel betrayed by our body. In order to realign mind and body, self and body, and self and the world, we need to be able to make sense of the suffering. The college football players attempted to attribute meaning to their experiences, yet the difference between the cultural beliefs and their personal experiences became clearer the longer they played. Injury experiences were in obvious contradiction to the cultural narratives of sport. In these instances, suffering replaced pain. The constructive force of pain had led to the formation of identities and a community; the destructive nature of suffering now threatened both identities and the collective.

Discussion

The narratives of pain among college football players are similar to the stories told by chronic pain patients. The findings point to some interesting sociological insights in regard to community formation and maintenance and the importance of narratives and bodily practices in forming collective identities. Communities are formed based on shared practices, views, and experiences. The football players are brought together by their shared experiences of pain; they form a "brotherhood of pain": pain is the rite of initiation; pain determines status within the community; pain maintains the collective bonds by isolating members from others who "do not understand" and by reinforcing commitment through the repeated infliction of pain.

Football socializes its adherents into what Goffman (1961) labels "deference" and "demeanor" to the institution. Playing through pain forms the "football self": a committed member of the team and the institution football. Practices of initiation include camps, conditioning, and mental toughness days. Being able to endure the pain means full initiation into the football team—the brotherhood of pain. Paying deference to the brotherhood means to show appropriate demeanor: living with pain, playing through pain, embracing pain as a constructive force. The target of the initiation practices is the body. The process of maintaining deference and the right demeanor is ongoing. Repeated inflictions of pain are important events in this process. The football body is punished constantly. The commitment to the institution of football is thus affirmed over and over again.

Exclusionary and inclusionary bodily practices regulate and affirm the new community. Cultural narratives play an important role in these processes and also tend to generate ambivalences. Respondents often recited the specific expectations and beliefs about pain within the subculture of football. However, they clearly had not internalized this pain model. Many of the beliefs and expectations directly contradicted their experiences. McNamee (2007) argues that the communal suffering in sport is "closely related to intense pain" (241) and experienced in different sports settings such as the weight room, boxing, rugby, or football. "Communities of suffering"—a term coined by Illich (1987)—are often found in the religious realm, but Fry (2006) asserts "that sport has its communities of sufferers" (253). Fry suggests that communal suffering exists in the form of "suffering on behalf of others," or solidarity emerging "out of a sense of suffering together" (250). Both in religion and sport, pain is often viewed as a positive experience.

It is quite possible that the pain experienced by the football players has a very different quality than the pain suffered by patients thrown into unexpected, involuntary, and unwelcome pain. The difference is that athletes' pain is a voluntary pain; they did not receive a medical diagnosis of chronic pain; pain is valued and deemed instrumental; pain is often suffered together and for each other. The majority of pain endured in football might not qualify as suffering with the exception of pain suffered as a consequence of a major injury. Suffering associated with an injury threatens the identity and integrity of the afflicted person.

One of the main differences between chronic pain patients and athletes is the collective experience of pain. Pain might be controllable and manageable because it is shared. "Good communities" are established as therapeutic tools. Jackson (2000) describes a treatment center designed for chronic pain patients who have not responded to other treatment options. The center incorporates "brotherhood, intimacy, mind/body fusion, wholeness, and integration into their treatment program"—all hallmarks of "good communities" and features we found among college football players.

Pain "un-makes the normal world" (Scarry 1985) and creates a new identity and a new community. Narratives play an important role, but they also generate ambivalences. The brotherhood of pain is formed through exclusionary and inclusionary bodily practices. Pain is the throb of the drum to which these athletes move "in a choreographed concert like dancers at an elaborate ball" (Aho and Aho 2009, 30).

Conclusion

Because of my interest in the experience of health and illness and in particular because I studied the experience of chronic pain, narrative as a topic and as a method became central to my research. Narrative now also provides a framework for future endeavors. I plan to look into narratives of different kinds of pain and suffering in different settings: letters immigrants wrote about their experiences in the United States to their families back in Europe, interviews with serial killers in mental health institutions in the 1950s, letters exchanged between early American and German sociologists about the struggles to establish the new discipline of sociology, and stories about the lives of wealthy women in isolated communities struggling to establish new identities. And as it is the nature of narrative, narrative research also provides me with an identity within my college and the larger institution. The identity as a researcher of narratives and utilizing narrative as a method connects me with scholars across disciplines in the social sciences, humanities, and fine arts. What connects us is the exploration of similar topics—culture, cultural expressions, existential angst and desires, and life experiences over time and across cultures. In particular, reading, constructing, presenting, or deconstructing identities—individual and communal—seems to be running through all our scholarly explorations. What also bridges our disciplines is the methodology. While every discipline developed their own terminology and tools, how we go about studying narratives is very similar in psychology, sociology, political science, English, literature, history, or music. It helped me in my research to borrow from other disciplines. Thinking in different terms at times got me out of a rut. Approaches and topics in other discipline have inspired me to pursue some new ideas.

Aside from enriching my research program, I believe narratives serve a similar function for us in the academic world as it did for the football players. We also form a peculiar subculture within our larger society; we have our own cultural narratives that provide meaning to our experiences, and these narratives are the basis for our identity and connect us as a community of academic scholars. Yet, in recent years, we have struggled to reconcile our traditional cultural identities as academics with the new market-driven model of higher education. The values and norms we were taught, then embraced and shared as professionals, do not seem to fit in this "brave new world" of "corporate U." The adaptation to the new standards is painful (and maybe impossible) as they appear to be in contradiction with the values in our subculture. Can we learn from pain experiences and the role of narratives in other groups? May I dare even point to the football players in my study? Could the shared pain that we without doubt all feel turn into a constructive force? Can the shared experience of pain bring us together and reinforce our community of scholars in the face of these external threats? Narratives, writing and sharing our experiences, could provide meaning to these experiences and form the basis of a strong community of scholars. Our shared collective experiences could make the frustration felt by us all more manageable.

References

Aho, James, and Kevin Aho. 2009. *Body Matters: A Phenomenology of Sickness, Disease, and Illness*. Lanham, MD: Lexington Books.

Berger, Peter L., and Thomas Luckmann. 1966. *The Social Construction of Reality: A Treatise in the Sociology of Knowledge*. Garden City, NY: Anchor Books.

Carr, Daniel B., Loeser, John D., and David B. Morris. 2005. "Why Narrative?" In: *Narrative, Pain, and Suffering*, edited by D. B. Carr, J. D. Loeser, and D. B. Morris, 3–13. Seattle: International Association for the Study of Pain Press.
Cassell, Eric J. 2004. *The Nature of Suffering and the Goals of Medicine*, 2nd ed. Oxford and New York: Oxford University Press.
Denzin, Norman. 1989. *Interpretive Interactionism*. Newbury Park, CA: Sage.
Edles, Laura D., and Scott Appelrouth. 2010a. *Sociological Theory in the Classical Era. Text and Readings*. 2nd ed. Thousand Oaks, London, and New Delhi: Pine Forge Press.
Edles, Laura D., and Scott Appelrouth. 2010b. *Sociological Theory in the Contemporary Era: Text and Readings*, 2nd ed. Thousand Oaks, London, and New Delhi: Pine Forge Press.
Foucault, Michel. 1978. *Discipline and Punish: The Birth of the Prison*. New York: Pantheon.
———. 1982. *The Archaeology of Knowledge*. New York: Pantheon.
Fry, Jeffrey P. 2006. "Pain, Suffering and Paradox in Sport and Religion." In *Pain and Injury in Sport*, edited by Sigmund Loland, Berit Skirstad, and Ivan Waddington, 246–260. London and New York: Routledge.
Goffman, Erving. 1961. Asylums: Essays on the Social Situation of Mental Patients and Other Inmates. Garden City, NY: Anchor Books.
Goffman, Erving. 1967. *Interaction Ritual*. Chicago, IL: Aldine.
———. 2007. "Asylums: Essays on the Social Situation of Mental Patients and Other Inmates." In *Sociological Theory in the Contemporary Era: Text and Readings*, edited by Laura D. Edles and Scott Appelrouth. Thousand Oaks: Pine Forge Press.
Hearn, Gesine. 2006–2007. "Illness without a Cause—Patients with a Cause: Online Self-Help/Mutual Aid Organizations for Functional Syndromes in the US and Germany." Special Issue on International and Cross-Cultural Issues. *International Journal of Self-Help and Self-Care* 5: 19–42.
———. 2010. "The Brotherhood of Pain: Persistent Pain among College Football Players." Paper presented at the Annual Meeting of the Pacific Sociological Association, Oakland, CA, April 7–11.
———. 2016. "Identities and the Internet." In *The Routledge Handbook of Medical Anthropology*, edited by Lenore Manderson, Anita Hardon, and Elizabeth Cartwright, 176–185. New York: Routledge.
Hughes, Robert, and Jay Coakley. 1991. "Positive Deviance among Athletes: The Implications of Over-Conformity to the Sport Ethic." *Sociology of Sport Journal* 8: 307–325.
Illich, Ivan. 1987. "Some Theological Perspectives on Pain and Suffering." Originally posted at the Institute for Theological Encounter with Science and Technology. Accessed October 10, 2015. Reprinted at http://backpalm.blogspot.com/2011/01/theological-perspectives-on-pain-and.html.
Jackson, Jean. 2000. *"Camp Pain" Talking with Chronic Pain Patients*. Philadelphia: University of Pennsylvania Press.
Küspert, G. 1992. "Studieren, und Was Dann?" *Widersprüche* 12 (43): 57–62. Offenbach/Main.
Leder, Drew. 1990. *The Absent Body*. Chicago: University of Chicago Press.
Lichtman, M. 2014. *Qualitative Research for the Social Sciences*. Los Angeles and London: Sage.

Loeser, John D. 2005. "Pain, Suffering, and the Brain: A Narrative of Meanings." In: *Narrative, Pain, and Suffering*, edited by Daniel B. Carr, John D. Loeser, and David B. Morris, 17–27. Seattle: International Association for the Study of Pain Press.

Mailis-Gagnon, Angela, and David Israelson. 2005. *Beyond Pain: Making the Mind-Body Connection*. Ann Arbor: University of Michigan Press.

McNamee, Mike. 2007. "Suffering in and for Sport." In *Pain and Injury in Sport*, edited by Sigmund Loland, Berit Skirstad, and Ivan Waddington, 229–245. London and New York: Routledge.

Scarry, Elaine. 1985. *The Body in Pain: The Making and Unmaking of the World*. New York and Oxford: Oxford University Press.

Weber, Max. 1968. *Economy and Society*, Volume 1. Berkeley, CA: University of California Press.

Wright, Mills C. 1959. *The Sociological Imagination*. Oxford and New York: Oxford University Press.

9 Narrative and the Performing Arts
A Symposium

Brian Attebery, Vanessa Ballam, Grant Harville, and Lauralee Zimmerly

How does narrative affect the practice and the teaching of musical or theatrical performance? In this symposium, English Professor Brian Attebery, who doubles as principal cellist in the Idaho State Civic Symphony, asked selected members of our performing faculty a number of questions about storytelling in their respective fields. Participating were senior lecturer in dance Dr. Lauralee Zimmerly; assistant professor of theater Vanessa Ballam, whose expertise extends as well to opera performance and production; and assistant professor of music and symphony Director Dr. Grant Harville, an experienced vocalist and composer as well as a conductor. Their discussion ranges from the nature of storytelling within their particular art forms to the ways performer and audience interact to create unique events that seem to transcend time.

Brian Attebery (BA): What are your first thoughts when I say the word "narrative?" Would they be different if I used the term "storytelling?"

GRANT HARVILLE (GH): *"Narrative" connotes more abstraction for me—it puts me in mind of concepts like sequence, process, cause and effect. "Storytelling" sounds much less formal, and is associated more in my mind with childhood. I imagine the difference reflects the contexts in which I generally hear the terms. "Narrative" shows up in academic papers; "story" appears in phrases like "bedtime story," "story time," "campfire story," and in reference to genres associated with popular audiences: horror story, ghost story, love story. In an objective sense,* Don Giovanni *is absolutely a ghost story (and a horror story, and maybe a love story), but would generally only be described as such by someone (a concert promoter, perhaps) who wanted to undermine opera's highbrow reputation.*

The performer/theorist distinction may play into the use of the terms. "Storytelling" implies agency in ways that narrative does not: narrative is something a piece possesses; a story is something that is told. Among academic musicians—music theorists who study narrative and how the term applies to music—"narrative" is much more common. Theorists (with some controversy) rarely consider performance in analysis; narrative remains a part of a piece independent of its individual performances, and regardless of whether it's actually being performed at that moment or, indeed, whether it ever has been. To a performer, whatever narrative a piece possesses exists in the execution. I once heard a performer describe the difficulties of performing a certain a work with the phrase "it's hard to make it tell a story."

One of Patrick Sheridan's solo albums is called Storyteller, and in the liner notes he refers to every piece as a "story," rather than the more conventional "piece," "work," or "song." Again, I think this stems from his mission to popularize his craft. Interestingly, he has two other albums called Lollipops and Bonbons—conceptions of musical works that are much more static, as a single, unchanging object. A bonbon, in particular, is designed to be experienced as one single, delicious event.

VANESSA BALLAM (VB): *Narrative to me is primarily plot, characters, setting and sequence of events—the facts if you will. Storytelling, in the field of drama, can mean the revelation of a story through a variety of theatrical conventions. In dramatic form, storytelling allows the artist to both show and tell the story to an audience simultaneously. Through this process of showing a story as well as telling a story, I feel that the audience is better equipped to draw their own conclusions about those facts.*

Storytelling also lends itself to interpretation. For example, in the dramatic perspective, a playwright initially determines which details of the narrative they desire to highlight, then the director through their concept will decide how they want to communicate this particular playwright's story based on their own ideals and experience, and next the actors do the same with the creation of their characters. What is so exhilarating about this process is that every production of the same play will inevitably tell a slightly different tale. Storytelling requires an artistic lens. David Ball claims that, "There is no single 'correct' interpretation of any good play."

I think Mark Twain best described the difference between narrative and storytelling when he said, "Don't say the old lady screamed—bring her on and let her scream."

BA: This project deals with the many ways different disciplines deal with narrative. Is that something you have thought about in connection with your own field? Would you recommend any specific works that discuss the nature and functions of narrative?

VB: *I feel that narrative has a fundamental relationship with my field of theater. What we inherently strive for as theater artists is to communicate stories. Additionally, many plays actually employ the technique of using a narrator within the production to aid the audience in their journey with the story. However, I treat all of my characters as narrators whether that is their defined role by the playwright or not.*

The work that comes to mind in regards to narrative in my field is Stanislavski's An Actor Prepares *and specifically his identification of the actor's through-line and how it is meant to connect them to the heart of* the narrative as a whole. Even the writing style of An Actor Prepares: though it is used as a textbook for actors, it is actually written as narrative. Also, David Ball's book Backwards and Forwards *is a wonderful manual for taking a narrative text, breaking it down, and putting it back together to ensure maximum effective story communication to the audience. This text is used frequently as a tool in script analysis both for actors and directors.*

LAURALEE ZIMMERLY (LZ): *My field is dance—more specifically, I work creatively in the area of Modern Dance though my technical/performance training is informed by many styles of dance including jazz, tap, and ballet. I will even throw my athletic training in as a movement influence on my art form. In dance we usually speak of the movement text of any particular work and whether the work stays true to the movement narrative. That narrative might be related to a specific linear story line or tale being told, or it might be a non-linear idea/message or an abstract display of pure aesthetic values. Some dances also use words—a verbal text that goes along with the movement text.*

There are some influential discussions of the use of narrative in dance. The earliest I can think of is Lettres sur la danse et les ballet *by Jean-Georges Noverre (1758), where he explains that ballets need to be presented in such a way as to move them away from spectacle toward emotional and physical expression. Other works that inform my current thinking include Sondra Fraleigh's* Dance and the Lived Body, Researching Dance *by Fraleigh and Hanstein,* Feeling and Form *and other writings by Suzanne Langer, and* Semiotics of Dance *by Blanatiu.*

GH: *Virtually everyone who pursues a degree in music is going to encounter narrative-like descriptions of music. Graduate students in music theory will almost certainly encounter studies where the relationship between music and narrative is discussed explicitly. For those of us with performance degrees, these encounters are much rarer, for some even absent altogether. But the vast majority of music analysis presents music in ways that are at least analogous to narrative: as a sequence of events that bear relationships with one another. A narrative understanding of music is either common or intuitive enough that even performers who don't consider narrative consciously often ask themselves questions that have narrative whiffs about them: Where's the climax of this piece? How do these passages relate? How do I get from here to there? What's that note doing? What do I want that note to do?*

BA: Storytelling is usually thought of as a function of language. Do we neglect the non-linguistic aspects of narrative? Does your art form bring those to the forefront?

VB: *I think often the non-linguistic forms of narrative are neglected. However, in my art form the non-linguistic aspects of narrative are often just as important as the linguistic. In fact, my perspective is that it's those non-linguistic aspects that demand our attention as theater artists* and require that we produce these narrative works live. Playscripts are meant to be performed and embodied, not just read.

GH: I'm not sure I can answer the first question, though it seems that in some fields (film, ballet) non-linguistic storytelling is common, and I'd be surprised if people weren't aware of it or studying it. Music is different from other art forms in that it is not only non-linguistic, it's non-semiotic. Other arts depend on the audience's ability to convert what they see or hear into something else. Words on a page, actors on stage or film, paint on canvas: none of these are the "thing itself." Abstract visual art exists of course, but humans have a remarkable ability to see symbols or patterns in randomness (like constellations). It actually takes a fair amount of work to produce a painting (for instance) that prevents any sort of representation from taking place in the mind of the viewer. Music is the opposite; it's virtually impossible to represent anything in music without giving the listener a lot of help. (There are a fair number of people who don't agree, but I haven't seen or read anything that has changed my mind.)

I do a bit whenever I do a music appreciation class where I play "Baba Yaga" from Mussorgsky's Pictures at an Exhibition for students who've never heard it before. When I ask them to describe the music, not a single person mentions a clock in the shape of a house standing on chicken legs. But they of course will immediately recognize a visual image of such an object, even though it's fairly bizarre, and even if it's not especially realistic—that is, the image can be substantially stylized or iconic while remaining recognizable. It has to go through some pretty severe distortion before they can't tell what it is. But it's virtually impossible to represent the object in tones.

Since language is by definition semiotic, narrative as it exists in music must necessarily be non-linguistic.

One caveat: virtually every listener will assign emotional content to music, calling it "sad" or "jolly" or some other emotion. There are some pretty substantial philosophical problems with such descriptions, but they're near ubiquitous and consistent enough to be interesting. (Most people who have listened to a lot of western music will ascribe similar emotions to a given work.) When I provided introductions to movements of the Shostakovich Fifth Symphony at our performance last November, it wasn't to suggest that the music describes the political situation the composer was enduring at the time, and it was only partially to educate the audience about the 1930s Soviet Union—there are plenty of people who know more about it than I do. It was largely to bring the audience into a receptive space, where they could connect on an emotional level with the music.

LZ: Does storytelling neglect the non-linguistic aspects of narrative? I guess that would depend on whether the story is read aloud as a performing art piece or read as a text on a page! As a written text, storytelling does exactly what it is supposed to do—breathe and animate words into images in one's mind through the beautiful constructs of language. As a person who rather responds to movement and visual stimuli, I never object to written texts being translated into visual forms of presentation (plays, movies, etc.), but I respond to those presentations in a different way than I respond to the written word. Yes, dance and other forms of performing art bring non-linguistic aspects of narrative to the forefront. The visual image making of dance generates a kinesthetic response to the experience: a bodily—felt, visceral feedback by proxy to the action of the performance one is witnessing.

BA: Does storytelling in music, dance, etc., require a parallel text in words? For instance, can a piece of music tell a story without a title or other verbal clues?

GH: I suppose it depends on whether you believe that the resemblance of musical features to narrative features qualifies musical works as narratives themselves, rather than merely analogues of narratives. If so, then no extra-musical association (title, program, etc.) is necessary, and in this case, absolute music carries (is?) the narrative itself. Music has events which influence each other, moments of high and low energy, surprises, climaxes—any number of features that have equivalents in narratives of other types—but these features derive from the notes themselves rather than any externally imposed story.

Which is not to say that imposing extra-musical (representative) content onto music hasn't been tried frequently: opera, song, program music are all attempts at this. This can certainly be done well, but even at its best, it remains artificial. The representations are not inherent to the music. The best one can achieve is plausibility—Wagnerian leitmotifs may make dramatic sense, but they must be explained and they aren't exclusive; that is, any number of other musical themes might serve equally well.

VB: In my field, storytelling does not require a text in words. Absolutely, music and dance—and I would add theater performances—can tell a story without a title, text, or verbal cues. Personal anecdote: this past spring while judging the Idaho State University One Act Competition, I was completely overwhelmed by the storytelling of a group who shared their narrative without uttering a word. In fact, all of the performers were masked and we knew nothing about the piece going in. Therefore, the communication of the story was completely left to the physicalization of the actors as well as their relationships with each other. This performance was for me the best storytelling of the entire festival and I was so pleased to have hundreds of high school students present to witness its success.

LZ: I would say that dance requires no verbal cues, though most dance works have some sort of title, even if it is just one word. Sometimes a dance will use the same title as the music that accompanies it. Keep *in mind that dance does not require a musical text either! You have inspired me now to entitle my next project "no associative words"—and to even have a blank program! In an academic setting, we most often include a title and a one-paragraph description of our work as we realize that some of our audience will be new-to-dance viewers and will need cues about how to view dance, especially modern dance forms. I suppose it depends on how astute your dance audience is. In most instances I would like to tell an audience to "Just watch . . . just feel . . . then think!" and to avoid trying to attach a story to the experience. That being said, some dances, such as classical ballets, world dance forms, and dance rituals tend to be more discursive in their telling of tales, and it might add some understanding to the movement text to have an accompanying verbal text, especially if the experience is outside of the viewer's vernacular.*

BA: What is the relationship between the more abstract aspects of performance (pure music, movement, stagecraft, etc.) and the narrative aspects? Are those ever in conflict?

LZ: *The relationship of all these components (music, costumes, sets, lighting, location, text, makeup—and performers, because individual performers bring nuance) must come together to work toward the intention of the artwork. If one aspect doesn't support the movement text, then it is considered extraneous. There is sometimes a component of creating dance that serves to showcase the bodily abilities of the performer—hopefully, you can seamlessly integrate that into the intention of the work because otherwise it becomes divertissement, a distraction that doesn't support the intent. Movement dramaturgy allows me as the choreographer/creator to reflect on the structure of the action I have designed and to understand its association to theater, to music—and to visual art as well since I consider myself an image-maker.*

VB: *Easy answer: not with a good director. Being a director myself, I have to view all of these aspects as vital components to the storytelling. What I teach, and what I strive to practice myself, is strategic and synergistic use of all the theatrical elements and conventions to clarify my story. If any element is not in harmony with this goal (i.e., if it's there just for the sake of spectacle or humor) then it must be addressed and adjusted. There's no reason for it. We are here to communicate a narrative. Thankfully, in my field we get to have the rehearsal and technical process to guarantee the harmonious interaction of all of these elements.*

GH: *To be clear, it's worth pointing out that I consider "pure music" to have narrative content, so I'm not contrasting narrative vs. non-narrative content but rather representative vs. non-representative content.*

To answer the question, yes, frequently. Bad text setting, where the words and music fail to integrate in some meaningful way, is one example. At least as common is program music where the composer privileges extra-musical content over the music, resulting in a theoretically appropriate depiction of the program but destroying the musical narrative. (Liszt's worst music has this failing.)

When musical and extra-musical content come into conflict, the music "wins." A good program or text cannot save bad music; the fact that most extra-musical programs are childishly simple doesn't prevent the music that goes along with it from being great. (In such cases, the musical narrative is generally more sophisticated than the extra-musical one.) Some of the best vocal music is set to incomprehensible lyrics or a ludicrous plot. Plenty of people listen joyfully to music in languages they don't know, or with words that don't make sense.

One place to observe the music-rules-the-text phenomenon is in a church chorus. Hymns, by definition, have verses, and while first and second verses usually correspond well to the musical phrasing, some of the later ones often don't scan well to the melody: the musical phrases don't line up with the verbal phrases. When choruses encounter this discrepancy, they virtually always breathe where the music breaks the phrase, not where the text does so, despite receiving no instruction to that effect (and sometimes receiving instruction to do the opposite).

BA: One of the functions of narrative is to measure and comprehend time. Time is also inherently part of performance (it has tempos and rhythms; it occurs in time; you can't return to earlier portions as you can with a written text). Does your sense of performance address those two ways of existing in time?

GH: *This is something I think I'd have to think a lot more about before I had something insightful to say. I will say that other people have tried, and at least one person would claim that music at its best happens outside of time. (It's worth mentioning that an imagined performance, where the events can happen at different rates from those of sounding performances and where the audience—the imaginer—can indeed return to previous events, is a no less valid mode of performance than any other.)*

Two books to check out: David Epstein's Shaping Time *and Markand Thakar's* Looking for the "Harp" Quartet.

LZ: *Yes, Dance is ethereal, ghostlike . . . you perform it and it is gone. You can't hang it on your living room wall . . . though I did once auction off a dance work at a fundraiser that I offered to do on a daily basis for a month in someone's home space! It sold but the buyer only purchased the idea of it, as he didn't want to spend the time to watch it daily! When we speak of time or timing in dance we do so as it relates to the energy and quality of movement that we are constantly shaping to communicate the intent of the work. We work with tempo, duration, momentum, accents, meter, breath and other natural rhythms, and stillness to communicate a movement meaning.*

VB: *In theater we are able to shift time quite easily with the use of theatrical conventions. We can stop time; we can jump forward; we can jump backwards; we can move in slow motion; we can have moments onstage*

Narrative and the Performing Arts 171

frozen while others are moving in real time. The possibilities are endless provided the conventions are clear, well established and consistent. And of course all of this must be based on and supported by the text.

BA: Are there particular sorts of stories that work best in your art form, such as fairy tales, tragic falls, slices of ordinary life? Sorts that don't work as well?

LZ: I work mostly in the abstract use of movement, so this is a difficult question to answer since I rarely work to tell a story as opposed to exploring a quality of movement. But I can see all of these sorts of stories being able to work in dance . . . and there are dances that do work to communicate using all of these literary structures. I do choreograph occasionally for opera and musical theater productions, and in those situations, you are given the musical score and a script of words to be sung and a narrative to follow.

VB: I'm likely biased, but I feel that a good director with a clear vision and understanding of his story can succeed with any type of text. But I feel it is the director's responsibility to have a very specific justification for telling this particular story to this particular audience. There has to be a reason why. I would say that audience members tend to respond best to stories with which they identify, and therefore narratives dealing with the human condition tend to resonate more.

GH: Because it's easier to apply emotion to music than other sorts of extra-musical content, stories that receive musical treatment tend be somewhat melodramatic or psychological, or to project the 'feeling' of a thing rather than the thing itself. It's hard to get specific—love or sadness or majesty seems to come pretty easily to composers, but the specifics have to be imposed. We may be able to hear love, but we probably wouldn't be able to tell just by listening if the couple in the music is Romeo and Juliet *or* Pelleas and Melisande.

Of course, there's no reason to assume that sadness (the human emotion) and sadness (the musical feature) are the same thing. In fact, it's harder to come up with similarities between the two than differences.

Musical narrative can certainly be intricate and sophisticated, but again it's hard to bring intricacy of extra-musical content into music. So plots that depend on complexity and specificity of events (murder mysteries, for example) tend not to work well. Lots of composers set myths, perhaps because myth is supposed to have a timeless, universal (rather than specific) quality.

BA: Do you think of narrative differently depending on whether you are creating a piece of art, directing others, or performing yourself?

GH: Not necessarily. The goal is always to pace the events appropriately, to make sure whatever processes and relationships exist in the piece are presented comprehensibly, and that stays constant as the role changes.

VB: I do think of narrative differently depending on what function I am performing. As mentioned in my last answer, as the director I need to take someone else's narrative and gain a sound understanding of the story, a *clear justification as to why I must tell this story*, and a detailed concept to share with my cast and creative team so that we may communicate it together.

As a performer within a theatrical text, I am responsible for my portion of the narrative, which is usually called the through-line. I'm also responsible for merging the playwright's vision, the director's vision, and my own personal vision of my character and their detailed role within the story.

As a creator of a new work it's a different experience, as I have absolute power in regards to the narrative instead of working to synthesize someone else's narrative and ideas with my own.

LZ: Absolutely—it depends on the project I am working on and whether I am choreographing for myself or for other bodies and whether it is a work of my own creation. I also love to collaborate with others on projects because of the analytical process and dialogue that ensues as you decipher what it is that you are creating and watch the magic as it unfolds and reveals itself. I also enjoy the process of embodying the ideas of others—to add my overtones to their project. I think in any instance there is a different kind of listening that occurs—to inner voices and other voices.

BA: Is narrative an important part of teaching in your field? How?

VB: Narrative is the basis of more or less everything that I teach in all of my classes at Idaho State University as well as the basis of my professional career, whether it be an acting class, a directing class, a musical theater class or even a survey of theater class. The heart of all of my techniques and methodologies is narrative: it all comes down to clear storytelling and how effectively it is being communicated to the audience. Theater is meant to hold a mirror up to society and we do that through the form of narrative.

GH: As I mentioned before, this comes up mostly in music theory when some sort of analysis is taking place. Boring theorists describe musical objects; better ones describe their relationships and progression. Virtually all analysis of vocal music will describe the relationship between the textual and musical narratives.

LZ: Yes—sometimes we refer to the "semiotics of the movement" or the "movement gesture," following through with a "movement idea" or "movement text," especially in dance composition or dance improvisation classes where we are working with dance students to find their unique movement voice. In teaching modern dance we are not so concerned with aesthetic codification of movement but more with an authentic emergence of movement where a motion doesn't necessarily signify anything definite (as sign language does) but rather arouses a variety of images for the user or spectator. In this way, dance movement strives to be translucent and evocative to the individual viewer and does not necessarily tell the exact same story to every observer.

In other dance traditions such as Indian classical dance, the stories told are derived directly from ancient texts, and there are gestural signs (mudras) that communicate meanings and reveal actions, relationships, and feelings related to the telling of the story. In this kind of dancing there are semiotic conventions and a movement code that is an alternative expression to the verbal/literal one and in some ways is more accessible to illiterate populations. So in dance, we cultivate narrative in a variety of ways from imitative to abstract.

BA: To what extent is the "story" of a performance something that the performer has control over? How much of the story does the audience construct?

LZ: *Dance, as a live performing art, is a dialogue among creator, performers, and audience. As a choreographer, I am looking for an opportunity to express and for an audience to perceive. I am looking to strike a chord rather than force a specific note, so I am willing to give the semiosis or construction of understanding over to individual viewers to form their own meaning. I am rather unconscious in my approach to art making, my motivation being spontaneous gesture or action, or exteriorized emotionality, or an interior image, or the flashing of life, or . . . the list goes on. As an artist, I have a way of interpreting the world, while those who witness my work have their own way of interpreting the dancing discourse.*

VB: *One of my favorite concepts from Stanislavski is what he calls* **Communion**: *the idea that before communicating the subtle nuances of the play to an audience, an actor must commune with the rest of cast. They must be fully aware of themselves and the relationships between their characters. To achieve full communion, the actor must use all of their senses and an actor should be sensitive enough to respond precisely to what the audience is giving back.*

An actor really only has control over his own performance. However, that actor's performance should be shaped and molded not only by the director but by his fellow actors and also by the audience on any given night. This is why I vastly prefer live theater over film and television.

Hopefully, through that effective communion the audience will also be able to construct a complete story for themselves.

GH: *The performer has a huge impact on the narrative. The performer can emphasize certain events (dynamically, agogically) and deemphasize others, thus establishing, even creating, relationships in the piece. The performer chooses the pace at which events unfold.*

Perhaps the greatest contribution the audience makes is to extra-musical content. As I've said, music doesn't carry objective extra-musical content well, but it's easy for audiences to impose their own extra-musical content on it, based on their own experiences. Someone who's seen Fantasia *is going to assign a different plot to* Rite of Spring *from someone who's only seen the ballet, or someone who's seen neither.*

BA: How do you think you formed your own sense of narrative, and especially the difference between stories that are effective versus ineffective or trivial versus profound? Was it from oral storytelling? Books? Other media? Do any specific examples come to mind?

GH: *Hm, not sure. I can say that I like works where things aren't spoon-fed to me, where the composer trusts the audience to get it without beating you over the head with it. I suppose reading Gene Wolfe has contributed to that some—a lot of authors seem crude in comparison—but I hated* Titanic *long before I liked Wolfe's* The Book of the New Sun. *I like works where beautiful passages/set pieces/images fit comprehensibly into the whole. I guess that's a sort of scale-independence: where the sentence is as good as the book, where the melody is as good as the movement. Brahms was good at that; Rimsky-Korsakov wasn't.*

LZ: *I rely on a variety of life's adventures to inform my narrative. I hope some of my work is profound and that some is trivial and fun! I trust that in either case it will be worthy of viewing on some level. Marion Scott, one of my choreography professors at UCLA, offered this axiom for creativity: "Trust Yourself, Don't Judge Yourself, Let Come What May," to which I have added "Tolerate Confusion." Don't put too many stipulations on your creativity or constantly edit or nothing will come about. Allow yourself some failures—not everything can be good. We have all burnt a turkey dinner or two along the way!*

Specific Examples?

- *I am a recreational scuba diver, so my world travels have allowed me to experience all sorts of oceans and seas. I have used this "otherworldly-underwatermotion" to inform a work I created called "subAqueous."*
- *"DueLLeague" was a duet I created with a colleague to explore the nature of working together while, at the same time, being competitors for salary, promotion, and funding.*
- *Oliver Sacks wrote a book called* The Man Who Mistook His Wife for a Hat *that told clinical tales from his days as a neurologist. He described one case study in which a man could not recognize his own leg as belonging to his body and would try to push it away from himself. This was an intriguing notion that inspired a movement text that led me to create a work entitled "This Is the Way It Is . . . and the Way It Is Always Going to Be."*
- *One of my recent works was inspired by a costuming concept. My mother had all these party dresses in her closet that she sewed in the 1960s. I used the memory of her making and wearing these dresses at parties along with a poem by Sonja Mesher: if the dress is ripped it can be mended, if it is shredded it can be lined with net for strength and longevity. dirty, will wash it, iron and air it, loosely bind into keeping, a collection, memory of those halcyon daze. will buy a suitable hanger.*

- *I raided my mom's closet and gave new life to these dresses by putting them on stage in a work I called ":: the dress ::." The work also used text projected on the backdrop comprised of quotes from the fashion industry of that period, such as "'Give a girl the right shoes and she can conquer the world.'—Marilyn Monroe." The work also served the purpose of getting my mom to clean out some of the stuff in her closet! (Come on, the dresses had been there since 1968!!!).*

VB: *I formed my own sense of narrative through live theater and specifically operatic rehearsal and performance from a very young age. I sat in on numerous operatic rehearsals as a child and I was fascinated with the idea that it only takes one person to communicate a story to an audience. I remember sitting in on a rehearsal for the opera* Carmen *and watching a very nice woman whom I had met transform herself physically and mentally to portray the role of Carmen in a rehearsal. It didn't matter that she was singing in* French! *Because of her specificity and embodiment of her given circumstances from the narrative, I believed her and I was transported to Seville, Spain, even at the age of five. She was much more interesting than the coloring book I had brought with me to the rehearsal.*

What I love about this realization is that, technically, a person doesn't even require a set or a costume to effectively tell that story. I learned that sets, lights, and costumes can enhance the story but what needs to be at the heart is truthful storytelling

I have always had a very strong sense of imagination, which I think is very helpful and effective for me as both a performer and a director in regards to my ability to successfully tell a story.

10 Stories and Objects
Narrative and the Construction of Connective Links in an American Quilting Guild

Sonja Launspach[1]

Linguistics studies language, and language is the medium through which society and culture are created. It is the medium through which most stories are traditionally told. Narratives have provided a rich ground for linguistics research and analysis. Aspects of narrative that researchers in the discipline focus on include what constitutes a narrative, the structure of narrative, and the functions of narratives in discourse.

I first became aware of narrative as a field of study in graduate school. During this period of my studies, I became acquainted with the theories of Barthes, Genette, Bauman, Propp, Bakhtin, and the Russian formalists, as well as the groundbreaking work by linguistic scholars such as Labov, Chafe, Polanyi, and Heath. In addition to these theoretical studies, I also presented a conference paper on narrative. More recently, I've explored the work of Fludernick, Bruner, Ochs, Norrick, Bamberg, De Fina, and Georgakopoulou.

Like many other scholars in linguistics, I collect language data, in my case, Conversation Analysis data, in order to explore a research question or set of research questions, or to examine language use in a particular context. Naturally occurring linguistic data is rich and can be examined from many different analytical viewpoints and levels of language. Throughout my various research projects, narratives are always present in the background, since they are part of the backdrop of all conversations and social interactions. So I have always had an awareness of narratives, even when I didn't always have an opportunity to foreground narratives as the primary object of study.

As a sociolinguist, I am interested in how language is used by speakers in everyday contexts and social situations. During the course of my research, I have been struck more and more by the centrality of narrative to our lives as human beings—how important stories are on so many different levels. Narratives are a basic component of social life. They play a key role in constructing individual identities and constituting social communities. Who we are is created through the stories we tell.

Part of my research involves investigating small group interaction, and one of the groups that I study is quilting guilds. Although my original investigation of the quilting guild focused on compliments, it was clear to me from the beginning that stories were a key part of the group culture. Communities, such as the quilting guild, use narratives in a variety of ways, including passing on accumulated wisdom, beliefs, and common values; sharing knowledge; creating and maintaining cultural practices; imparting lessons; and providing models for accepted behavior.

Quilting is an everyday act of creation, both verbal and material. Stories are a form of verbal art that provides links to the quilts, a form of crafted art. Thus stories are an important social and cultural resource that functions in the quilting guild on several different levels—most centrally, they serve to promote the group's core activities—creating quilts and creating a community centered around the act of quiltmaking.

Stories are used to form connective links at different levels of discourse. For instance, stories in the quilting guild function to (1) construct a connection between the quilter and the quilted object, (2) construct a connection between a quilter and other quilters—as quilters—creating that specific identity for the women, and (3) construct a connection between the quilter and the quilting community as represented by the local quilting guild. This chapter will focus its discussion on the relationship between the stories and the quilted objects (objects because modern quilters make more than just traditional quilts).

Quilting Culture and the Quilting Guild

Quilting has long been a communal activity. Women have practiced it individually and in groups in various guises from Japan to Zimbabwe. Some of the earliest quilted objects date from before the first century CE and have been found in Asia. Most of the evidence suggests that quilting was brought to Europe by the returning crusaders, although some quilted objects were probably brought into Europe by traders earlier than that (Colby 1971). Quilting, then, spread to the United States through colonization.

The United States has a long history of quilting and associated traditions and practices such as the quilting bee. Quilting became more prevalent in the late eighteenth and nineteenth centuries when women were no longer responsible for spinning, dying, and weaving the fabrics used by their families. After commercial fabric became readily available, quilting traditions spread across the continent with the westward movement, and quilting thrived until the middle part of the twentieth century when quilting was considered "old fashioned and dated" (History of Quilts 2009). However, in the 1970s, quilting experienced a revival, and out of this revival, the quilting guild emerged (Cerny, Eicher, and Delong 1993; Langellier 1992; Ronning 1991).

Quilting guilds share some of the characteristics of other craft guilds, such as a formal organization, but they have also developed other more egalitarian characteristics more in keeping with the needs of this new generation of quilters. They focus on promoting the craft/art of quilting and have developed both formal and informal methods of teaching and support for quilters (Quilts 2013). Many different aspects come together to shape the cultural and discourse practices within a quilting guild. For example, group norms and values such as egalitarian organizational principles, group solidarity, and cooperative interactional styles work together to determine the types of interactional strategies used by the women in the guild (Cerny 1992; Cerny et al. 1993; Langellier 1991).

One reason that quilting guilds use egalitarian principles that emphasize solidarity as a group norm is that many of the women who join quilting guilds learn to quilt as adults, from other women in the guild, rather than learning as children from mothers, aunts, or grandmothers, as had been the case in the past. Group values that stress community and connection create an environment where women are recognized for their particular talents and each contributes to the group; no one is directly criticized and each person's work or contribution is praised and encouraged (Cerny 1992; Langellier 1991). This preference for stressing community provides a supportive environment for newcomers where beginners' work is always encouraged and praised (Ice 1993). In addition, many guild members see the guild as a place that nurtures intergenerational relationships in a time when families are more and more scattered, allowing older women to stand in lieu of family members as teachers and mentors as they pass on shared knowledge and quilting lore to newer women in the craft.

Another group value, creativity, is central to quilting culture. "Quiltmaking is a quintessential form of 'everyday creativity,'" the type of creativity that encompasses the creative expressions of ordinary people in a variety of media (World Quilts 2013b). Women's creativity in the guild is regularly shared and recognized in show-and-tell events, workshops, and quilt shows. As part of both individual and communal expressions of creativity, quilters acquire and share knowledge about quilting tradition and sewing practices. Even though modern quilters often use different tools and techniques to make quilts, they are still cognizant of and feel a connection to the long history and traditions of quilting. This connection with the past is actualized in daily practice by the creation of links between objects, between techniques, and between quilters.

In quilting guilds, members come together because they share a passion for quiltmaking and for learning about quilting techniques, traditions, and history. These two aspects, a shared interest and continued learning (not necessarily formal learning), categorize the quilting guild as a community of practice. A community of practice is characterized by mutual engagement, a jointly negotiated enterprise, and a shared repertoire. The women in the guild meet regularly (mutual engagement). Their joint enterprise is, of course, the quilts and quiltmaking. The shared repertoire consists of common ways of speaking about quilting, the vocabulary of the craft, as well as the interactional norms for the group—what to say, how to say it, when to say it, and who to say it to.

In the quilting guild, as in many other communities of practice, members learn through participation. When new members join the guild, they need to learn the socially accepted quilting practices and shared repertoire. In quilting guilds, the context of socialization is both collective and individual in that individuals draw upon the collective knowledge of the community to create quilts that express their personal experiences (Cerny et al. 1993). Thus, as new members enter the guild, they need to develop competence in both how to quilt and how to talk about quilting. Learning how to quilt takes place both by observing and by being shown techniques individually and in workshops. Learning how to talk about quilting happens interactionally.

These two aspects, a shared interest and continued learning, form the core of many of the social practices within the quilting guild. As a community of practice, the quilting guild provides an excellent interactional context to explore how narratives are used to construct and reinforce community practices. In constructing narratives, the quilters draw upon the interactional resources of quilting traditions and practices.

Narrative is deeply embedded in quilting culture on several different levels. First, the quilt itself is a story. How it was made, by whom it was made, for whom it was intended, and for what occasion is one story. Second, the patterns tell stories; the names themselves conjure up images: Cross and Crown, Ohio Star, Log Cabin, Robbing Peter to Pay Paul, Star of Bethlehem, Flying Geese, Rocky Road to Kansas, Jacob's Ladder, Tree of Life, and Aunt Sukey's Choice. Third, the fabric itself can tell stories. Many traditional patchwork quilts are made from scraps, so each piece of fabric started as something else before it ended up in the quilt and has its own story—who wore it and on what occasion.

The women tell stories to each other as they sew their blocks and quilt together. The women in the quilting guild I studied told several different types of stories: personal experience narratives about daily life unrelated to quilting, story rounds on quilting topics, exemplar stories, how I did it stories, situating narratives, and covert value stories. These narratives emerge spontaneously as part of the ongoing talk about the various quilted objects they had brought to share and discussions of quilting practices.

While the quilting narratives, like many conversational narratives, are built around a tellable event, the tellable event in these narratives deals with some aspect of quilting rather than some aspect of the narrator's daily life. The stories are related to various types of quilting practices. Since the focus of the guild is creating quilts and other quilted objects, such as jackets, wall hangings, and pillows, the object itself is central to the discourse. Talk in a quilting guild will always, on some level, be related to the objects under construction. This relationship between talk and objects also extends to narrative.

However, few studies, if any, have examined the central role of talk/discourse in creating and maintaining quilting culture. While Fitzpatrick's

(2007) work studied the acquisition of literacy in a quilting guild, she did not analyze the discourse from a linguistic perspective. This study fills that gap by analyzing the role(s) of narratives to construct links between the quilted objects, material culture, and social and cultural practices of the group. Specifically in this chapter, I will present two stories that represent two different connective links between quilter and object: alignment frames and covert values.

My analysis of the stories will encompass two levels: discourse and structure. Central to my research in the larger project are the functions these stories perform for the group. How do the stories create and recreate group norms? How are they used to teach group quilting practices, and in this case, how do they connect to quilted objects on display? Since discourse functions are signaled through structure, the structure of the narrative is equally important. The linguistic elements the quilters use, tense, repetition, reported speech, and the order of the clauses as well as how the women combine these structures all contribute to the meaning(s) of each narrative. Speakers make creative use of the linguistic resources at their disposal, and the quilters combine these resources to construct narratives that serve important individual and cultural/group functions.

Data and Methodology

The Pine Creek Guild is a formal organization located in the southeastern United States. It collects dues, has regular meetings, has a resource library, and sponsors a yearly quilt show. The women meet every other Tuesday evening at a local school. Individuals bring in projects and works in progress to share, give demonstrations of different techniques, or work together on joint projects. There were an average of ten people present at the sessions I attended. The women in the guild were white, middle class, and ranged in age from late twenties upward to sixties.

When I first approached the members of the quilting guild to do an ethnographic study of their guild meetings, I was told I could do so only if I already knew how to quilt and would participate in the group's activities. They made this stipulation because they had had someone earlier try to study the group who had asked dumb questions and otherwise made a nuisance of him or herself, and the women did not wanted to repeat that experience. Since I knew how to quilt and had already participated in a quilting group when I lived in the Midwest, their request did not present a problem. In essence, the quilters were placing me in the role of a participant observer, although none of them had ever heard of such a thing. Being a quilter and being a researcher situated me in an in-between space. I was both an insider, since I was an experienced quilter, and an outsider, since I was not a member of their community. As a participant observer, I attended the quilting guilds meetings, shared my own quilting works in progress, and at the same time, I recorded the guild meetings and videotaped the technique demonstrations.

Over a three-month period, I collected eight-and-a-half hours of audio and videotape.

Since narrative is an integral part of conversation, for this study, I'm using Conversation Analysis (CA) as my methodological framework. One of the main goals of CA is to understand how ordinary people use talk to organize their social worlds. Conversation Analysis focuses on identifying the methods and social and linguistic resources people use in conversation to contribute to conversations, to interpret what others say, and to decide how they should act based on the interactional context. Through conversation, we talk our lives into being. If analysts look at how talk-in-interaction is organized, we will see how social practices are organized. How speakers organize and structure their talk provides the researcher (and speakers) with insights into the strategies used in every day social interactions to negotiate with others and accomplish goals. It reveals the unconscious social rules that let us communicate with each other through spoken language. Extending this type of detailed analysis from individuals to groups, such as the quilting guild, will allow us to uncover how groups utilize different kinds of verbal practices and interactional strategies to maintain the coherence of the group and group norms.

As part of an exploration of conversation structure, researchers in CA have examined the mechanics of how narratives naturally emerge as part of the conversation. (Goodwin 1984; Jefferson 1978; Sacks 1972, 1974, 1978). More recent studies on narrative have explored the structural components of narratives (Labov 1972; Labov and Waletzky 1967; Ochs 1997), analyzed the social functions of narratives in different contexts (Harris 2005; Holmes 2005, 2006; Majors 2004), and examined narratives as performance events (Bauman 1986; Langellier 1999; Langellier and Peterson 2004). Research has also focused on how narratives in conversation function to create different types of identities for speakers (Norrick 2000; Ochs and Capps 1997, 2001), and function to demonstrate and reinforce shared values—especially group values (Baynham 2011; De Fina 2008; Norrick 1997; Ochs and Taylor 1995). In addition, other studies emphasize the importance of listeners to the construction and meaning of narratives in interaction (Johnstone 1990; Norrick 2000; Ochs and Capps 2001; Tannen 1978).

Narrative Analysis

As a resource, narratives can be employed by both individuals and groups to transmit shared meanings and experiences (Bruner 2010; Phillipsen 1989). Quilting guild members can use narratives to create socially situated meanings around objects and activities relevant to the cultural practices of quilting (Carbaugh 1990). Exploring community-specific uses of narratives can give us insight into socially situated community practices of quilting and the construction of a shared group identity. While stories perform a variety of functions in a quilting guild, this chapter will focus on only one: the formation of connective links. Each narrative has a corresponding quilted object or practice with which it is linked, and all of the features in the narrative are being used to present the quilted object and/or technique within a specific context and purpose.

Another thing that facilitates the predominance of narrative in this community of practice is an interactional norm for long turns. In the guild, speakers often either take an uninterrupted long turn supported by backchannel tokens (hmm, uhm) or a series of shorter turns prompted by questions from their listeners, allowing them to remain as the main speaker over a longer stretch of talk. This use of the floor probably developed as a means to facilitate the joint enterprise of this group—creating and sharing knowledge about quiltmaking and other quilting practices. This contrasts with other types of conversational interactions, where prospective narrators usually need to request a long turn (Goodwin 1984; Norrick 2000; Ochs and Capps 2001).

The two stories that will be discussed in this chapter are part of a larger data corpus. They are both told by Lisa.[2] Outgoing and well liked, Lisa is a "core" member of the guild. She often travels to other states to attend classes and symposiums on quilting. Based on her long-term membership and extensive variety of quilting experiences, she frequently assumes a central role in discussing and sharing quilting techniques. The two stories presented represent two different examples of the way that narrative is used to construct connections between the quilting objects and the women. The first, a situating narrative, provides an alignment frame for viewing quilting blocks made with a new technique, while the second, a covert value narrative, functions as a means to express shared norms and experiences that are not valued positively outside the quilting culture. Since narrative works at both an interaction level and a structural level, the chapter will include both levels as part of the analysis.

Situating Narratives: *THIS IS A STORY*

Situating narratives are used to create a frame for both seeing/perceiving and understanding the elements of quilting presented in the narrative. They prepare and situate the quilted objects or quilting practices for the listeners. Furthermore, situating narratives are embedded within a larger interactional frame. Each frame contains two elements: (1) the narrative, and (2) the expansion and integration sequence, which follows the narrative. In this particular story, the narrative provides the necessary contextual information for seeing the quilting blocks, as well as connecting a new technique to a familiar setting, thus legitimizing the technique for the listeners. The discussion will focus on how the narrative situates the objects and communicates the stance of the narrator as well as briefly describes the negotiation of the integration of the new quilting technique presented in the narrative into the group's knowledge base and quilting practices.

Lisa told this narrative during the guild meeting's show-and-tell activity. Show and tell is a tradition in quilting culture. Each woman shows what she

Stories and Objects 183

is working on by putting her blocks (or quilt top) out on a table and the rest of the group comments on her work. In this particular show-and-tell event, Ellen has asked Lisa to show what she's working on. At first, Lisa claims that she hasn't done anything new, but then she concedes. She does have a project she can share—but it's not one that she considers new. However, instead of taking out her quilt blocks to share, Lisa launches into a narrative. The narrative is given in (1). (Transcription conventions can be found at the end of this chapter).

(1) (L=Lisa, A=Anne)
1 L: This is a story now.
2   you got to listen,
3   to the story.
4   this lady comes down,
5   and looks into our room
6   where we're quilting at Thomson house.
7   °Oh I used to quilt.
8   (name) says oh she does beautiful work.
9   but she never comes down. (1.2)
10   to visit us.°
11   ((louder)) and everybody seems to understand t<u>oo</u>,
12   I don't know why they understand.
13   but they understand.
14   °and finally she says that she's made this quilt from strips,°
15   and I've been thinking,
16   you know I need to use up some of my strips,
17   an (whatnot)
18   and so we finally force her to g<u>o</u> up,
19   and get her quilt.
20   and she comes down with this <u>rea</u>:lly n<u>eat</u> quilt. ((louder))
21   <u>a</u>ll scraps.
22   <u>a</u>ll different colors.
23   and <u>e</u>very single piece of f<u>a</u>bric in there,
24   is something else that she has made.
25 A: Oh, uh-huh=
26 L: =Over the y<u>ea</u>rs.
27   an' so I thought that's how I'm using my scraps,
28   so (.)
29   I came home and,
30   one block a day
31   every since two weeks ago.
32   I have been (.) [ma::: ((laughter)) ((puts blocks out))

The narrative recounts a past experience Lisa has had quilting at Thomson House.³ In the narrative, Lisa uses the narrative to situate the quilt blocks and the techniques used to make them. She uses the different background elements of the story not only to orient her listeners to the setting but also to situate the blocks/technique within a familiar context, the weekly quilting session at Thomson House, as well as to introduce a new solution to a common dilemma: how to use up fabric scraps. In addition to providing a context for the blocks themselves, the narrative also serves to introduce the technique—an innovative approach to using scraps—to the group.

The story provides a frame or schema for the other women to view and assess the quilt blocks. Thus the story is crucial to understanding the quilt blocks since it guides the viewers in the appropriate way to "see" the quilt blocks before they even see them. The narrative's function in the group doesn't end there. Situating narratives provide a starting point for both discussion and negotiation of the idea/viewpoint relative to the quilted objects represented in the narrative by the narrator. In the talk that follows the presentation of Lisa's quilting blocks, the expansion and integration sequence, the group uses the narrative and the quilted objects together to expand on the elements in the narrative and on the blocks. Thus the narrative functions as a means to both represent and share new knowledge—knowledge which can then be integrated into the group's practices.

The talk following *THIS IS A STORY* is divided into the following parts: (1) Lisa's "How I did" it sequence. (2) Expansion on sewing techniques. (3) Expansion on design elements. (4) What to do with blocks using this technique. The expansion and integration sequence gives the women a discursive space to negotiate how this new approach will be integrated into both their personal quilting knowledge and the group's collective knowledge. Further, this interactional segment gives the other group members an opportunity to challenge, expound on, or transform the specified identity for the objects/technique established by the narrator.

The story then becomes a bridge that connects the original quilter's experiences/technique to a new context and a new set of quilting blocks as well as providing/contributing new quilting knowledge to the quilting guild. Different structural elements in the narrative also work together to build the connective function of narrative content.

- Original quilter—>Lisa—> to audience
- Original quilter's technique—>Lisa's blocks—> potential use of technique by Lisa's audience.

Thus the situating narrative forms connections between the quilted objects and quilting practices on both an individual and group level.

Covert Value Narratives: *WE CERTAINLY DO*

Covert value stories allow quilters to acknowledge and secretly value aspects of quilting culture that are often represented negatively outside the quilting guild, especially by family and non-quilting friends. For most quilters, quilting is a creative passion, yet it is often misunderstood. "Because in contemporary life quilting is not a necessity (and indeed may be a luxury), it is not always legitimated as an activity worthy of time, space, and resources" (Stalp 2006, 121). Unlike men, women are pressured to put family responsibilities before their own creative endeavors, thus creating an internal conflict for many quilters.

One conflict that can arise is over the acquisition of quilting supplies. Many quilters feel they have to justify or hide their quilting supplies—especially the fabric stash. The fabric stash is a central element in modern quiltmaking. The stash represents a quilter's creative process on several levels—first, it provides the raw materials for quiltmaking and second, selecting, collecting, and curating the fabric and other quiltmaking supplies is a creative process in and of itself (Stalp 2006). While a fabric stash is a vital part of a woman's identity as a quilter, she must often contend with misunderstandings and misrepresentations about this part of the quilting process by non-crafting family and friends.

Because of this, the stash is a source of many types of stories among quilters and these narratives function as a way for women to value their stash by expressing a positive orientation toward this key component of modern quilting, while at the same time, resisting the negative perceptions of those outside the group. Thus covert value stories allow the women to celebrate certain aspects of quilting culture, and at the same time, they acknowledge the problematic attitudes of non-quilters with whom the quilters interact in their daily lives

The story discussed here is told by Lisa as part of a story round on fabric collecting, and it is the second story in a sequence of three. The stories about fabric come after Ann has complimented one of Lisa's fabrics and Lisa's admission that she only bought a few yards as well as her regret that she didn't buy more. This prompts Nancy to read a list of excuses for buying fabric from a book. Her reading of the list is followed by the two other stories on fabric collecting. The story Lisa tells is a retelling of a story from an article in a quilting magazine, so this is a story about a third person rather than one drawn from her own personal experience.

(2) (L=Lisa, H=Hannah, A=Anne, GP=group)
1 L: All right.
2   have-have yall read the-the. (1.0)
3   oh gosh I think it was Patchwork Pattern.
4   well if you have you're gonna have to help me,
5   cause I don't remember the whole thing.
6   but it was an a:rticle about someone, who had come into a who:le bu:nch of fa:bric.
7   (1.6) a::nd (.) the reason she had come into this whole bunch of fabric,
8   is (.) that (.) she was the friend of somebody in a quilt guild,

9	and (.) th<u>a</u>t (.) particular person was a friend of a woman who d<u>ie</u>d.
10	'kay-it was long-you know,
11	so she didn't even know this woman.
12	but she was writing about her.
13	(0.8)
14	and after she d<u>ie</u>d.
15	an she says obviously this woman did not intend to die.
16	(.) when she did.
17 GP:	Laughter
18 L:	Because her husb<u>a</u>nd would start cleaning out the stuff,
19	and he (0.7) open up a drawer an there would be a couple of pieces of lingerie on the top,
20	an underneath ((smile in her voice)) it was a stack of fabric.
21 GP:	Hahha.
22 L:	He said he found fabric beh<u>i</u>nd ((smile in voice))
23	the soup c<u>a</u>ns in the k<u>i</u>tchen. [hahha
24 GP:	[Laughter
25 H:	[Oh my.
26 L:	Everything all the drawers were all neatly. (0.5)
27	you know placed.
28	and every dr<u>a</u>wer.
29	((hits the table)) an every kitchen cabinet.
30	((hits table)) an every bathroom cabinet.
31	((hits table)) had fabric stuck hbehhhinhd [hahahah
32 A:	[Uhummm hahhaha
	(6.4)
33 H:	We know people like th<u>a</u>t don't we.
34	[maybe not quite that baə::d.
35 A:	[We certainly do.
36	(1.3)
37	we certainly do.

The story presents a humorous account of a widower finding his wife's fabric stash concealed all over the house. The story is divided into several parts. The beginning of the narrative sets the scene and clarifies the relationships between the woman writing the article and the woman who died (lines 6–9). In lines 18–27, Lisa uses repetition and delay to set up her listeners for the climax (lines 28–31). The last part (lines 33–37) depicts evaluation of the story. Although, Lisa is the main storyteller, her listeners participate in the storytelling event with their laughter and encouraging comments. The final evaluation of the story is done, not by Lisa, but by Anne and Hannah, two of the other quilters in the group.

The evaluation of the story connects the events in the story back to this particular quilting group. This is a story told in the third person about a stranger to the women in the group. However, at the end of the story, there is a shift from the third person to the first person, "we"—connecting the type of experience related in the story to these quilters. Next, in lines 33–34, Hannah acknowledges that they know people who hide fabric from their spouse, but she mitigates the negative view of this in line 34, "they/the people they know are not as bad." Ann's agreement overlaps with Hannah's remark. These final lines (lines 33–37) show an affiliation with the practice of collecting/hiding fabric—both collecting lots of fabric and having to hide it.

This is a funny story. In some ways it is an inside joke—only another quilter would understand, and find funny, why one would have to hide their fabric stash in the pantry. The humor is used to celebrate the woman's creative solution to conceal how large her stash was; at the same time, it highlights the ridiculousness of the situation. Thus both the use of humor and the story itself highlight and interrogate the tensions between quilting values and outsider attitudes toward quilting practices. The story frames fabric collecting as a contested activity in the intersection between quilting culture and values, and the social values and behaviors expected of women in their mundane lives. This type of narrative is one resource the community has to negotiate the tension between the values of the quilting community and the role restrictions placed on women, especially the restrictions on women's leisure time.

This type of story, one that expresses covert values such as attitudes toward collecting fabric, connects and reaffirms values toward the raw material needed to create quilts and other quilted objects. Like many of the narratives told by the quilters, covert value narratives provide ways of expressing links between the material objects necessary for quilting, such as the fabric, and quilting practices/culture. This story also illustrates the interconnections between women who quilt, even when they don't know one another.

- Woman writing story is—> connected to friend—> who is connected to someone in a quilting guild
- Quilting Guild member—> connected to woman who died

Structural Elements of Narrative

Narratives, like all speech acts, are put together in very specific ways. The various ways the linguistic elements can be arranged are resources for the quilters (and all speakers) to communicate meanings in the stories effectively. The quilters make use of two fundamental types of resources to create narratives: 1) social/discourse resources of the community and 2) the linguistic resources available to the narrator. These linguistic resources include syntactic elements, tense, interjections, asides—or stepping out of the story world—repetition, choices of details, reported speech, and gestures, as well as raised pitch or volume. This section will discuss the narrator's use of foreshadowing, evaluative comments, parallel syntactic structures, and reverbalization.

Foreshadowing

Foreshadowing, as its name implies, is used by narrators to hint at what's to come as well as to build anticipation and suspense.

This is a Story

In line 8, Lisa's positive evaluation foreshadows her later description of the original quilter's work. Lines 14–16 also foreshadow the main point of the story—the use of scraps.

(1)
8   (name) says oh she does beautiful work.
14 finally she says that she's made this quilt from strips. {softer}
15 and I've been thinking,
16 you know I need to use up some of my strips,

We Certainly Do

In the lines 14–16, Lisa sets up expectations for her listeners by hinting that there was something the dead woman did not do or expect.

(2)
14 and after she di*ed*.
15 an she says obviously this woman did not intend to die.
16 (.) when she did.
17 GP: laughter

Evaluative Comments

Evaluative comments are an important part of all conversational narratives. They keep the audiences' interest; they focus listeners' attention on certain elements of the story, and they provide the answer to why—why the narrator is telling the story. According to Norrick (2000), evaluative comments "serve to signal the teller's attitude and cue the hearers' expectations" (35). Evaluative comments can occur anywhere in the narrative and different story elements can be used to evaluate the ongoing action of the story.

This Is a Story

Lisa uses evaluative comments such as those in lines 11–16 to delay the description of the actual quilt in the story as well as to set up, for her listeners, her connection to the quilt. In line 14, she sandwiches a key piece of information between two sets of evaluative remarks.

(3)
11 ((louder)) and everybody seems to understand t<u>oo</u>,
12 I don't know why they understand,
13 but they understand.
14 and finally she says that she's made this quilt from strips. ((softer))
15 and I've been thinking,
16 you know I need to use up some of my strips,

We Certainly Do

Lisa uses evaluative comments and repetition of the phrase "a whole bunch of fabric," in lines 6–7, to focus her listener's attention on fabric collecting. Next, she uses lines 10–12 to provide a context of what comes next in the story, as well as to remind her listeners of the circuitous set of relationships between the woman who wrote the article and the woman who hid the fabric.

(4)
6 but it was an <u>a</u>:rticle about someone, who had come into a wh<u>o</u>:le b<u>u</u>:nch of f<u>a</u>:bric.
7 () a::nd (.) the reason she had come into this whole bunch of fabric,
(5)
10 'kay-it was long-you know,
11 so she didn't even know this woman.
12 but she was writing about her.

Parallel Structures and Repetition

In narrative, parallel structures and repetition are a key grammatical component of narrative and perform many different organizational functions. Both repetition and parallel structures occur on several levels: words, phrases, clauses, groups or units of information, and theme. They can be used to "accentuate central events," create "dramatic effect," and "highlight evaluations" (Norrick 2000, 59, 61, 63).

This Is a Story

In lines 18, 19, and 20, Lisa uses parallel syntactic verb phrases to focus her listener's attention on the original object/the woman's quilt. Here the repetition of the verb phrases functions to create dramatic effect.

(6)
18 and so [we$_{NP}$] [finally force her to g<u>o</u> up,$_{VP}$] (and NP VP)
19 and [get her quilt.$_{VP}$] (and VP)
20 and [she $_{NP}$] [comes down with this r<u>ea</u>:lly n<u>ea</u>t quilt.$_{VP}$] (and NP VP)

Next, in lines 22–24, she describes the fabric in the quilt using both parallel noun phrases and lexical reverbalizations.

(7)
21 all scraps.
22 all different colors. (elaborates on scraps)
23 and every single piece of fabric in there, (recharacterized as scraps of different colors)
24 is something else that she has made.

In line 23, "all" is replaced by "every single piece," while the terms "scraps," "different colors," and "piece of fabric" all build up to the climax in line 27 (an' so I thought that's how I'm using my scraps). Lisa uses syntactic parallelism and the repetition of short phrases to create suspense, build the description of the object, and delay the climax of the story. In this way, she heightens the dramatic effect, and, more importantly, this grammatical foregrounding keys her listeners into the most salient point—the unexpected use of scraps.

We Certainly Do

This story utilizes repetition and parallelism on two levels: (1) syntax and (2) story elements. Storytellers often repeat events several times in a row to build suspense. Repetitions of threes also serve to focus the attention on the third element as the story gradually builds up to it—here the third element in excerpt (8) is "all the drawers." The listeners' attention is focused on the drawers and what's in them. Of course, by this time in the story, the listeners expect the drawers to contain fabric. This set of repeated elements in excerpt (8) also sets up the final repetition in the resolution of the story, which immediately follows in lines 28–31 (except 9).

(8)
9   and he () open up a drawer an there would be a couple of pieces of lingerie on the top,
20 an underneath {smile in her voice} it was a stack of fabric.
21 GP: hahha.
22 L: he said he found fabric behind ((smile in voice))
23 the soup cans in the kitchen. [hahha
24 GP: [laughter
25 H: [Oh my.
26 L: everything all the drawers were all neatly. ()
27 you know placed.

Lines 28–31 are the resolution of the story, the climax. Here Lisa uses the parallel syntactic structure "and NP." She substitutes a different noun phrase for drawer in each line. She uses this structure (as well as hitting the table with each line) to emphasize the point of her story—that this woman had hidden fabric everywhere in her house.

(9)
28 and every dr<u>a</u>wer. (and NP)
29 {hits the table} an every kitchen cabinet. (and NP)
30 {hits table} an every bathroom cabinet. (and NP)
31 {hits table} had fabric stuck hbehhhinhd [hahahah

The structural elements of the narrative function on an unconscious level to guide the listener toward key parts of the story as well as allow the narrator to tell a good story by building suspense and keeping the audience involved in the telling. Further, structural elements are often imbued with culturally relevant meaning. As such, they provide the quilters with ways to construct narratives that function to positively reinforce the connective links so essential to quilting culture and practice.

Discussion

Through the analysis of these two narratives, we can clearly see the important role narrative plays in connecting quilted objects with quilting practices, in connecting quilting values with women's experiences, and in connecting the material means to make quilts with the creativity and knowledge that quilters need for quiltmaking. Situating narratives provide quilters with a way to "set the stage" for their quilted objects. They position the listeners in specific relationships with the quilted objects and provide a discursive space for the exploration and negotiation of the points of view introduced in the narrative with their own and the group's body of quilting experiences and practices. Covert value narratives also provide a space for negotiation. They, however, provide quilters with a way to stay connected to the values of the quilting community in the face of misunderstanding and hostility from non-crafting family and friends. They can also, as this narrative does, connect women across a wider quilting community through their dissemination in quilting magazines.

Connection is only one of the many group values in the quilting guild. The guild, like all communities of practice, needs engagement to function successfully. Groups, since they consist of individuals, have access to the linguistic resources of their members. Within this situational context, narratives are one linguistic resource that quilt groups can exploit. Indeed, quilters draw on different levels of resources—regional discourse norms, community discourse norms, and structural elements to create/construct their narratives within the talk. Furthermore, the group's goals and values may intersect; that is, a narrative might be used to accomplish more than one interactional goal at a time.

In this interactional context, narrative types like the ones discussed here, carry social meanings beyond the content of the story itself and its socially situated function in the talk. Stories become bridges that connect objects, knowledge, experiences, values, and practices. Since the structural elements of the narrative can also be imbued with culturally relevant meanings, they provide the quilters with an additional resource to construct narratives that positively reinforce the connective links so essential to quilting culture and practice. Thus guild members can use narratives to create socially situated meanings around objects and activities relevant to the cultural practices of quilting (Carbaugh 1990).

This study enriches our knowledge of the way narratives can be used to construct group culture. Specifically, analyzing the role(s) of narratives to construct links between the quilted objects, between material culture, and between social and cultural practices of the group contributes to the growing body of knowledge on narrative use by groups. Moreover, the centrality of the quilting object to the talk and the link between the narrative and the object of the narrative is one key aspect that makes these functions of narrative so different from its uses in other groups. Thus the quilters' use of this rich interactional resource to construct community practices and reinforce community values sets this community's use of narrative apart from other uses of conversational narratives.

This chapter has discussed some of the diverse functions of narrative within a specific group—the quilting guild. Since conversational narratives are basic to communication, we could extend our analysis of the group functions of narrative to other groups, including the academic community, positing that narratives would function in similar ways within the academic community. Scholars like everyone else tell stories, and these stories can be used to convey an understanding of what it means to be a scholar (and a teacher) within a particular academic discipline. These narratives would also provide insights into the process of research and the creation of new knowledge as well as construct speaker identity(s) and group identity(s), demonstrate and reinforce shared academic values and academic practices. In addition to their communicative functions within a specific academic field, the study of narrative from a multidisciplinary perspective would promote a richer understanding about the complex nature of narrative and its role in human communication. For example, I taught a seminar on narrative (Spring 2015) that introduced the students to narrative theories from social psychology, folklore, linguistics, and narratology and to the applications of those theories to different types of narrative texts. This multidisciplinary approach encourages the formation of connective links between the different conceptualizations of narrative among the different disciplines.

Transcription Conventions

Characteristics of Speech Delivery

    :   a colon indicates a lengthened sound, usually a vowel
    .   a period indicates a stopping fall in tone

,	a comma indicates a continuing intonation
?	a question mark indicates a rising intonation
!	an exclamation point indicates an animated tone
—	a single dash indicates an abrupt cut off
—	multiple dashes connect the syllables or strings of words to give a stammering quality
a	an underline indicates emphasis
CAP	capital letters indicate that part of the utterance is louder than the surrounding talk
o	a degree sign indicates that the talk is softer

Continual Utterances

| = | when two utterances are adjacent without overlap they are linked with equal signs |
| [| a bracket indicates overlapping utterances |

Intervals between Utterances

(0.1)   silences are timed and marked in tenths of a second in parentheses

Transcription Doubt

( )	empty parentheses indicate that part of the utterance could not be deciphered
(xx)	uncertain words are enclosed in parentheses
(( ))	indicate transcripter's descriptions

Notes

1 This work was supported by an Idaho State University Humanities and Social Sciences Research Committee grant [grant no. HF 11-4F].
2 All names are pseudonyms. This includes personal names, the guild name, and Thomson House.
3 Thomson House is the senior citizen's home where some of the guild member go and quilt with the older women in one of the common rooms every Tuesday.

References

Bauman, Richard. 1986. *Story, Performance, and Event: Contextual Studies of Oral Narrative*. Cambridge: Cambridge University Press.

Baynham, Mike. 2011. "Stance, Positioning, and Alignment in Narratives of Professional Experience." *Language and Society* 40: 63–74.

Bruner, Jerome S. 2010. "Narrative, Culture, and Mind." In *Telling Stories: Language, Narrative, and Social Life*, edited by Deborah Schiffrin, Anna De Fina, and Anastasia Nylund, 46–49. Washington, DC: Georgetown University Press.

Carbaugh, Donal. 1990. "Toward a Perspective on Cultural Communication and Intercultural Contact." *Semiotica* 80: 15–35.
Cerny, Catherine. 1992. "A Quilt Guild: Its Role in the Elaboration of Female Identity." In *Uncoverings 1991*, edited by Laurel Horton, 32–49. San Francisco CA: American Quilt Study Group.
Cerny, Catherine, Joanne Eicher, and Marilyn DeLong. 1993. "Quiltmaking and the Modern Guild: A Cultural Idiom." *Clothing and Textile Research Journal* 12: 16–25.
Colby, Averil. 1971. *Quilting*. New York: Charles Scribner's Sons.
De Fina, Anna. 2008. "Who Tells which Story and Why? Micro and Macro Contexts in Narrative." *Text & Talk* 28: 421–442.
Fitzpatrick, Caroline. 2007. *Women's Voices, Women's Quilts: A Study of Discourse Practices in a Pennsylvania Quilting Guild*. PhD. Diss., Indiana University of Pennsylvania, Pennsylvania.
Goodwin, Charles. 1984. "Notes on Story Structure and the Organization of Participation." In *Structures of Social Action: Studies in Conversation Analysis*, edited by J. Maxwell Atkinson & John Heritage, 225–246. Cambridge: Cambridge University Press.
Harris, Sandra. 2005. "Telling Stories and Giving Evidence." In *Sociolinguistics of Narrative*, edited by Joanna Thornborrow and Jennifer Coates, 215–237. Amsterdam: John Benjamins.
"History of Quilts in American Folk Art." 2009. Quilting-in-america.com. Accessed July 2015. http://www.quilting-in-america.com/History-of-Quilts.html.
Holmes, Janet. 2005. "Story-Telling at Work: A Complex Discursive Resource for Integrating Personal, Professional, and Social Identities." *Discourse Studies* 7: 671–700.
———. 2006. "Workplace Narratives, Professional Identity, and Relational Practice." In *Discourse and identity*, edited by Anna De Fina, Deborah Schiffrin, and Michael Bamberg, 166–187. Cambridge: Cambridge University Press.
Ice, Joyce. 1993. "Women's Aesthetics and the Quilting Process." In *Feminist Theory and the Study of Folklore*, edited by Susan Hollis, Linda Pershing, and M. Jane Young, 166–177. Chicago: University of Illinois Press.
Jefferson, Gail. 1978. "Sequential Aspects of Storytelling in Conversation." In *Studies in the Organization of Conversational Interaction*, edited by Jim Schenkein, 219–248. New York: Academic.
Johnstone, Barbara. 1990. *Stories, Community and Place: Narrative for Middle America*. Bloomington, IN: Indiana University Press.
Labov, William. 1972. *Language in the Inner City: Studies in Black English Vernacular*. Philadelphia, PA: University of Pennsylvania Press.
Labov, William, and Joshua Waletzky. 1967. "Narrative Analysis: Oral Versions of Personal Experience. In *Essays on the Verbal and Visual Arts*, edited by June Helm, 12–44. Seattle, WA: University of Washington Press.
Langellier, Kristin. 1991. "Contemporary Quiltmaking in Maine: Re-Fashioning Femininity. In *Uncoverings 1990*, edited by Laurel Horton, 28–53. San Francisco CA: American Quilt Study Group.
———. 1992. "Show and Tell in Contemporary Quiltmaking Culture." In *Uncoverings 1992*, edited by Laurel Horton, 128–147. San Francisco CA: American Quilt Study Group.
———. 1999. "Personal Narrative, Performance, and Performativity: Two or Three Things I Know for Sure." *Text and Performance Quarterly* 19: 125–164.

Langellier, Kristin, and Eric Peterson. 2004. *Storytelling in Daily Life: Performing Narrative*. Philadelphia, PA: Temple University Press.

Majors, Yolanda. 2004. "'I Wasn't Scared of Them, They Were Scared of Me': Constructions of Self/Other in a Midwestern Hair Salon." *Anthropology and Education Quarterly* 35: 167–188.

Norrick, Neal. 1997. "Twice-Told Tales: Collaborative Narration of Familiar Stories." *Language in Society* 26: 199–220.

———. 2000. *Conversational Narrative Storytelling in Everyday Talk*. Amsterdam: John Benjamins.

Ochs, Elinor. 1997. "Narrative." In *Discourse as Structure and Process*, edited by Teun van Dijk, 185–207. New York: Sage.

Ochs, Elinor, and Lisa Capps. 1997. "Narrative Authenticity." *Journal of Narrative and Life History* 7: 83–89.

———. 2001. *Living Narrative Creating Lives in Everyday Storytelling*. Cambridge MA: Harvard University Press.

Ochs, Elinor, and Carolyn Taylor. 1995. "The 'Father Knows Best' Dynamic in Dinnertime Narrative." In *Gender Articulated" Language and the Socially Constructed Self*, edited by Kira Hall and Mary Bucholtz, 97–120. New York: Routledge.

Phillipsen, Gerry. 1989. "Speech and the Communal Function in Four Cultures." In *Language, Communication, and Culture: Current Directions*, edited by S. Ting-Toomey and F. Korezenny, 79–92. London: Sage.

Ronning, Kari. 1991. "The Contemporary Quilt Revival, 1970–1990." In *Nebraska Quilts and Quiltmakers*, edited by P. C. Crews and R. C. Naugle, 167–207. Lincoln, NE: University of Nebraska Press.

Sacks, Harvey. 1972. "On the Analysability of Stories by Children." In *Directions in Sociolinguistics*, edited by John Gumperz and Dell Hymes, 325–345. New York: Holt, Rinehart and Winston.

———. 1974. "An Analysis of the Course of a Joke's Telling in Conversation." In *Explorations in the Ethnography of Speaking*, edited by Richard Bauman and Joel Sherzer, 325–346. Cambridge: Cambridge University Press.

Sacks, Harvey, Emanuel A. Schegloff, and Gail Jefferson. 1978. "A Simplest Systematics for the Organization of Turn-taking for Conversation." In *Studies in the Organization of Conversational Interaction*, edited by Jim Schenkein, 7–55. New York: Academic.

Stalp, Marybeth. 2006. "Hiding the (Fabric) Stash: Collecting, Hoarding, and Hiding Strategies of Contemporary US Quilters." *Textile* 4: 104–125.

Tannen, Deborah. 1978. "The Effect of Expectations on Conversation." *Discourse Processes* 1: 203–209.

"World Quilts: The American Story, Everyday Creativity." 2013a. Worldquilts.quiltstudy.org. Accessed July 2015. http://worldquilts.quiltstudy.org/americanstory/creativity/everydaycreativity.

"World Quilts: The American Story, Groups and Guilds." 2013b. Worldquilts.quiltstudy.org. Accessed July 2015. http://worldquilts.quiltstudy.org/americanstory/creativity/guildmovements.

11 The Currency of Stories
Anthropologists, *Nawaals*, and the Strange World of Academe

Elizabeth Cartwright

All stories have currency. They circulate like gold coins, from hand to hand; they are hoarded; they are polished; they are deployed, and they are coveted. Stories have played a particular role in anthropology over the decades. Stories come back home with anthropologists who have gone out to the field; we use them to illustrate our points, gain prestige in our discipline and to make departmental parties much more mythic, at least in our own minds, than those of the other, less swashbuckling, social sciences. Our stories change over the years as we tell them to students and others, like all stories do, but for the anthropologist, they remain proof that we were *there*, proof that we looked beyond our own culture(s), proof that there are other ways of seeing in the world. We use our stories to justify our existence in academe—we systematically codify and analyze them too. What counts are the insights about others and about us as we interact as humans that come from and through our stories; we illuminate very different corners of the human experience, sometimes, it is true, but it is human, nonetheless. Our stories are the meat of our discipline, told around campfires real and metaphorical; they are our aces in the hole. We take our stories very seriously. I quote here from a narrative I recorded in Oaxaca, Mexico. Esperanza, an older woman in the village told me about her pregnancies:

> Like me when I had my three babies, Esperanza said. They had problems. They were *nawaals*. They were born with *tripa* (the umbilical cord) all around their bodies. The *nawaals* were born onto a bed of dry leaves, so they died of hunger. There was nothing to eat, and they all died. Esperanza didn't go get a *curandero* because she didn't believe that they were *nawaals*. Then they died, she said sadly. In the cemetery once a man came up to me, Esperanza continued. He was a *nawaal*. He said, You, why didn't you bring your babies here to be cured? I could have cured them. They were *nawaalitos* (little *nawaals*), the three of them. Esperanza was shocked. Why didn't you tell me? she asked him. You should have come to my house to tell me so that they wouldn't have all died. He replied, I didn't know if your husband Leno would want me to. He is very *bravo*, (very angry and fierce), that's why I didn't come.

After they had died, he told me that they were *nawaals*. I didn't know that they were *nawaals*. If I would have known that they were born *nawaalitos*, I would have tried to cure them, Esperanza concluded.

I first learned about *nawaals* very early in the medical anthropology fieldwork that I was carrying out in rural Oaxaca, Mexico, between 1995 and 1997 (Cartwright 2001). The majority of my research took place in the village of San Pedro Amuzgos—a village of about four thousand inhabitants in a remote part of the semi-deciduous rain forest bordering on the state of Guerrero. My initial research activity included doing household-based interviews to document the most common illnesses in the community as well as gathering ethnographic descriptions of daily village life. During the interviews, I encouraged individuals to tell me stories about what had happened during their most recent illness events. These illness narratives about *nawaals* were collected during that process.

Illness narratives are a foundational manner of gathering data for medical anthropologists and have been used extensively over the last twenty-five years in our discipline (Cartwright 2007; Kleinman 1989; Mattingly and Garro 2000; Ning 2005). Illness narratives are rich sources of cultural information that illustrate how people understand the functioning of their bodies within their particular cultural, social, environmental, and ideological contexts. Individuals use illness narratives to describe their illnesses to their families and friends, and they use them to communicate with their healers. Illness narratives are based on individual's unique understandings of how their bodies work—their ethno-physiological concepts. They attend to pains and discomforts while simultaneously attesting to the social and cultural context of the lived experience of the sufferer. These narratives often have moral components that illustrate what is considered to be "right" or "wrong" in a given situation; they give credit to those who are seen as behaving in the most culturally acceptable manner, and they blame those who are "in the wrong" (Price 1987). They are a rich source of data for understanding what matters most to people, especially when it comes to their health and well-being.

Amuzgan Illness Narratives

After completing a couple dozen ethnographic interviews with families in my research field site, San Pedro Amuzgos, I decided to broaden the sample and get out to the more isolated households in the rugged hills that surrounded the village. On our first trip out to this area, I was accompanied by my partner Mark and by a sixteen-year-old high school student named Rosa. We went out to the *cuadrilla* (district) of Guadalupe, as Rosa had relatives there—a situation that would facilitate us getting interviews in this out-of-the-way place that had few, if any, foreign visitors. The tiny village of Guadalupe was known for its violence and high numbers of robberies, and for the fact that many people there spoke little or no Spanish. Rosa was both our guide and interpreter when the interviews were in Amuzgo, the language of the local inhabitants.

We caught a ride in the back of one of the small passenger trucks (*pasajeros*) that periodically left San Pedro Amuzgos and rode it up the highway a few miles to the turnoff to Guadalupe. We then walked the remaining three or four miles into the community; most people walk the entire way from San Pedro Amuzgos by a small footpath to save the bus fare—it takes about an hour and a half to walk depending on how much one is carrying.

Nestled in a deep-green valley surrounded by brilliant red cliffs, the adobe huts clung to the sides of the steep hills in a most precarious fashion. We arrived at a household that was teaming with children, dogs, and chickens. There were a couple of adult women sitting outside, and Rosa indicated that this was a good place for us to start our interviewing. The mother of the family brought out a couple of little wooden chairs that she placed next to the outside adobe walls of the house—in a somewhat vain attempt to keep us out of the broiling late afternoon sun. My first question was the usual *is anyone in the household ill at this time, and what do they have?* Rosa, who verbally translated back into Spanish from Amuzgo as I took notes said,

> The woman says her teenage daughter is a *nawaal*. She had an attack a few days ago while she was attending school. In the middle of the day, her daughter ran out of her class and ran all the way home along the footpath. When she got home, she collapsed. She died for a little while. Her mother ran and got the *curandero de nawaals*, and he revived her. She's not really been well since. She's aggressive and uncontrollable. Her mother doesn't know what to do for her. The girl says she's a *nawaal de tigre* (tiger *nawaal*, or spirit animal). Other than that, no one is sick right now.

I had not ever heard of a youngster being possessed in this way; in fact, at that point I was quite confused. I asked Rosa to explain to me one more time what was wrong with the girl. She said that a *nawaal* is someone who is like anyone else, but when you make them mad, they are likely to get exceptionally mad at you. Sometimes a couple of them will choke another child or they may try to get back at you for something you've done to them by turning into their animal and coming in the night to frighten you; *espanto*, or fright is another very common and serious illness. Not everyone is a *nawaal*, only some people are born that way, Rosa told me. The person will tell others that they are *nawaals*. The mothers and other family members may suspect it and will ask the person again and again what is wrong with him or her. The child or young person will at some point tell them that he or she is a *nawaal*. The fourteen-year-old in the interview family went to school and did normal things. A person can be a nawaal of any kind of animal. "It's as if the animal takes over the whole person." Rosa said. "They turn into the animal, then they go out at night. They are very large animals, and they will come and give you *espanto*."

Rosa could name eight people who were *nawaals* that she knew in San Pedro Amuzgos and in Guadalupe. One of the *curanderos* in San Pedro was a *nawaal*. He was reportedly a very good *curandero* and had cured Rosa of a bad case of fever and her inability to eat. She had been sick for a long time, and finally her mother called him to come do a cleansing (*limpia*). He came and did an egg *limpia*, and she was fine. She said that there are a lot of *nawaals* in Guadalupe, and that over the past few years, several of the ones that she knew had died from drinking too much. She said her grandfather was one. I asked her if it wasn't difficult to live with a *nawaal*. "Yes," she replied, "The mothers will realize that the child is doing a lot of bad things and not listening. They do their best to try to find out from the child if it is a *nawaal*. The child knows and they will tell her," Rosa assured me.

The interview continued with the mother of the adolescent *nawaal* describing when her daughter would get attacks and what had happened over the last couple of years with her illness. As we were talking about *nawaals*, a deep rumbling could be heard coming up the valley. The ground began to tremble, at first just perceptibly and then with increasing violence. The tile (*teja*) roof clattered as the house swayed back and forth. Earthquakes are not uncommon in this area, but they are much feared as the heavy roofs often collapse into the interior of the houses and the adobe walls crack and crumble. The señora's eyes opened wide as she saw me grabbing at the air to steady my chair. Rosa jumped away from the wall of the house that she had been leaning on while doing the interview. There was an odd silence as the rumbling died away in the distance. We continued the discussion of *nawaals* after making sure that the roof was still intact. More evident than the cracks in the adobe were the crumbling foundations of my perception of reality.

The subject of *nawaals* came up time and again in the interviews and in conversations with people both in town and in the *cuadrillas*, both indigenous and *mestizo*. To clarify the concept just a little, I will give a composite description of this condition. The fluidity of real-life definitions should be kept in mind. In general, a *nawaal* is understood to be a person who is born with two hearts—the heart of a person and the heart of an animal. The animal can be a tiger, hog, *onza* (a spirit feline of great strength), or a snake. To be born a *nawaal* is a serious thing. It is considered to be a life-threatening condition that often has a strong social stigma attached to it. To be cured of this condition may be very difficult or even an impossible endeavor. I met several people who had been diagnosed as *nawaals* during my stay in Amuzgos. Often, this illness manifests at birth or during childhood for the first time. Many children are said to die of this condition. Some children don't start exhibiting signs and symptoms until they are five or six years old, while others recognize that they are *nawaals* during adolescence or even adulthood. Some are eventually cured; some die violent deaths, and some become particularly powerful healers or particularly feared witches. As one resident of San Pedro Amuzgos described it to me,

> There are months and phases of the moon when the animal takes over the person. The animal inside starts moving and agitating and takes over the actions of the person. This begins at conception. The baby and the animal are in utero at the same time—each in the womb of their respective mother. The baby and the animal are born at the same time, often but not always in close proximity to one another. When the animal is born, it covets the baby's heart. So it comes into the house and robs the heart out of the newborn baby, leaving part of its animal heart in the baby's chest. Often a baby who is a *nawaal* will be born with a very long umbilical cord. The cord will be wrapped around the neck and under the arm and may actually be inserted back into its own umbilicus.

Linkages between nature and people become blurred; the lines between species become fuzzy. As an anthropologist, I believe understanding these different conceptualizations of reality is fundamental to understanding the actions and decisions that people make.

Conversations about *Nawaals*

I was told repeatedly that the medical doctor cannot cure a person who is a *nawaal*. This illness is only cured by a special *curandero* (who is also a *nawaal*) who uses many *limpia de huevos* (egg cleansings) among other treatments. In the case of being a tiger *nawaal*, the afflicted baby may be taken to the top of the mountain where the tiger lives to ask the tiger permission to let the spirit of the baby go free. If the baby is not cured, it will be known as a *nawaal* from that time forward. Often *nawaals* die while they are very young. The mother needs to admit publicly that the baby is a *nawaal*, as it is this recognition that allows the curing to take place. If the child is older, the child must say that they are a *nawaal*. I was told that the mother will know that her baby is a *nawaal* because she can feel it moving in the womb when she is only eight to twelve weeks pregnant. This is a baby that will be born with two hearts. Usually a baby moves in the womb around five months, according to Esperanza, who was describing this condition to me:

> When a *nawaal* is born, it whines a lot. It cries and cries. The mother may try to breastfeed it, but it will reject the breast. The baby's eyes will be wide open, like it is frightened. That is because the animal is always in front of it, looking at it. The animal doesn't let it sleep or eat. The animal wants to take it back to its cave where it lives.

The baby and the animal are spiritually and physically interdependent. If the baby is not doing well, neither will the small, newborn animal. The baby may cry and cry, Esperanza told me, until the mother bathes it with leaves of the lemon tree and *aguardiente* alcohol. As the baby calms down, so does the animal. When the baby is hungry, the animal is hungry. And when the babe breastfeeds some of the milk goes to the animal. Later, when the human and their *nawaal* are older, the dangers that one encounters will affect the other. If a hunter shoots the tiger *nawaal*, the person who has part of this animal's heart will also suffer. Esperanza continued,

> The adult will cry out, "They're killing me; they're choking me," because their animal is being hurt. If their animal gets a paw caught in a trap, the person's hand will swell up and turn green. If the animal is killed, you'll see the sign in the dead person—the marks of the machete, bullets or where they choke them. I saw a man with these marks just the other day, Esperanza told me.

To cure this illness, you must do cleansings with eggs. Esperanza, who had lost three babies to this condition, told me that one does a *sopla* (blowing out of the disease) seven times to rid the baby of the animal heart. With this type of curing, a baby can get well. It will be left with just its good heart and the animal heart will go out of its body.

There are other signs at birth that a baby may be a *nawaal*. When babies are born with a lot of hair, this is a sign that they are *nawaals*. "When babies are born with lots of hair in the US the grandmas call them *changitos* (little monkeys)," I said. To which Esperanza replied, "*Nawaals* are born there too. It's just that you don't know what they are. They put tubes down their throats, but it doesn't do any good. You don't have people that know how to cure them, so they die." Mothers in the village were particularly afraid of having a baby that was a *nawaal* of a snake, as these children will never walk; they will never stand, and they vomit all the time. They were also reported to hurt all the time, and they do not want to be held.

In this case, the *curandero* of *nawaals* will be called to do *limpias* and to pray. After the cleansing and the praying, the *curandero* will fall into a deep sleep. His *nawaal* will go in the dream and find the *nawaal* of the animal. He will ask it to let go of the person. This is a dangerous and expensive treatment—prices quoted to me were up to six or seven hundred pesos. (In the village. a laborer can earn ten to fifteen pesos a day, if they can find work. 7 pesos = $1 U.S.) Families sometimes wait years in order to amass adequate monies to pay for this cure. Tiger *nawaals* are perhaps the most common. Much of the village violence is blamed on them, both when they are children and as they grow into adults. Uncured, this illness is one that changes and takes over more and more of one's life as the years pass.

Learning to be a Nawaal

If the "nawaalness" of a person is not apparent at birth, then usually it is not fully diagnosed until the afflicted person can actually say that they have the disease. In other words, sometimes one learns to be a *nawaal*. It is a process of revelation that occurs over time, taking years to manifest fully and to be accepted by the patient and the family. This is a description of an evening chat I had with Esperanza. Her three babies had died from their undiagnosed *nawaal* condition fifteen years prior to our conversation. None of her children lived past infancy. Esperanza's eight young nieces and nephews lived next door to her—their presence was ubiquitous in her small house. They dropped by for a chat or for a tortilla or, if they were quite lucky, for a tamale. Esperanza and her husband gave them lots of attention. The tiny Pancho was their clear favorite; they let him use his small machete to cut on pieces of firewood and kept an eye on him while his parents, who were schoolteachers, were at work. He was often over at their house, even long after dark and despite the fact that he lived at least a half a kilometer away. Because the condition of being a *nawaal* seemed to be so socially stigmatized and unpleasant, I was shocked when I heard Esperanza asking him if he was a *nawaal* that evening.

After teaching English class to the junior high school students, Mark and I went down the hill to Esperanza's house. In the black night, the candle flickered on the wall of the adobe kitchen that Mark and Leno had constructed the week before. Esperanza made hot sweet coffee, and we ate fresh sugared bread from the bakery on the top of the hill. Small Pancho was playing on the dirt floor. Suddenly, he started pulling his shirt over his head and making claws with his hands. He growled. I pretended to be afraid. He growled, and I peeked out from behind my hands, quickly hiding again. The conversation then went something like this:

> He's tiny, but he's fierce, said Esperanza as she knelt down beside him. You know, she said, he has always been like this. Every once in a while he just acts like an animal. I think he may be a *nawaal*. I was surprised at this evaluation of the much-adored nephew. Pancho, are you a *nawaal*? Esperanza asked him as she cuddled him in her arms. Are you a lion, or a serpent or a snake or a rat? No, he shook his head, no *tia* (aunt). She turned to me and said, I think he's an onza-lion. You are a *nawaal* aren't you Pancho?

Esperanza spoke in a serious manner. Pancho listened attentively. After asking him a couple more times, she desisted. It seemed that he was less and less sure with his negative response each time she asked. Her final comment was for him not to mention that he was a *nawaal* to the other children in his first-grade class.

I asked Esperanza what would happen if he told his classmates, and she replied that they would tease him and that the teacher might single him out or taunt him. The stigma of being a *nawaal* seemed to evolve along with the behavior of the person and the interpretation of that behavior by those in the community. The social implications of being a *nawaal* are an interesting combination of Goffman's two distinct types of stigma—those that you are born with and those that you acquire during life (Goffman 1963). The process of internalization and changes in self-esteem take place if the person begins to engage in violent behavior or if the person becomes a very adept *curandero*, another trait of being a *nawaal*. The person's social identity is "spoiled" in that people fear their violent tendencies, yet the option for success as a healer also remains open to them. Esperanza's husband was a tiger *nawaal* when he was young. He was cured over forty years ago. Still, his reputed fierceness was the reason that the *curandero* gave for not approaching Esperanza about their children's condition.

Treating the *Nawaals*

Thus far, my descriptions of *nawaals* have been among families that would call themselves indigenous. This illness is widely accepted in the community, even among the *mestizo*[1] families. Their discourse is tinged with disbelief, but only just slightly. They turned down the volume of their speech when we talked about this subject; they told stories of their neighbors first and only later in our relationships did they talk to me about this condition in their own families. How much of this is because they wished to seem more modern when talking to me and how much of this had to do with a lack of belief on their part is difficult to assess. However, they took the idea of *nawaals* seriously enough to engage in their treatment and to suggest it as a possible cause of illnesses that may occur in their own families.

Ana owned a pharmacy on the main street of the town. She was from one of the larger, more successful *mestizo* families in town. She spoke English, as her family had hosted several American exchange students when she was in high school. One of her sons was currently living in New Jersey. She was well read, and we often spent evenings discussing European history or Mexican politics. One evening she started to discuss a *mestizo* neighbor's health problems. Her neighbor, she said, was a *nawaal*. Ana began to recount the story:

> I've known my neighbor friend since we were kids. We went to school together. A few years ago, she became very sick. She couldn't sleep at night and would scream and scream. We could hear her while we were in our house. I went over to her and asked her what was wrong, why she was screaming. She told me, It's because I'm a *nawaal de tigre*. I said, How is that possible? I don't understand? She looked at me and shook her head. I can't explain it to you, she said. It's just how it is. There are a lot of small tigers all around me, and they are fighting me and they won't leave me alone. She kept getting worse and worse. Finally, they sent a *curandero* to see her. He was a special one that knew how to cure a person of being a *nawaal*. We were all in the room with her waiting for the *curandero* to arrive. The *curandero* told us to leave because he had to be alone with her. He had her lay down, and then he started praying and praying. He then shot two shots over her with his gun—in

the form of a cross over her as she was resting on the floor. He came out of the room; he was covered with sweat and had urinated all over himself. He said that he had seen the tiger and that he had scared it into a dark corner. He told us that we couldn't see the animal, only he could. Ever since then, her neighbor had been fine, Ana concluded.

Ana said that there are things that she just could not explain, but she believed that something was happening and that it was beyond her comprehension. She went on to say that a couple of years later, late in the night, a young man about seventeen years old was brought to see her husband who was practicing medicine in the village at that time. His family had carried him there—he was screaming and screaming. Ana began recounting this episode:

> She said that first, she had asked him what was wrong, and he said, I am a *nawaal* of a snake. He screamed and writhed about. His family asked Ana and her husband to cure him. We didn't know what to do, Ana told me. So her husband gave him a shot of pain medication to calm him down. Ana then went to the church and pounded on the door. It was probably one o'clock by that time, she told me, and the door was locked tight. Finally, an old church worker opened the door. She asked him for some holy water. So he filled the glass, and she took it home and told the family to go get some camphor. When they brought it back, Ana took her scissors and put them in the form of a cross and put the camphor around them in the shape of a circle. Then she sprinkled holy water over him and told him he was better. He left with his family. Ana gave them her scissors to use in case he had another episode. She concluded by saying that she thought that *nawaals* were something that the devil sends (*algo diabolico*).

Thoughts

So for the moment, the boy's pain was assuaged. Between the Neomelubrina (the anti-inflammatory, anti-fever drug) and the holy water, a cure, however temporary, was affected. Ana did not know if he recuperated or died, but the role that she and her husband played was successful in that the symptoms subsided, and he did not die while he was under their care. Cures are invented on the spot. If it is perceived that they are effective, they continue. The literature carefully describes sacred tools passed down through generations—the specialized armamentarium of traditional healers. Reality shows individuals grasping at straws and in this case, reaching for the nearest implement that might pass for a cross. On that particular night, there was a pair of scissors at hand. This is not to say that off-the-cuff improvisation are less effective. Like a jazz riff, they are a variation on a theme; they support the main idea. It takes us a little further along the road to healing. It is a performance in the desperation of the moment.

Nawaal Redux

So as I bring back my stories and you, the reader, read them, what does that mean in our commodified world of the university? Am I, the professor, providing a service, a return on investment, something that I can put on my annual faculty evaluation? Should I be supported by state dollars and students' tuition—the value of which goes up every year as their loans accrue unpayable interest? Is what I do considered still to be a viable profession? There are those who would argue that it is not.

And yet when our particular corner of the university put out the call to professors to discuss "narrative," we all came with our stories—albeit in many shapes and sizes, amassed for many intents, but in the end, stories were something that meant a great deal to all of us. Stories have provided us with a way to think through the bigger meanings of what we do, and they show us that learning is about opening up our ears and our hearts. It is about hearing other tellings of what it is like to be a human, now, in the past, and, perhaps, in the future.

Note

1 Locals refer to themselves as belonging to two groups: *gente de la naturaleza* (people of nature—Indians) and *gente de razon* (people of reason—non-Indians or mestizos). Both groups used these terms in conversations, and much of village life is separated along these lines. Of the approximately four thousand people in the village, about half belong to each group.

References

Cartwright, E. 2001. *Espacios de Enfermedad y Sanacion: Los Amuzgos de Oaxaca, Entre la Sierra Sur y Los Campos Agricolas de Sonora*. Hermosillo, Sonora, Mexico: El Colegio de Sonora.
———. 2007. "Bodily Remembering: Memory, Place, and Understanding Latino Folk Illnesses among the Amuzgos Indians of Oaxaca, Mexico." *Culture, Medicine and Psychiatry* 31 (4): 527–545.
Goffman, Erving. 1963. *Stigma: Notes on the Management of Spoiled Identity*. New York, NY: Simon & Schuster.
Kleinman, Arthur. 1989. *The Illness Narratives: Suffering, Healing, and the Human Condition*. New York: Basic Books.
Mattingly, Cheryl, and Linda C. Garro, eds. 2000. *Narrative and the Cultural Construction of Illness and Healing*. Berkeley, CA: University of California Press.
Ning, Ana M. 2005. "Games of Truth: Rethinking Conformity and Resistance in Narratives of Heroin Recovery." *Medical Anthropology* 24 (4): 349–382.
Price, Laurie. 1987. "Ecuadorian Illness Stories." In *Cultural Models in Language and Thought*, edited by D. Holland and N. Quinn, 313–342. Cambridge, UK: Cambridge University Press.

Section III Summary: An Author Conversation

Gesine Hearn, Sonja Launspach, Grant Harville, and Elizabeth Cartwright

Gesine: I recall how we came up with the title for this section [Performing Bodies, Creating Stories] together. From what I remember, it was clear to us that bodies and what these bodies were *doing* was central to the narratives we each were exploring. Also, what the bodies of those involved were doing shaped their sense of who they are, how they related to others, and how others perceived them. So "performing" bodies are central for shaping identities of "performers."

Sonja: Yes, Gesine, the common thread that seems to flow through these different chapters is the link between performance and identity. In most of the chapters here, the narratives are used to perform some type of identity construction: being a football player, being a *nawaal*, or being a quilter. Performance theory and the related concept of performativity describe the presentation of self in the world, either through some type of semiotic signal (dress, behavior, etc.) or through discourse/talk. Talk is the central resource we use to create and navigate our social worlds. When we tell a story to someone else, we engage with the narrative on two levels: the level of the story itself and the level of telling the story—the act of narration.

Gesine: I think the word "performing" is possibly a little ambivalent when applied to sick bodies as in Liz's paper. However, I think it can be argued that "illness" (my perception of my ailment) or "sickness" (others' perception of my ailment) is a "performance"—a private as well as a public presentation of one's condition. In the case of the football players, their bodies are central to their being. It is all about their bodies: how they perform, if they can perform, to prepare them to perform, how coaches see them, how fans see them, how other students see them. They get noticed because of their bodies. They pay attention to their bodies in a way that other people with other jobs and responsibilities do not. They are their bodies. In a similar way, this can also be applied to the quilters. Bodies do something (quilt) and thus become someone (a quilter).

Sonja: As I see it, Gesine, it's in the act of narration that performativity comes into play. The narrator enacts the story using gesture, tone, changes of pitch or volume, as well as facial expressions to embody the different characters in the story they are telling. The chapter focused on the performing arts addresses performance and bodies in a more everyday sense—actors becoming characters, dancers performing movement, musicians playing music. Except in the theater (plays), the notion of narrative for me seems more abstract and nebulous, although perhaps one could argue that these acts of performance for both performer and audience are embedded in the larger social narrative of going to the theater.

Grant: As someone in the performing arts and who is a teacher, one thing the material in this section brings is just an awareness of how I use narrative when I teach. I tell stories all the time, because students remember them. The issue with "parable-based" education is that it's both powerful and not necessarily rigorous. It's easy to tell a compelling story that's not true, or to try to fit facts into a story when reality is more complicated than the story allows for. In any case, I think it's important to understand the power of stories in education, and also to recognize the resulting responsibility we educators have to use them as a force for truth rather than deception or oversimplification.

Liz: Being involved in this project has given me some time and space to think about narratives in my own work and in the work of others, in a variety of fields, including the world of arts and performance. I recently heard an interview with Hans Zimmer who has an extensive background in writing music for motion pictures. He commented on how he is sometimes approached to create the music for a film and given a small kernel of the overall idea of the film—a father and son taking a trip, or whatever. He then works that idea a bit, and then shares what he's done with the screenplay writer, who listens to the music and uses it as inspiration to move the narrative forward.

In his work on *Interstellar* with Christopher Nolan, Zimmer would get a bit more of the narrative each time they interacted, and he used those ideas to modify his musical score; in effect, the musical composer and the screenplay writer co-constructed the written/heard narrative. This interests me as it shows how different forms of communication can be interwoven into a coherent narrative that bridges the worlds between words and notes. Providing a foundation for a director's flight of fancy is a film composer's most important task, and, in a recent article in *Slate* magazine, Nolan described Zimmer's score as reflecting "the tightest bond between music and image that we've yet achieved." I think he's right, at least as far as the intellectual content of the film is concerned. And this leads me to wonder what other kinds of sensorial bridges build narratives. Is there a natural, multidimensional element in all narration? In the embodied recollections that pain narratives evoke? In the tactile remembrances of crafters remembering patterns and stitches and the feel of the cloth?

Sonja: Very thought provoking. At the same time, I would have to say that my understanding of narrative and identity really hasn't really changed as a result of this book project. I would say the chapters in this section have given me examples of other kinds of identities narrative can construct, for example, those associated with pain and illness. I find the whole concept of the *nawaal* and its function in those communities fascinating. It is interesting to see how the relationship between narrative and identity plays out in the context of different cultures or different subcultures. The chapters reaffirm the centrality of narrative as a means of constructing both individual and group identities, a basic assumption in narrative study in linguistics.

Grant: One thing that I would say this book project has changed for me is it has allowed me to engage the "academic" side of my discipline more than I generally do. I don't want to overstate the distinction between the two, but as a rule, we doctor of musical arts folks (a degree explicitly intended for performance) generally focus on practice rather than research or analysis: becoming knights rather than experts on knighthood, so to speak. Certainly, we've spent lots of time in both the practice room and the library, but probably at the opposite ratio of the musicologists and theorists. It's not that performers never consider narrative but that they are more likely to elucidate such considerations through performance, perhaps subconsciously, rather than discussion or prose or seminars.

As a conductor, I probably live as close to the performance/academic intersection as most performers, but the vast majority of my collaborations are, nonetheless, with other performers rather than scholars: orchestra with chorus, music with dance, etc. This project represents a relatively rare sojourn for me into academic collaboration.

Gesine: My involvement in the narrative project has made me more aware of the interdisciplinary overlap in narrative research and how my research actually fits nicely into this kind of research. The involvement in this particular chapter has made me ponder even more the connection between narrative, bodies, and identities. My research prior to the football project also centered on this connection—patients with chronic pain syndromes sharing their stories and shaping their identities as sufferers utilizing online organizations and platforms. I now see possibilities of extending this line of research to other topics that have interested me for a while—immigrants, convicts in mental institutions, wealthy women raising their children in small isolated "elite" communities. Listening to the talks in the narrative colloquium lecture series sponsored by the College of Arts & Letters and talking to the authors of chapters in this book section has actually helped focus my research and created a path to future projects.

Sonja: Yes, Grant and Gesine. As scholars, we are lifelong learners, and this project and the narrative colloquium lecture series have provided opportunities to learn about what other fields do with narrative and to become more aware of the many parameters of narrative. Any kind of multidisciplinary dialogue provides space for new ideas and new perspectives on familiar objects or concepts. Since my chapter discusses a selection of narrative types and their functions from a larger research project, my research in this particular chapter hasn't really been impacted by what I've learned from other participants in the project. However, after I finish researching the quilters' narratives, I will be able to branch out and explore narrative in different ways in future projects.

Conclusion: Narrative Diffusion

Paul Sivitz

The preceding chapters illustrate how narrative unifies diverse disciplines, thus contributing to the identity of Idaho State University's College of Arts & Letters. In many ways, the present text is part of the College prosopography: elements that a group of people have in common, thus creating a collective biography. This book represents only a fraction of the College's engagement with narrative. Faculty and graduate students from every department participate in the Colloquium on Narrative, produce scholarship, and use narrative in the classroom. In other words, diffusion of narrative is central to academic life in the College. Moreover, this dissemination moves us beyond the walls of the university (and further out of our silos).

The Humanities Cafe features College faculty making their research accessible to the public. Held about six times per academic year at a local microbrewery restaurant, participants discuss their projects in relation to the year's overall theme. Members of the public at large, as well as university faculty and students, routinely fill the space to standing room only. We, as a College, want to change the prevailing (and all-too-often stereotypical) narrative of the "ivory tower academic." Engaging with the broader community in this informal atmosphere also has the effect of putting the "public" back in "public university," albeit defined in a slightly different fashion. In another forum, the Human Library, local residents are encouraged to share their own narratives, with the College not only cooperating but also facilitating.

The international Human Library project began in Denmark as a way for community members to learn about their neighbors. The overall theme of the undertaking is "never judge a book by its cover." At Human Library events, human "Books" can be "checked out" by a small group of three or four "Readers" who then hear a "Chapter" from the Book's life. After the fifteen-minute chapter is complete, Readers interact with the Book, asking questions pertaining to the Chapter. Readers then move on to another Book. Here in Pocatello, the Marshall Public Library started their own Human Library. Staff members from the Marshall had heard about the Colloquium on Narrative and contacted the College. They attended a colloquium session, and then requested our input on the planned Human Library. As the director of the colloquium, I have been the advisor to the library for their project. Events are held several times per year at the library and at ISU. While the Marshall Public Library program is local, the connections between the College of Arts & Letters, the academic community, and narrative are regional, national, and international.

The College of Arts & Letters' inaugural Conference on Narrative in April 2016 attracted paper proposals from universities in Utah, Chicago, New York, Israel, Bangladesh, and Idaho. Faculty and graduate student presenters from literature, history, film studies, biblical studies, and communication reflected the broad reach of narrative. Furthermore, the importance of narrative across these diverse fields is illuminated by the willingness of scholars to travel to a relatively rural location to present their papers.

Throughout the process of assembling this book, authors were encouraged to examine each other's chapters to further understand their colleagues' approaches to narrative across disciplines. While we, the editors, did not want authors to change their individual writing styles, we hoped that this sort of "universal access" would encourage contributors to adopt particular elements of methodologies they found appealing. Although it is difficult to quantify whether this has been successful, we are pleased that it has opened (in-person) dialogues among the writers. Authors' willingness to engage with the process has doubtlessly made this text better.

Technology has, of course, made it possible to diffuse narrative instantaneously. The twenty-four-hour news cycle, the Internet, and the ubiquitous cell phone contribute to this phenomenon. We often are led to believe that these narratives are complete, or at the very least, at a point where new details simply add to the existing story but do not change its essence. Obviously, this simply is not the case. The transmission of information does not necessarily correspond to a narrative, but can appear to be one. Furthermore, living, breathing characters—villains, heroes (and soon-to-be heroes), victims, and bystanders—as well as non-human actors such as animals and the environment, make this illusion even more real. In the discipline of history, nothing can be "historical" unless a generation (i.e., twenty to twenty-five years) has passed since a particular event took place. While new evidence might materialize—either in an attic or some long-forgotten government storage closet—that overturns a narrative (i.e., the "facts"), the story is considered finished. As the present volume illustrates, the work of our "root" disciplines starts with a completed (but not always historical) narrative, regardless of how that narrative will be used. We take those stories and digest, analyze, and transform them. Those transformations become public policy, art, literature, and music, historical analysis, health policy, understanding of the human condition, and political theory, to name a few.

As my fellow editor, Brian Attebery, noted in the introduction to this volume, "Narrative runs through everything human beings say and do." The stories that we present to each other, to our students, and to the public, often follow the defined path of narrative: a beginning, a middle, and an end. But the narrative of the College of Arts & Letters at Idaho State University, and our counterparts throughout the academy, continues without conclusion.

Contributors

All contributors to this book are members of the College of Arts & Letters at Idaho State University.

Brian Attebery/English

Vanessa Ballam/Theater

Elizabeth Cartwright/Anthropology

James R. DiSanza/Communication, Media, & Persuasion

Zac Gershberg/Communication, Media, & Persuasion

John Gribas/Communication, Media, & Persuasion

Grant Harville/Music

Gesine Hearn/Sociology

Alan Johnson/English

Kellee J. Kirkpatrick/Political Science

Thomas Klein/English

Sonja Launspach/English

Nancy J. Legge/Communication, Media, & Persuasion

Mark K. McBeth/Political Science

Raphael Chijioke Njoku/Global Studies

Terry Ownby/Communication, Media, & Persuasion

Paul Sivitz/History

Kandi Turley-Ames/Dean, College of Arts & Letters (Psychology)

King Yik/Global Studies

Lauralee Zimmerly/Dance

Index

1984 103
the 5 Cs 10

Abiakam, J. 36–7
Actor Prepares, An 165–6
Adiga, Aravind 59–61, 66
aesthetics 1, 93
African studies 33, 34, 36
agency 33, 87, 164
Altman, Rick 4
Animal's People 66
anticolonialism *see* nationalism
anthropology: autoethnography 68–80; medical 196–204; participant observation 180
Apple corporation 98–9, 103–4
Arcadia 54
Aristotle 93
artificial insemination *see* assisted reproductive technologies
assisted reproductive technologies (ART): artificial insemination 113, 114, 118; costs of 120–1; history of 113–15; insurance coverage of 121–2, 123; in vitro fertilization 113, 114, 118, 121, 122–3; regulation of 115, 119, 120–3; surrogacy 113, 114, 115, 122

backstory 19–20
Barthes, Roland 70–1
Bartram, John 132, 133, 134, 138
baseball 77–8
basketball teams: Cleveland Cavaliers 105–6; Miami Heat 105–6
Berkenhout, John 139
Biscotti, Steve 101
body politics 116; *see also* gender; social norms

Bombay *see* Mumbai
books *see* texts
branding *see* rhetoric
Britain 22–4, 49–50, 130–9; *see also* London
Brocchus, Aelius 23–5
Brown, Louise 113, 114
Burke, Kenneth 94, 99, 103, 104, 106, 145
Butler, The 68–9

Carmen 175
Cave, Edward 133, 134
CDC (Centers for Disease Control) 112, 113, 114–15, 119
cell phones 20–1, 47, 103, 212
Cerialis, Flavius 23–6
Chatterji, Bankimcandra 54–5
Chaudhuri, Nirad 64
cinema *see* texts
cities 34–5, 48, 52–3, 55–6, 58–64, 105–6
civil rights 68–9
cliffhanger 21, 27
Clinton, Hillary 104
codex *see* texts
coding, analytical 76
coherence *see* rhetoric, narrative coherence of
Colden, Cadwallader 134, 137
Colden, Jane 137–8
Collinson, Peter 133, 134, 136–8
colonialism 31–43, 54–5
communication, asynchronous 18–28
communication, organizational: and corporate image 98, 103–4; and crises 98–102; and leadership 96–8; *see also* rhetoric
communication, scientific 129–40

Index 215

communication studies 91–107
conversation analysis 176
Corax 93
creativity 164–75, 178–9, 185
critical thinking 8–10, 52, 57–8, 60, 65, 107
Cub Scouts 78
curanderos 196, 198–201, 203–4
cursus publicus 23

darshan 56–7
Del-Zio, John and Doris 114
Dhoom 3 63–4
Don Giovanni 164

economics 31–43, 59, 66
Ehret, Georg Dionysius 138
Ellis, John 137
embryos, personhood status of 122
England *see* Britain

Fairey, Shepard 104–5
family, social construction of 117, 122
Fertility Clinic Success Rate and Certification Act of 1992 (FCSRCA) 115, 119
festivals 48–9, 168
fidelity *see* rhetoric, narrative fidelity of
films *see* texts
Fisher, Walter 94–5
folktales *see* texts
football 99–102, 154–60
football teams: Baltimore Ravens 99, 101
franking, postal 131
Franklin, Benjamin 131, 133

Garden, Alexander 132, 138
gender: construction of femininity 35–40, 116–17; construction of masculinity 31, 37–8; Victorian ideals of 37–8
Gentleman's Magazine 133, 134
globalization 47–8, 52–3, 58, 60–1, 64
Goodell, Roger 99–102
Gronovius, Johann Frederick 134, 138
guilt-purification-redemption cycle *see* rhetoric

Habermas, Jürgen 132
heroes 7–8, 95, 96, 99, 105–6
holidays *see* festivals
homo narrans 94

Human Library Project 147, 211–12
Humanities Cafe 147, 211

IBM 103–4
identity: group 84–5, 95–8, 102–6, 152–60, 176–92; political 7–8, 51, 56, 57, 68; self 7–8, 32–4, 50–1, 68–9, 73–9, 83–4, 112–13, 130, 185; *see also* nationalism
Igbo 31, 35–9, 42
India 47–66; *see also* Mumbai
infertility: history of 113–15; medicalization of 114, 117–19; narratives of 112–13, 115–16
intimacy 18–28, 160; *see also* asynchronous communication
in vitro fertilization *see* assisted reproductive technologies

James, LeBron 105–6
Jobs, Steve 98–9, 104
journals *see* texts

Kapoor, Raj 52, 53, 57, 58–9
Kennedy, John F. 95
Kuhn, Thomas 130

Lagos 34, 38, 41
languages: Amuzgo 198; Bengali 54–5; English 54–5, 58, 61, 134–9; French 175; German 138; Hindi 50–1, 53, 55; Latin 25, 26, 134–9; Urdu 55, 57
Lepidina, Suplicia 24–7
letter-tablets, Roman *see* texts
letters *see* texts
liberal arts disciplines 9–10, 12, 51
Life 70
limpias 199, 200–1
linguistics: alignment frames 180, 182; conversation analysis 181; discourse analysis 180; evaluative comments 188–9; foreshadowing 188; parallel syntactic structures 189–91; reverbalization 189–91; structural analysis 180; use of humor 187
Linnaean classification system 135, 137
Linnaeus 132, 136–9
Lister, Martin 136
literacy 26, 32, 35, 84, 132, 180
London 23, 51, 53, 132–8; *see also* Britain
Lyotard, Jean-François 143–4

magazines *see* texts
Man Who Mistook His Wife for a Hat, The 174
marriage 36–9
material culture 176, 185–7, 192
Mbadiwe, Dr. Kingsley Ozurumba 37
micro-coordination 20, 23
motherhood 112, 116–17
Mumbai (Bombay) 48, 52, 56, 59, 64; *see also* India
music lyrics *see* texts
Mussorgsky, Modest 167

Narayan, R.K. 55
Narrative Policy Framework 5–6, 111, 120
narratives, types of: collective 152–3; covert values 184–7, 191; dance 166–75; dramatic 165–75; historical 129–40; illness 197–204; musical 164–75, 208–9; ontological 116; personal 20–7, 68–80, 151–61, 179; public 91–108, 143–8; public policy 5–6, 116, 120–3; situating 182–4; sports 154–60; *see also* texts
narratology 1, 3, 17, 192
nationalism 54–6, 58–9; *see also* identity: political
nawaals 196–204
NBA (National Basketball Association) 105–6
New Criticism 1, 145
newspapers *see* texts
network, epistolary 130–40
NFL (National Football League) 99–102; *see also* football
Nigeria 31, 34–43
Nike (sports apparel company) 105
Njoku, Nathan 38–9
novels *see* texts

Oaxaca 196–204
Obama, Barack 104–5
O'Donnell, Norah 99–102
Orwell, George 103

pain: and communal suffering 159–61; and initiation 159; mental 156–8; physical, 151–60, 197
Palmer, Janay 99–102
Panchatantra 48
pantoum 72
paradigm shift 130–1, 134

pastoralism 53–4, 55
Philosophical Transactions 133–5, 139
philosophy, Greek 92–4
photographs *see* texts
photojournalism *see* texts, photographs
Pictures at an Exhibition 167
plays *see* texts
plot 2, 6, 119
poems *see* texts
political science 5–8, 111, 116, 120
postal service 131, 133–4
postmodernism 5, 70–1, 72, 143–4, 154
postsecondary education 8–9, 27, 43
public policy 5, 115, 120–4

quilting: fabric stash 185–7; guilds 177–92; Pine Creek Guild 180–91

Ray, John 135–6
Reagan, Ronald 95
research poetry 68–80; *see also* texts, poems
rhetoric 6, 24–5; and aesthetics 93; and branding 103–4, 105–6, 108; and the guilt-purification-redemption cycle 94, 99, 106; and identification 94, 95, 102–7; and logic 93, 94; narrative coherence of 94–5, 99, 100–1, 106, 107; narrative fidelity of 94–5, 99, 101–2, 104, 106, 107; persuasive 93
Rice, Ray 99–102
Royal Society of London 133, 134–5, 139
Rushdie, Salman 51, 53, 58–9

Sabatier, Paul 5
Sacks, Oliver 174
salutations 21–2, 23, 25, 36
Satanic Verses 53, 58
Scott, Sir Walter 54
screens 18–19
semiotics 71, 74, 80
sense of presence 18–28; *see also* asynchronous communication; intimacy
Seven Years' War 130, 134
Severa, Claudia 24–7
Sheridan, Patrick 165
Short Message Service (SMS) *see* texts
Shostakovich, Dmitri 167
Shree 420 52–3, 57

Sidney, Sir Phillip 53–4
Sinha, Indra 66
skepticism 27, 144, 146–7
social constructivism 154
social norms 35–41, 113–14, 116–17, 178, 181, 191–2, 202–3
sociology 153–4, 159
software, quantitative analysis 76
sophists 93
Southern United States 74–5, 76–8
space program (US) 74–5
Stanislavski, Konstantin 165–6, 173
STEM disciplines 5, 9
stereotypes 50, 60, 152

tablets, electronic 18, 83, 103
technology: digital 10–11; medical 112–15, 117–19; publishing (printing press) 54; space program 74, 103–4; writing 18–23, 26–8; *see also* cell phones; tablets; screens; texts
text messages *see* texts

texts: art exhibits 71–2; books, nonfiction 137–9; codexes 18; films 49, 52, 56–9, 63–4, 68–9; folktales 48; journals, scholarly 133–5, 139; letter-tablets, Roman 22–8, 83; letters 36–7, 129–41; magazines 47–8, 70, 106, 133–4, 185–6; music lyrics 49, 53, 54–5, 57, 58; newspapers 131; novels 19, 35, 40–1, 49–51, 53–6, 58–63, 174; plays 34, 35, 39–40, 41, 52, 168; poems 1, 41, 52–4, 57, 61, 63, 68–80, 85–6, 174–5; photographs 70–1; text messages 18, 20–23

victim blaming 102
villains 7–8
Vindolanda 22–8

White Tiger, The 59–63
Wolfe, Gene 174
Wunderkammer exhibition 73–8

For Product Safety Concerns and Information please contact our EU representative GPSR@taylorandfrancis.com
Taylor & Francis Verlag GmbH, Kaufingerstraße 24, 80331 München, Germany

www.ingramcontent.com/pod-product-compliance
Lightning Source LLC
Chambersburg PA
CBHW050632300426
44112CB00012B/1770